CULTURE *and* CONDUCT

An Excursion in Anthropology

Richard A. Barrett

University of New Mexico

D0840114

Wadsworth Publishing Company
Belmont, California
A Division of Wadsworth, Inc.

To Dottie

Anthropology Editor: Sheryl Fullerton
Production Editor: Hal Humphrey
Designer: Detta Penna
Copy Editor: Susan Caney-Peterson

Printed in the United States of America
1 2 3 4 5 6 7 8 9 10—88 87 86 85 84

ISBN 0-534-03034-3

Library of Congress Cataloging in Publication Data

Barrett, Richard A.
Culture and conduct.

Bibliography: p.
Includes index.
1. Ethnology   2. Culture.   I. Title.
GN316.B377   1984   306   83-14836
ISBN 0-534-03034-3

Credits and acknowledgments appear on page viii.

Preface

This book provides a brief introduction to cultural anthropology, but it is not a textbook. A text is one that sets forth the basic principles of a discipline and summarizes its conventional wisdom. In a typical anthropology text there are chapters on subsistence techniques, language, kinship systems, social organization, and the like.

Here a different tack is taken. The reader is introduced to anthropology by examining some of the fundamental ideas and insights that the discipline has to offer. Rather than focusing on topical divisions, each chapter deals with an intellectual problem or application of anthropological ideas. The aim is to arouse interest in these questions and to engage the reader's intellectual curiosity. The book is therefore a treatment of ideas, not a catalogue of information.

The organization is as follows. The first two chapters deal with the special features of cultural anthropology that set it apart from other academic disciplines. The third introduces the notion of culture, the dominant concept of our discipline and the master concept of this book. It is this chapter that sets the stage for virtually everything that follows, since it highlights a discussion that is carried forth, in various guises, throughout. This is the question of the degree to which humans are most profitably viewed as products of their culture or, contrarily, as producers of it. As the reader will learn, this probably is not a question that can be resolved in either/or terms. All social life is made up of what have been termed (Moore 1976) processes of situational adjustment (coping with circumstances, adaptation) as well as processes of regularization (the imposition and confirmation of cultural form). Consequently in Chapter Four we see that as societies and individuals strive to adjust to changing circumstances, a new cultural inventory emerges that facilitates this adjustment. These processes do not continue indefinitely, however, since once cultural forms appear, new forces come into play that serve to perpetuate them. Hence the theme of cultural persistence that is the subject of Chapter Five.

Chapters Six and Seven also develop ideas that are only broached in Chapter Three. The power of culture over the individual is brought out particularly in the treatment of symbolical themes in Chapter Six. There it is demonstrated that many aspects of everyday behavior are subject to rules and principles of which the average individual is only vaguely aware. In Chapter Seven, however, there is an effort to show that individuals can never be thought of as mere creatures of their culture, and we examine some of the reasons why deviance and nonconformity are tolerated, even encouraged, in most societies. Chapter Eight is an epilogue in which certain of the ideas developed in earlier chapters are placed in the context of contemporary debate.

A final feature of the book deserves comment. Many of the examples and arguments relate directly to our own Western society, more perhaps than is common in an introduction to anthropology. This is so because I have wanted to show how the insights of anthropology bear upon our own lives. It is very easy for readers of anthropology to accept the explanations of other peoples' customs without applying very much of it to themselves. Those people over there can be made to appear very different from us. But it is just as true that we learn about ourselves by studying others. We see that our ways of doing things may not differ fundamentally from the way they are done elsewhere. And, more importantly, we begin to view our own culture not as a natural taken-for-granted reality, but as the artifact it really is.

Acknowledgments

The inspiration for this book came many years ago when, as an undergraduate, I read Peter Berger's *Invitation to Sociology: A Humanistic Perspective*. Here was a book that presented a provocative introduction to sociology by concentrating on the seminal ideas and food for thought that sociology has to offer, and that specifically avoided the topical and descriptive approaches characteristic of the texts of the day. Stimulated by Berger's treatment, I thought that something like it should be attempted for cultural anthropology. Years later, while on sabbatical leave from the University of New Mexico, I sketched out a plan for the book and began filling it in. I am grateful to the university for the time and freedom that enabled me to begin the project.

The works of certain scholars have profoundly shaped my thinking, yet the references to their books in the text do not properly attest to the influence. They are: Thomas Kuhn, *The Structure of Scientific Revolutions;* Elvin Hatch, *Theories of Man and Culture;* Marshall Sahlins, *Culture and Practical Reason;* and Mary Douglas, *Natural Symbols*. The book would have been very different had I not read each of these works.

I also want to thank those who have given me advice and encouragement. Carol Joiner was a constant intellectual companion with whom I discussed most of the ideas in the book, and she contributed many of her own. Gary Logsdon was a wonderfully sympathetic listener. My colleague Harry Basehart read the manuscript and made suggestions that led to significant additions, and I am grateful. My wife Dottie heard it all many times, and bore up well.

Contents

Credits and Acknowledgments

Page 6: Excerpt from Elizabeth Marshall Thomas, *Warrior Herdsmen.* © 1972
Vintage Books. Reprinted with permission of Alfred A. Knopf, Inc.

Pages 16-17: Excerpt from Alice Marriott, *Greener Fields: Experiences Among
the American Indians.* Thomas Y. Crowell Co., 1953. Reprinted with permission of the author.

Page 50: Excerpt from Edward Norbeck, "Changing Japan: Field Research,"
from *Being an Anthropologist: Fieldwork in Eleven Cultures,* George D. Spindler, ed. Copyright © 1970 by Holt, Rinehart and Winston, CBS College Publishing. Reprinted with permission.

Page 67: Excerpt from Ruth Bunzel, *The Pueblo Potter: A Study of Creative
Imagination in Primitive Art.* Columbia University Press, 1929. Reprinted
with permission.

Pages 71, 143, 168: Excerpts from Erving Goffman, *Behavior in Public Places:
Notes on the Social Organization of Gatherings.* Copyright © 1963 The Free
Press of Glencoe, a Division of Macmillan Publishing Co. Reprinted with
permission.

Pages 103, 189, 190: Excerpts from Thorstein Veblen, *Imperial Germany and
the Industrial Revolution.* Copyright 1939, 1966 by The Viking Press, Inc.
Reprinted with permission.

Pages 125, 126, 127: Excerpts from Edward M. Weyer, *The Eskimos: Their
Environment and Folkways.* Yale University Press, 1932. Reprinted with
permission.

Pages 131, 132: E. E. Evans-Pritchard, *Witchcraft, Oracles and Magic among
the Azande.* Clarendon Press, 1937. Reprinted with permission of Oxford
University Press.

Pages 210-211: Excerpts from Eric R. Wolf, *Sons of the Shaking Earth.* University of Chicago Press, 1959. Phoenix Edition. Reprinted with permission.

Chapter 1

The Anthropological Enterprise

The average person has only a vague notion of what cultural anthropology is about. I am aware of this from contact with students in the introductory course, and also from some experience with the general public. When I board a plane my seating companion frequently asks what I do for a living. I reply that I am a cultural anthropologist and this is generally followed by "Oh," or "How interesting." There is usually a brief pause and then the companion says something to the effect that he (or she) has always been interested in the study of ancient societies. This is my cue, and I take the opportunity to deliver a short lecture on the difference between *archeology*, which does in fact concentrate on ancient or prehistoric societies, and *cultural anthropology*, which deals overwhelmingly with living peoples that are accessible to firsthand observation and study.

The error made by my traveling companion is a natural one, since both archeology and cultural anthropology are considered subfields of the larger discipline of *anthropology*, the study of humankind. There are in addition two other subfields: *physical anthropology*, the study of the human as a biological being; and *linguistics*, the scientific study of human language. It was not uncommon some years ago for those who called themselves anthropologists to write more or less authoritatively about all four branches of the field. But the enormous growth of the discipline in the past twenty years, plus the increasing specialization of the component subfields, has made it difficult for a single writer to do justice to the entire subject. I will not even make the attempt; I deal exclusively here with cultural anthropology, my own field of expertise.

Cultural anthropology is sometimes referred to as *social anthropology* or, alternatively, as *ethnology*. While it is true that anthropologists consider that each of these terms refer to slightly different subject matters, for the purposes of this book the terms may be considered virtually synonymous. Thus I will occasionally refer to my cultural anthropological colleagues as ethnologists and sometimes as social anthropologists without implying any basic differences among them. Regardless of the terms employed, cultural anthropology is the comparative study of human culture and society. Wherever men and women form into social groups, as tribespeople in New Guinea, as Bedouin nomads, or even as street junkies in New York City, they are of potential interest to cultural anthropologists.

In the remainder of this chapter the characteristics that distinguish anthropology from other academic disciplines are summarized and described.

Fieldwork

As mentioned above, anthropologists tend to deal with societies on the basis of "firsthand observation," and this is one of the important keys to the field. In fact what the layman does know about cultural anthropology usually stems from this characteristic. He or she has perhaps read occasional articles in *Newsweek*, *National Geographic*, or the daily newspaper about an anthropologist who lived for a year in igloos and tents among the Eskimo; or about one who wandered about northern Mexico in the company of an Indian medicine man; or, more sensationally, about a woman who became a nightclub stripper in order to obtain firsthand information about the underworld of pimps and prostitutes in San

Francisco. Through articles of this kind, the general public is made vaguely aware not only that such animals as cultural anthropologists exist, but also that they are willing to go to extraordinary lengths to gather information about other human societies.

What the public does not generally know is that this is an essential part of the training of nearly every cultural anthropologist. Any student who intends to become a member of the profession is expected to live for a year or more with some people until he has a satisfactory understanding of their society and culture, or at least of the facets of their way of life that he deems worthy of detailed investigation. This is what anthropologists term *fieldwork*, and it is without doubt the outstanding characteristic of the discipline; much that is valuable and distinctive in anthropology derives from the tradition of original fieldwork. When an anthropologist writes about a people, it is with the assuredness that comes from intimate association. He has learned their language, participated in the humdrum daily round, eaten their food, observed their ceremonies, and, normally, established lifelong friendships. He is not merely an outside observer of a foreign way of life. He has made an effort, albeit temporary, to accommodate himself to that way of life and to gain understanding from the experience.

It is true that there are some cultural anthropologists who have never undertaken fieldwork, but their number is extremely small. One reason is that graduate departments of anthropology typically make fieldwork a condition for granting the doctoral degree. Only under special circumstances are Ph.D. candidates allowed to write "library" dissertations, i.e., those based on information collected by others. But perhaps the principal reason that there are so few who have not undertaken fieldwork is that they bear a stigma within the discipline. Those who have not been through the challenge of fieldwork are never thought to have properly earned their stripes. And in the competition for jobs and professional status, there is a clear preference for those who have demonstrated a capacity for effective fieldwork. Cultural anthropology is the only discipline among the social sciences that makes this a virtual requirement for professional status. Many sociologists also do fieldwork, and some employ approximately the same battery of techniques as anthropologists. But it is not a requirement in sociology as it is in anthropology, and no sociologist is considered a second-class member of the profession simply because he has never spent a year in the field.

The tradition of original fieldwork is of such crucial importance to anthropology partly because of the kinds of societies that anthropologists have studied. From the beginnings of academic anthropology in the late nineteenth century up until the 1950s, the primary attention of anthropology was concentrated on what may be called *tribal societies*: the American Indians, various peoples of Africa, the island societies of the Pacific, and so forth. Since the 1950s this focus has shifted dramatically, and anthropologists are now as likely to be studying a counterculture commune in New Mexico, or the social organization of a Tokyo bank, as they are to be roaming the Kalahari Desert with the Bushmen. But more of this change later.

Given the fact that anthropology began as the study of societies that were small in scale, preliterate, and exotic (from the European point of view), it was necessary to devise appropriate means for obtaining information. Since there were almost no written sources on these peoples—no literature, no documented history, not even reliable census information—anthropologists found it expedient to gather the primary data themselves. And so began the tradition of participant observation fieldwork, fostered in the early part of this century particularly by Bronislaw Malinowski in Britain, and by the students of Franz Boas in America.

This tradition that began almost from necessity has been retained even though anthropologists now investigate various types of modern communities that could more conveniently be studied using other techniques. The reason is, of course, that participant observation fieldwork has become virtually indispensable. Anthropologists have learned that by living with the people themselves, they can achieve a level of understanding that would be impossible by any other means. People tend to develop relationships of trust and confidence with someone who shares their life and becomes a familiar presence. They will open up with such a person in ways that they would never do with strangers. It is also a means by which anthropologists discover aspects of the society that remain concealed to all but those who live there. It was only after one anthropologist was bitten by a centipede that he learned of the native medical lore that existed in the community where he was living. And almost every field-worker has had the experience of some accident or trivial encounter that opens up totally unexpected perspectives on the culture he has been studying for months. These are the rewards of extended fieldwork, and they are unlikely to accrue to those who do not make a similar commitment. As one ethnologist (Downs 1973: 322) has expressed it:

> To find out about man, you must go among men. There is no other way. It is perhaps the most important contribution anthropology has made to science, this simple idea.

Cultural Relativism and Subjective Understanding

It is not my intention to discuss the technical or methodological aspects of fieldwork here, since that is a subject of the following chapter. Something should be said, however, about a perspective that is closely allied to the tradition of fieldwork and that has become one of the hallmarks of the anthropological approach. This is the effort anthropologists make to achieve dispassionate but at the same time empathetic accounts of the societies they investigate. Above all, they strive to prevent their own culturally determined values from prejudicing their evaluations of the culture in question.

This is of special importance in anthropology because of the variety of cultures dealt with. Anthropologists frequently encounter societies in which attitudes, values, and standards of appropriate conduct differ radically from those of the anthropologist's own society. They thus find themselves witness to practices that, if judged by the standards of American or European culture, would be nothing short of revolting. The Dani, for example, a tribal group of western New Guinea, practice the custom of cutting a finger from the hand of the close female relatives of every man who dies. It is a standard part of their mourning rituals, and by the time a woman is old she may have only one or two fingers left on each hand. The Dodoth tribesmen of Uganda painfully pry out the lower front teeth of young girls because it is thought to make them attractive. An anthropologist recorded the following description (Thomas 1965: 88–89):

> When the family spontaneously decided to extract the lower teeth of all the little girls in the dwelling (except the baby, whose milk teeth had already been extracted), the operation was performed in Rengen's court. Her son Akral sat in her day house with one of his weeping little half-sisters between his knees. Her twenty-three-year-old son Akikar, mild and impassive, placed a stick as a bit in the girl's mouth, and while Akral held the girl tightly, Akikar expertly hooked out the lower teeth with an awl. They were second teeth, deeply rooted, and as they came, cracked loudly, and the smell of blood filled the air. The little girl screamed that she was dying, and vomited red foam.
> . . . her sister, begging and crying, her hands pressed over her mouth, was captured by Rengen, who firmly handed her over the heads of all the seated people to Akral, who gripped her with his knees. The weeping little girl began to scream: "Akikar, help me!" Akikar dispassionately pried open her jaw and forced the bit into her mouth. He worked carefully, the extraction took only a moment, but she struggled so much he nearly pierced her palate with the awl. She moaned hysterically when it was over and her teeth lay on the ground.

This is powerful, yet it probably never seriously occurred to the anthropologists, either among the Dani or the Dodoth, to condemn or interfere. Such a course would, in the first place, be impolitic and would certainly make the anthropologist's presence unwelcome at such events in the future. More importantly, it is simply not the mission of anthropologists to attempt to reform the society. Their task is to achieve understanding: to discover the meaning that these practices have for individual participants and to determine the part that they play within the context of the culture as a whole. This in no way implies, of course, that they endorse the customs they describe. There is hardly an anthropologist in the world who approves of hacking off little girls' fingers or of prying out their healthy teeth. But that is not the issue. The issue is whether or not objective description and interpretation of such customs further the aim of understanding human cultures in all their variety. Most members of the profession agree that this neutrality is a *sine qua non* of successful anthropological research.

There are two important means by which anthropologists strive for this level of detachment. Most subscribe to what is known as *cultural relativism*, and they also attempt to achieve a subjective understanding of the societies they study. Cultural relativism is the belief that any particular set of customs, values, and moral precepts are relative to a specific cultural tradition, and that they can only be understood and evaluated within that particular milieu. Thus Eskimo marriage practices, religious beliefs, and artistic expression all "make sense" if we place them in the context of their surrounding circumstances and historical tradition. They make much less sense if we wrench them out of their natural setting in order to contrast them with our own customs. The Eskimo practice of infanticide, for example, would appear in our society as a callous and atrocious custom. But if the practice is viewed within the context of traditional Eskimo life, a different light is shed on the matter. In the absence of effective means of birth control, infanticide was one method of limiting population in a situation of harsh environment and narrowly limited resources. Overexpansion of the population could, and frequently did, mean hardships and even famine for the entire community. Thus families did not characteristically retain more children than they could provide for, and by eliminating unwanted infants they were thought to contribute to the welfare of the ongoing community. And so it is with most customs that on first impression appear extreme: there is usually a logic to them when placed in appropriate context.

What cultural relativism means in practical terms, therefore, is that anthropologists tend to adopt a very tolerant
attitude toward all manner of foreign customs and beliefs.
They strive to avoid any suggestion of *ethnocentrism*, which
is the tendency to evaluate other cultural practices from the
vantage point of one's own culture. This is not to suggest,
on the other hand, that all societies must be treated sympa-
thetically. There certainly exist moribund or pathological
social systems that would be difficult even for anthropologists to defend; the examples of Nazi Germany and certain
criminal subcultures in the United States spring to mind. But
the occasional tendency for anthropologists to treat other
cultures with excessive approbation, to the extent that they
have sometimes idealized them, is less cause for concern
than the possibility that they will misrepresent other societies
by viewing them through the prism of their own cultures.

Another and more important means that anthropologists
employ to eliminate ethnocentric bias is the attempt to understand other cultures from the inside, to view them to a certain
extent from the natives' point of view. This is what is known
as *subjective understanding*. The idea is simple: the anthropologist attempts to assimilate the outlook of his informants
to such a degree that he can begin to perceive the world as
it appears to them. It involves mentally placing himself in
their circumstances, comprehending their logic and value
orientations, and in the light of these, assessing their behavioral choices. Some very sensitive portraits of other peoples
have been produced by anthropologists who have followed
this technique. It can be especially useful when the investigator deals with a culture that accents values and behaviors
that run counter to those cherished in the enthnographer's
society.

The potential difficulties can be illustrated by the situation, say, of a female American anthropologist who under-
takes a study of the role of women in traditional Middle
Eastern society. If the community selected for study has not
been deeply influenced by recent social change, our anthropologist will likely discover that the women are permitted
few of the freedoms that Western women take for granted.
The rules of decency in Muslim society require that proper

women spend most of their lives sequestered in the home; when they do appear in public they must cover their heads and bodies completely with a bulky garment. They can have no contact, not even a conversation, with any male who is not an immediate relative. In addition, the men consider women their moral and mental inferiors, and it is believed that they require the guardianship and protection of males— first of their fathers and brothers, then of their husbands— throughout life.

Elizabeth Fernea, accompanying her anthropologist husband, encountered just these circumstances in her residence among the women of a small village in Iraq. Prior to her visit she had little familiarity with Middle Eastern culture, and, as one would expect, had no particular sympathy for the above-mentioned restrictions and attitudes concerning women. Since there was no sanctioned role for an independent and unfettered female in the village, Fernea found it expedient to adopt the *abayah* (the covering garment and veil) that the other women wore, and to limit her social life to the company of the women and children in their walled-in seclusion. After a trying apprenticeship she succeeded in developing rapport and friendship with many of the women, and later produced a sensitive account of the world of Muslim women as viewed from within. Not surprisingly, she developed a certain appreciation of a way of life that had initially appeared rather forbidding. By attempting to view the situation from the point of view of the participants, by understanding how they perceived their circumstances, and by gaining insight into their pleasures and satisfactions, she was eventually able to describe the society with warmth and sympathetic detachment. She has a comment for those who have never viewed this world from the inside and judge it by outward appearances (Fernea 1965: 313):

How many years would it take, I wondered, before the two worlds [the West and Middle East] began to understand each other's attitudes towards women? For the West, too, had a blind spot in this area. I could tell my friends in America again and again that the veiling and seclusion of Eastern women did not mean necessarily that they were forced against their will to live lives of submission and near-serfdom. I could tell Haji [an Iraqi friend] again and again that the low-cut gowns and brandished freedom of Western women did not necessarily mean that these women were promiscuous and cared nothing for home and family. Neither would have understood, for each group, in its turn, was bound by custom and background to misinterpret appearances in its own way.

The degree to which Fernea came to appreciate the society she studied is in no sense unusual. The average anthropologist leaves the field experience with a sense of profound respect for the culture and the people among whom he has lived. This is almost inevitable if the anthropologist begins to assimilate the native point of view. Since most people in most societies find their own culture a satisfying way of life (indeed, most think it is the "natural" and best way), and since most are willing to defend it against all outsiders, the anthropologist tends to become a defender as well. He cannot help but perceive that the culture affords rewards, satisfaction, and security for those who have grown up within its confines and are only familiar with that way of life.

But even in situations in which this is not true—when, for example, they deal with subcultures that are despised in the larger society—anthropologists are still able to describe them with detachment and empathy. In recent years anthropologists have explored various of the less seemly aspects of American life, such as violent city street gangs (Keiser 1969), alcoholic tramps (Spradley 1970), and heroin addicts (Agar 1973). While none of the authors has praise for these subcultures, still, by attempting to place themselves in their informants' shoes, they have written at least compassionate accounts of these peoples. Ruth Benedict (1946) even proved that it was possible to do the same for her country's enemy, Japan, at a time when the United States was swept by anti-Oriental war hysteria.

Indeed, some anthropologists have been so taken by a people studied that they have identified with them strongly and have even tended to perceive the environment as the natives do. Colin Turnbull, for example, has written various warm and sympathetic accounts of the Congo Pygmies, a people he has lived among and greatly admires. In the same studies, however, he presents a decidedly unflattering portrait of their village-dwelling neighbors with whom the Pygmies maintain mildly uncordial relations. The contrast in his treatment of the two groups is so sharp that it is difficult for the reader not to suspect that the Pygmies' view of the villagers influenced Turnbull's characterization of them. In this Turnbull is not alone; more than one anthropologist has permitted the natives' viewpoint to pass for a more objective appraisal of the same reality. But despite occasional excesses, the attempt to see the world as it appears to the people studied is an invaluable tool in anthropology; it is a safeguard against ethnocentrism and a means of developing a degree of empathetic understanding of any ongoing society.

Comparative Perspective

Up to this point I have dealt with some of the approaches that anthropologists utilize in collecting information and in describing the people they study. But anthropologists are not content merely to describe; they are also interested in comparison. If there is one characteristic that virtually all members of the profession agree is distinctive of the discipline, it is this *comparative perspective*.

Comparison is important because anthropologists aim to understand human culture in the broadest possible terms. They are interested in the simplest hunting and gathering bands as well as in modern industrial civilizations. In fact, any human society is grist for the mill. This significantly differentiates anthropology from the other social sciences— sociology, psychology, economics, political science—which have dealt overwhelmingly with European and American societies, or at least those that are within the mainstream of Western civilization. Anthropologists pride themselves on their *holistic* approach to mankind, meaning that they deal with cultures from every corner of the earth and with humankind as an all-inclusive category. (Holism in general anthropology also refers to the fact that humans are dealt with as biological as well as cultural beings, and that all human cultures, prehistoric as well as living representatives, are of equal concern.)

The advantage of this broad perspective is that it serves as a check on those who would generalize about all of humanity on the scanty evidence from our own or Western societies. While it is easy to suppose that our own customs and institutions are "natural," anthropologists can usually cite some society, and sometimes many, in which things are done very differently. This is even true in regard to physiological processes common to all people, such as aging, sex, and the consumption of food.

Take, for example, the aging process and how it is regarded in different societies. A friend of mine recently passed his fortieth birthday, an event that sent him into a mood of depression because "he suddenly realized he was getting old." I chided him, saying that he should be happy to have made it to age forty. Unwilling to be consoled, he said that his feelings were natural and that "nobody can look forward to old age." But regardless of how normal this seems to him as an American, his feelings might be considered odd in other societies. Japanese peasants, for example, not only look forward to the restful years of old age but have even been known to speed the process along. The following is taken from an anthropological study of a Japanese community (Beardsley 1959: 63–64):

> Increased longevity does not guarantee a youthful appearance in elderly persons. Rather, men and women begin to look elderly very soon past age fifty, though vigorous and hearty a few years earlier, with a spring in their walk. The rapidity of aging, it may be suspected, is not solely a matter of physiological change but reflects a social situation encouraging the mature person to reach out gladly and thankfully to old age rather than to fear it. . . . To enter old age early is to enjoy its advantages longer. Accordingly, without conscious awareness, people take up the mannerisms of old age rather than carry on those of the middle years past age fifty.

So here we find a people pretending to be old before their time—just the opposite of the tendency for middle-aged and elderly Americans to try to appear fifteen years younger than they really are.

A similar cultural variation can be found in sexual practices. What Americans consider the normal mode of heterosexual intercourse might be considered aberrant elsewhere. Writing about a people of the central Pacific, an anthropologist notes some remarkable differences (Murdock 1965: 301):

> The normal, routine posture assumed by the Trukese in copulation is one that is not even mentioned in Kinsey or, to my knowledge, in any other occidental work on sexology or pornography. It probably has never even been approximated by any native-born American couple, however experimental.

It would be wrong, however, to leave the impression that the comparative focus in anthropology is limited to a kind of cultural nitpicking in which all generalizations about human society are shown to be false. If such were the case it would be an unworthy and unscientific endeavor, since one of the goals of the discipline is to seek regularities that are valid in a wide range of cultural contexts. The knowledge of hundreds of human cultures that anthropology possesses can, and should be, the starting point for such generalizations.

An example will make the point. The data that anthropologists have compiled on relations between the sexes in the known societies of the world are an invaluable source of information for those interested in the question of male-female relations in our own society. Is the inferior position of females in relation to males in the United States and in other Western countries a product of a specific kind of society? Or is the relationship between the sexes that we are familiar with quite general? Margaret Mead wrote a famous book in 1935, *Sex and Temperament in Three Primitive Societies*, in which she argued that cultural conditioning can produce a situation in which our stereotypical sex roles can be nearly reversed. Her description of male and female among the Tchambuli, a tribal people of New Guinea, portrayed the women as the dominant and managing partners, while the males were emotionally dependent on the more aggressive females.

Unfortunately, Mead's study has remained ever since virtually one-of-a-kind. The overwhelming testimony of ethnological literature leads to a very different conclusion: that in fact male dominance has been characteristic of almost every society on earth. While it is true that women in many societies wield considerable power in domestic affairs, the public sphere, in which individuals vie for positions of leadership and authority, is almost always controlled by males. The near universality of this fact does not mean, of course, that it is inevitable, or that it cannot be altered in the future. But it would seem to indicate that the cause of the condition is rooted in fundamental differences between human males and females rather than in specific economic or political arrangements. The social engineers of the future should at least be cognizant of this corpus of information on sex role differences if they aspire to make meaningful changes.

Almost any hypothesis that is offered about human society can be tested against the ethnological record, which is the body of information on human societies compiled by anthropologists. Is it true, for instance, that human beings are innately aggressive, as a number of writers have recently contended? Then how do we account for the large number of remarkably peaceable hunting and gathering groups that anthropologists have described? Can one say that all enduring societies have some form of religious expression? To answer, of course, one must first know what is meant by the terms *enduring society* and *religious expression*. Generally speaking, however, the evidence from all known societies since Neanderthal would suggest that religious expression is in fact universal.

Anthropologists are therefore inveterate comparativists because they control a body of knowledge that includes all accessible cultures of the globe. If one is to speak sensibly about humanity in general, they believe that one must have more than the knowledge attainable through observation of American, European, or selected Asiatic societies.

Distinctive Subject Matter

This discussion of the importance of comparison has led me to touch upon what, to any outside observer, is certainly the most distinctive feature of the discipline, namely, its concentration on exotic or tribal peoples. Just a glance at anthropological literature reveals names of societies (Kpelle, Yanomamo, Yurok, Fulani, etc.) that the average person has never heard of. There was a time, in fact, only about fifty years ago, when anthropologists even defined their subject matter in these terms. Anthropology was thought to deal with "people without historic records" (Boas in Hymes 1969: 36), while sociology and the other social sciences were said to deal with "modern" societies. These definitions are no longer suitable. The spread of industrial civilization to formerly remote areas has brought about the disappearance or transformation of most of the small-scale societies that anthropologists traditionally investigated. Partly as a result of this situation, anthropologists have expanded the range of their subject matter to include peasants, the urban poor, minority groups, rural American communities, and the like.

Despite this change, there remains in anthropology a strong preoccupation with exotic societies (i.e., those most unlike our own). If given an everything-else-equal choice between studying a Denver street gang or a tribe in New Guinea, four out of five anthropologists would probably opt for the latter. This is due in part to a romantic syndrome in anthropology; the discipline has always attracted persons who are not wholly satisfied with their own way of life and seek the challenge of the strange and the unknown.

But romanticism is far from the whole story. There have always been sound scientific reasons for the preference for exotic societies. As already noted, the past century has witnessed an unprecedented destruction of tribal peoples; their languages and aboriginal way of life have either been lost forever or they remain a faded memory in the minds of a few elderly men and women. Thus from the beginnings of the discipline, anthropologists have been concerned to record the available information on these peoples before it becomes irretrievably lost.

Viewed in this light, the concern with exoticism can certainly be justified. Anthropologists have performed an invaluable service in recording the details of social life, native economies, myths, and technology of peoples that future generations will be unable to observe under anything like aboriginal conditions. I will even hazard the guess that scholars of a hundred years from now will wish that anthropologists had done more, rather than less, of this "cultural salvage" work.

And what about descendants of these peoples? Will they not appreciate a perspective on their past? For societies without written records, the anthropologist's account will someday be the best and perhaps sole chronicle of what they once were. Many anthropologists of the future may in fact relive Alice Marriott's experience as she began fieldwork among the Kiowa Indians in the 1930s. On her first night with an Indian family, her Kiowa host, Mr. Camp, suddenly announced (Marriott 1953: 65–66):

"Now," he said, "when you ready, we start writin' book about the Indians". . . .

I sat and stared at him, and he saw my astonishment and answered it. "Long time now I been thinkin' somebody ought to write down ole Kiowa ways so these little young ones can know. I try, no good. I don' know English good enough. My daughter, she been to college, but she too busy social workin' for Indian Service; never got time to write for her ole dad. Now you come. We got plenty time, like in old days, when was storm, people sit by fire and tell history stories from far-back times. We do that now."

He was dynamic. He was forceful. He was an answer to prayer. . . . "All right," I said, "where shall we begin?"

"You wait here," he ordered abruptly. "I got to get the record, make sure we go right when we talk." Again he departed into the other room.

While I waited for his return, I tried to decide what "record" he could mean. The women had placidly returned to their quilting; the children and the puppies frolicked around my feet. Nobody seemed to be surprised by what was going on; nobody seemed surprised when Mr. Camp reentered the room with an outsize volume, bound in shabby green cloth and stamped with dulled gold, in his arms.

"There," he announced, laying the volume on the table, "that's Mr. Mooney. He wrote about us Indians long time ago. Now when we don' know for sure what happen' we look him up in Mr. Mooney."

James Mooney was an anthropologist who had studied the Kiowa in the 1880s and had written the book that Mr. Camp brought into the room. Thus Marriott found herself recording a Kiowa version of Kiowa culture as interpreted at various points by a deceased anthropologist!

This anecdote illustrates why one writer (Richardson 1975) has referred to the anthropologist as a kind of epic poet for mankind. Only the anthropologist has been interested in the human story as told by these otherwise forgotten and downtrodden peoples. And it is their story, by the way, that tells us about life as it was prior to the urban and industrial revolutions, a way of life representing well over 90 percent of all human history. Thus Richardson asks, if the anthropologist had not been motivated to preserve parts of the story for later generations, who else would?

Microscopic Focus

A final characteristic that distinguishes the work of anthropologists is their preference for conducting research in contexts of very small scale. This is of course related to the tradition of firsthand fieldwork. The demand that anthropologists reside with a group of people and become intimately acquainted with their way of life clearly sets limits to the size of population that can be studied. One anthropologist (Hsu 1969: 6–7) has even suggested that the maximum number of people who can be dealt with by means of face-to-face interaction is about six hundred individuals. It is usually not possible to become acquainted with a greater number in the span of a year or more, simply because good personal relationships take considerable time to develop. In fact the figure six hundred is probably too high. Many excel-

lent ethnographies have been written that elicited information from far fewer. The fine study by Elliot Liebow (*Tally's
Corner*) of streetcorner blacks in Washington, D.C. was based
on the lives of only about twenty-four men; and many of the
classics of American Indian ethnography were constructed
largely on information provided by tiny numbers of elderly
informants.

This is not to say, of course, that anthropologists never
undertake studies of greater scope. Analyses of whole nations
and of broad periods of time have also been written by
anthropologists. Benedict's *The Chrysanthemum and the
Sword*, Wolf's *Sons of the Shaking Earth*, and Geertz's *Agricultural Involution* are examples of an extensive literature
of this kind. But even these authors insist that it is the anthropologist's attention to intimate details, to particular lives in
particular places, that allows them to reach from the part to
the whole. One of the above authors (Benedict 1946: 10–
11) has remarked that the "trivial habits in daily living
. . . thrown large on the national screen, have more to do
with that nation's future than treaties signed by diplomats."
And another (Geertz 1973: 21) speaks of anthropologists
approaching their broad interpretations "from the direction
of exceedingly extended acquaintances with extremely small
matters."

Thus one of the strengths of anthropology as a discipline
is that the information grows out of minute observations of
commonplace events. The fieldworker immerses himself in
the lives of others, he studies their daily routine and everyday cares. He comes to know this material so well and so
intimately that it becomes second nature. The sacrifice, of
course, is the larger focus and the statistical aggregates of
the other social sciences. These are more than compensated
for, most anthropologists believe, by the intimate, small-
scale, and qualitative types of information that have become
the hallmarks of our science.

Suggested Readings

Briggs, Jean L., *Never in Anger: Portrait of an Eskimo Family*. Cambridge: Harvard University Press, 1970.
    As a doctoral student studying the Eskimo, Briggs allowed herself

to be adopted into an Eskimo family. She lived intimately with them for almost a year and a half and produced a remarkably insightful portrait, both of the Eskimo and of her own attempts– and frequent failures–to live up to Eskimo expectations. It is one of the most revealing portrayals of the trauma in fieldwork of anything in the anthropological literature.

Fernea, Elizabeth W., *Guests of the Sheik: An Ethnography of an Iraqi Village*. New York: Anchor Books, 1965.
The author is an American woman who accompanied her archeologist husband to Iraq, where they resided in a small village. Fernea vividly describes the adjustment she made to a way of life radically different from her own. We witness her initial shock and then the gradual growth of understanding as she tries to view the people in their own terms.

Liebow, Elliot, *Tally's Corner: A Study of Negro Streetcorner Men*. Boston: Little Brown, 1967.
An anthropologist describes the lives of Black streetcorner men in inner-city Washington, D.C. Liebow "hung out" with these men and took part in their lives, and the result is an intimate and perceptive portrait of the men as husbands, fathers, friends, and lovers. The book is an impressive demonstration of the applicability of participant observation research even in urban situations.

Richardson, Miles, Anthropologist—The Myth Teller, *American Ethnologist*, Vol. 2, No. 3, 1975, pp. 517–32.
One person's view of what it means to become an anthropologist in late twentieth-century America. He tells us something of his personal background, his experiences as a practicing anthropologist, and then tries to say what it all means. The account is humorous, the language poetic, and a message comes across.

Turnbull, Colin, *The Forest People*. New York: Simon and Schuster, 1961.
A thoroughly charming account of the Pygmies of the Ituri Forest of Zaire, Africa, by an anthropologist who knows them well. The book flows like a novel, yet it is full of information about the Pygmies and their way of life.

Chapter 2

The Fieldwork Experience

It should be clear from the discussion in Chapter One that fieldwork is of paramount significance for cultural anthropology; the very personality of the discipline is influenced by the special manner in which anthropologists collect their primary data. But the effects are not limited to the quality of the data produced; it may plausibly be argued that fieldwork has considerable impact on the character of anthropologists as well. The fact that the average professional spends many months and even years living in isolation from his own society, while attempting simultaneously to develop a sympathetic understanding of another, often radically different, social system cannot help but leave an imprint on the individual's character and outlook.

Some of the consequences are positive, others less so. One author (Bohannan 1963: 7–8) maintains that the process provides anthropologists with a kind of "stereoscopic social vision," enabling them to view the world through two or more cultural lenses at once. They can thus think and perceive in the categories of their own cultures, but are able to shift gears, so to speak, and view the same reality as it might be perceived by members of the societies they have studied. This intellectual *biculturism* is extremely important to anthropologists. It makes them continually aware of alternative ways of doing things and prevents them from taking the customs of our own society too seriously. The impact of fieldwork can also be observed in the virtual obsession that many anthropologists develop for the people among whom they have worked. Some can barely discourse for ten minutes without mentioning "their" people; and every department has at least one individual who teaches a course on "Peoples of Africa" or "South American Indians," which in reality becomes an extended discussion of the group that the professor lived among in 1955.

Since fieldwork does have very considerable significance both for the discipline and for its practitioners, it will be worthwhile to devote some attention to it, looking at the methods and techniques employed, as well as at the peculiar advantages and disadvantages of the approach.

It is always difficult to discuss fieldwork in general terms because the kinds of communities that anthropologists deal with are so varied. The problems encountered among the Bushmen of the Kalahari desert would seem to bear little resemblance to those faced doing fieldwork among the upper classes of a Spanish town. The advice one would offer to an anthropologist setting out for the Kalahari might include information about food supplies, camping equipment, snakebite, and truck maintenance, none of which would be remotely applicable to the student who heads for provincial Spain.

Despite these obvious differences, there are certain things that are common to the field experience almost everywhere. All fieldworkers must make their presence acceptable to the people they study, select trustworthy informants, find satisfactory means of recording and classifying information, and continually subject their provisional interpretations to empirical test. It is these general aspects of fieldwork that are dealt with in this chapter, though it should be kept in mind that the observations will not apply to every case.

Preliminaries

No anthropologist gets into the field by simply desiring it. Many months of study and planning go into the initiation of a research project. Since fieldwork is generally expensive, particularly when conducted in foreign countries, the potential fieldworker must depend on outside sources of financing. This is generally accomplished by submitting a proposal of the projected study to one of the many agencies that support scientific research, such as the National Science Foundation, the National Institutes of Mental Health, the Social Science Research Council, or the Ford or Rockefeller foundations. The scientific merit of the proposal is then evaluated by panels of scholars who lend their services to these agencies to select the proposals that are most deserving of financial support.

Thus long before a proposal can be submitted, the investigator must do a considerable amount of preliminary research, reading the theoretical literature and acquainting himself with the geographical region and the people to be studied. On the basis of this work a concrete research problem is outlined and the various methods to be employed in the investigation are specified in the proposal. It is especially important that a realistic relationship be drawn between the kinds of data sought and the specific techniques to be employed in gathering the information.

The anthropologist also attempts to learn the language of the people. This is sometimes impossible, since anthropologists occasionally go to areas in which either the languages are unrecorded or there are simply no facilities available for instruction. In such cases they must plan to pick up language skills as the investigation proceeds, perhaps using interpreters in the initial stages.

Another matter of importance is to secure permission from the appropriate authorities of the country where the research will be conducted. This is an increasingly thorny issue for anthropologists, since in the last ten years certain Third World countries have literally closed their doors to social science research within their borders.

Community Selection and Initial Adjustment

Once financial support and permission from local authorities have been obtained, the fieldworker is ready to proceed to the location to initiate the investigation. Unless he or she has been there before, however, it is generally necessary to spend a number of days or even weeks in a reconnaissance of the local region to determine the communities or districts that are most suitable to the requirements of the study.

Certain considerations are of a purely scientific character; but there are practical concerns that also must be taken into account. If the ethnographer is accompanied by family members, particularly small children, the accessibility of medical services becomes an important consideration. Is there a convenient residence available? In some areas of the globe, the seemingly simple matter of obtaining food can present almost insuperable obstacles. In the Arctic, among the Eskimo, for instance, unless the anthropologist intends to subsist mainly on raw fish and bannock (unleavened barley flour bread), most food supplies must be airlifted in at considerable expense. Even in highly civilized countries housekeeping tasks may require hours of labor every day, making servants a virtual necessity.

The experience of one anthropologist and his wife in a peasant village in India gives an inkling of some of these problems. Their original intention was to be self-sufficient: as the ethnographer expressed it, "to live totally without servants, depending upon locally available food supplies and vitamin tablets" (Beals 1970: 38). But once they set about getting their first meal—under the astonished gaze of more than twenty trying-to-be-helpful villagers—they discovered that they were incapable of performing even apparently simple chores like lighting a primus stove and fetching clean water from the creek. The anthropologist admits that (1970: 38)

> in a surprisingly short time, we were painfully aware that we had achieved an almost legendary reputation for incompetence. We could not get water, we could not make fire.

> We seemed totally unable to get food or prepare it properly
> once we had it. Already exhausted by such simple tasks as
> getting water . . . [my wife] was in no shape to scrounge
> around for foodstuffs or to endure the routines of cookery
> that involved six to eight hours of hard work on the part of
> highly skilled local women.
>
> Within a few days, we were begging the Gauda [village
> headman] to find us a servant.

As this example makes clear, anthropologists are not free
to reside just anywhere. They do not possess the same skills,
medical immunities, or digestive tracts as the natives, and
they must therefore make special arrangements for their own
and their families' physical comfort and safety. Practical
matters of this kind generally weigh heavily in the eventual
decision to remain in one place rather than another.

But the matter is more complicated still, since the selection of community does not reside entirely with the ethnographer. The people of the community have a voice in the
matter as well, and must at least *allow* themselves to be
studied. There are anthropologists who have been ignored,
politely asked to leave, or even bodily expelled from communities that they had hoped to study. Some peoples will
simply not cooperate with anyone who inquires into their
customs and beliefs. This is true of many of the Pueblo
Indians of New Mexico, who will not permit ethnographers
to reside in their villages for the purpose of conducting an
investigation. The anthropologist Leslie White, who spent
years studying the Keresan Pueblos, could only do so by
engaging informants in absolute secrecy and interviewing
them far from the village (White 1962: 7). Fortunately, cases
of this sort are rare. Most peoples of the world respond to
the sudden appearance of an anthropologist with considerable civility and hospitality, even when, as is normally the
case, they do not fully comprehend his purpose.

There can be little doubt, however, that the reception an
anthropologist is given generally has an important bearing
on choice of community. In this initial period the investigator
finds himself in alien surroundings, usually speaking the

language poorly, if at all, and desperately in need of some reassurance that the people are going to like and accept him. When, therefore, certain individuals extend some uncommon kindness it tends to make a deep impression. I must admit that this was important in my own fieldwork in rural Spain. In the spring of 1967 my wife and I visited various communities that seemed equally attractive on practical and scientific grounds. The ultimate decision to reside in the village of Benabarre was due to the fact that I met two men there whom I liked immediately and believed would become trusted friends.

Once the ethnographer settles in a community, the problem arises of how to explain his presence there. Among some peoples this is no problem; the American Indians, Australian aborigines, and certain other societies have been so thoroughly studied that anthropologists have become like features of the natural landscape. But this is not true of most peoples of the world. The arrival in a remote Peruvian, Spanish, or Egyptian peasant village of a foreigner who announces the intention of living there for several months is a sensational and unprecedented occurrence. Since most of the villagers have never heard of anthropology, this explanation cannot be very helpful.

What they do perceive, however, is that the newcomer asks a lot of questions and writes the answers down. He is also wealthy by local standards, perhaps owning a car and bringing cameras, a tape recorder, a transistor radio, and the like. Who then is paying him to do this? In peasant Spain the notion that anyone would actually pay someone to write about a peasant village strikes people as ludicrous. A book about Madrid or Barcelona, yes, that they could understand; but to pay thousands of dollars for a book about an insignificant peasant village? Who would be that crazy? I once had the following conversation with a peasant in the Spanish community where I worked. He asked,

"But who is supervising you?"

"There is a professor at the University of Michigan who is my supervisor."

"How does he know you're here in this village and not [at some resort] on the Costa Brava?"

"But if I were there, how would I write a book about this village that my supervisor expects?"

"How would he know? You already know more about this village than he does."

"Then you think I could just make it all up?"

"I don't know. All I know is that nobody would trust a Spanish student to do what you're doing."

"Why not?"

"Why not!? Because he wouldn't stay in any American village. No sir! He would just take the money and go to New York [City] and have a good time!"

Thus the fact that the fieldworker engages in activities that by local standards appear both illogical and uneconomical makes it difficult for him to be accepted at face value. Rumors inevitably arise to the effect that he is not what he claims to be; that he is perhaps a spy of some sort (either Communist or CIA), or maybe even an agent cunningly hired by their own government to collect local tax information. There is usually very little that a fieldworker can do to prevent such rumors, except to act in a friendly, open manner that invites trust. However, as the fieldworker establishes increasingly intimate relationships with members of the local population the rumors tend to subside, especially since many of the topics of greatest interest to the ethnographer (e.g., kinship, childhood socialization, myth, and ritual) are not what people expect from a spy. Furthermore, if the anthropologist is accompanied by family members this also tends to counter such rumors, for, people reason, would even a political agent risk the safety of his own family?

The period of initial adjustment is frequently a very difficult one for the fieldworker. Various anthropologists have confessed that they have suffered periods of intense anxiety and depression in the early stages of their work and even experienced doubts about their ability to carry out their projects. One ethnographer became so anxiety ridden that it led to alarming symptoms (Wax 1971: 71–72):

There was no one I could talk to in any meaningful fashion . . . and after almost two months I began to see myself as a total failure. The anxiety I suffered was so agonizing that

I still find it hard to describe. Every time I returned to my stifling room after a series of futile "interviews," I sat down and cried. . . . Meanwhile, I fought a losing battle with an obsessive desire to eat. For several weeks I alternately stuffed and starved myself. Finally I surrendered and ate almost all the time. . . . I ate in a kind of desperation—until the sweat rolled down my face and body. In three months I gained thirty pounds.

Though there may be multiple reasons for the anxiety and depression that afflict many fieldworkers, a principal cause is certainly the disorientation occasioned by lack of meaningful social contacts. The ethnographer has temporarily cut ties with his own society, and it frequently takes considerable time to establish any meaningful human relationships in the community where he is living. For this period he is in "social limbo," as Wax (1971: 19) has expressed it, and anthropologists are no more exempt from the serious consequences of estrangement from society than are others.

Once the fieldworker gains acceptance and friendship in the community, the anxiety and depression tend to decrease and sometimes disappear altogether. The experience of Hortense Powdermaker in Lesu provides an excellent example. She has revealed how she experienced a sudden feeling of panic when left alone (i.e., without other Europeans) on a south Pacific island. She decided she must have been completely mad to have come in the first place and resolved to give up her work entirely and return home. But then various of the natives came to visit her with gifts of food and offers of friendship. Her panic subsided as quickly as it had arisen because, as she says (1966: 59),

I was no longer alone. I had friends. . . . No more thoughts of madness or leaving entered my mind. Several years later I learned that a definition of panic is a state of unrelatedness.

This period of initial stress may last for only two days or for three months, depending on the relative difficulty of establishing rapport. Indeed, some anthropologists report no complications whatever, while others (Kobben 1967: 46; and Briggs 1970) have been under considerable stress throughout the entire experience.

Participant Observation

Even during the period of initial adjustment, fieldworkers take careful notes of everything observed and told to them, even though most perceptions at this stage are likely to be naive and uninformed. Nevertheless, it is important to record as much as possible in this period because it is then that the distinctiveness of certain customs and behavior strike the fieldworker with greatest force. Also, since fieldwork procedures are best learned by doing them, it is advisable to work out the problems of observation and recording of data as early as possible.

The term that anthropologists use to describe their principal research methodology while in the field is *participant observation*. As the term suggests, the ethnographer aims to participate to some extent in the general life of the community and to observe the society from this internal vantage point. The degree to which anthropologists are able to actually participate in community activities varies widely, depending on the rapport established, the permissiveness of the society, the temperament of the ethnographer, and a number of other factors.

In certain instances, as in the case of Leslie White mentioned above, the ethnographer is not allowed even minimal participation. In other societies it may be possible for the anthropologist to camp, hunt, and fish much as the natives do, and to accompany them wherever they go. But even in the latter case, despite a few rare exceptions, anthropologists do not attempt to take up native life nor are they considered by the people to be "just like them." The notion to the contrary probably derives from the fact that fieldworkers have occasionally been adopted into the tribe and given a place in the kinship system, and some have even been prevailed upon by the people to remain with them forever. But these tokens of friendship and esteem—and they are usually little more than that—do not imply that the fieldworker has become a native any more than an honorary degree from a university signifies that the individual so honored has earned a Ph.D.

In the vast majority of cases the fieldworker not only does not become closely integrated into the society, but remains a conspicuous visitor at best. His presence is constantly encumbered by pencils, notepads, cameras, sunburn, and nagging diarrhea, all of which are reminders to everyone that he is an outsider, and a tenderfoot to boot. Even when an ethnographer studies his own society, and is therefore not set apart in appearance, he is still usually perceived differently. This was brought home to William Whyte in his study of an Italian streetcorner gang, the Nortons, in Boston (1955: 304):

> At first I concentrated upon fitting into Cornerville, but a little later I had to face the question of how far I was to immerse myself in the life of the district. I bumped into that problem one evening as I was walking down the street with the Nortons. Trying to enter into the spirit of the small talk, I cut loose with a string of obscenities and profanity. The walk came to a momentary halt as they all stopped to look at me in surprise. Doc shook his head and said: "Bill, you're not supposed to talk like that. That doesn't sound like you."
>
> I tried to explain that I was only using terms that were common on the street corner. Doc insisted, however, that I was different and that they wanted me to be that way.

Far from being a hindrance, however, the role of marginal observer is a necessary concomitant of successful research. The anthropologist is there to ask incessant questions, to take down life histories, and in certain societies to film rituals and even calculate the crop yield per acre. These are highly unconventional activities from the native viewpoint and they take up a great deal of the fieldworker's time. Yet if he should forego them in the desire to "fit in," or to be thought a proper native, he would abort his true mission— which is to collect meaningful information on the people he studies. The fieldworker must simply accept the fact that his activities set him apart, and that children may laugh at him

and others consider him a strange bird. But the benefits of
the outside observer role are too great to be relinquished.
As Berreman has expressed it (1968: 347):

. . . while some ethnographers pride themselves on having
adopted the way of life of those they have studied and having been accepted into their society, successful research is
most often the result of being viewed and accepted as a
trustworthy, interested and sympathetic outsider. This has
advantages in that an outsider can be naive. He can ask
blunt, embarrassing, trivial or simple-minded questions, he
can do or say the wrong thing, he can repeat his queries
and pursue his interests ad nauseum, he can consort with
people of every status and reputation. Such behavior would
not be tolerated in an insider, yet it may be crucial to the
research. The outsider derives the benefit of an immunity
borne of difference and ignorance.

For many of the same reasons, anthropologists do not
normally assume false identities (i.e., pretend to be something other than ethnographers) in order to gain acceptance
in a community. Once a fieldworker assumes a particular
role, he must accept the obligations and limitations of that
role. If he masquerades as a schoolteacher, for example, he
must live up to the expectations that people have of teachers,
which may mean that the boundaries of appropriate conduct
are rather narrowly drawn. There may be individuals school-
teachers should not be seen with, certain places they should
not go, a specific pattern of interaction followed with parents
of their pupils, and so forth. By assuming such a well defined
identity, the anthropologist is transformed into an "insider,"
with the result that the rules, regulations, and mores of the
society apply to him in a manner that may drastically curtail
his activities. Quite apart from these practical difficulties,
there are in addition serious ethical objections to disguising
one's intentions and thereby gaining ethnographical information under false pretenses. All things considered, it is by
far the best strategy to openly declare oneself an ethnographer (or some equivalent that the people can understand)
from the beginning. This not only redounds to the long-term

benefit of the fieldworker, but also avoids the resentments that can arise from dissembled research.

In my effort to dispel the notion that anthropologists become just like natives, I may have left the reader wondering what participation in the culture actually entails, or indeed, if the term "participant observation" is itself a misnomer. It is not. Fieldworkers do participate in the society in the sense that they live in the community and share many aspects of the life with the people. This includes learning their language, eating their food, listening to their stories, and joining in everyday conversations. But most importantly, this participation also entails learning to function properly within the context of the culture.

When a fieldworker begins work in an unfamiliar society, he generally finds that he does not know how to behave appropriately. He often makes embarrassing blunders and violates rules of etiquette that can cause people to become angry and upset. These rule violations can be seemingly trivial things, such as mistaking the meaning of a gesture or using the left hand to pass food to someone. In certain societies, for example, it is a flagrant breach of decency to ever mention the name of a deceased individual. An anthropologist working among the Yanomamo Indians of Venezuela once uttered the name of a woman who had recently been killed in a raid. The man he was talking to "flew out of his chair, raised his arm to strike me, and shouted: 'You son-of-a-bitch! If you ever say that name again, I'll kill you!' " (Chagnon 1968: 13).

Fortunately, anthropologists are generally treated more indulgently. The errors they commit are either overlooked, cause mild embarrassment, or become a source of amusement, as if they had been performed by an irresponsible child. In fact, many ethnographers have initially been regarded in just this fashion: as helpless children who must be patiently instructed in the rules of decent behavior.

However, if the ethnographer does his job properly he gradually develops some feel for the social context. He learns to address people correctly, to avoid tabooed subjects with certain individuals, to reciprocate in precisely the right amount for favors received, and if unduly imposed upon, to fly into a towering rage just as the natives do in similar circumstances. The time may even come when whole weeks may pass without a serious misstep or blunder, and the surprise or amusement that formerly accompanied his actions turns to approval and even admiration—a sure sign of progress. He may even be rewarded with that ultimate, but jovial, compliment that he is "almost a Japanese now," or "a peasant like us," or "a true Kiowa"—a simple form of flattery that is certain to caress the anthropological soul. This, then, is a part of what is meant by participation: the ethnographer strives to become sufficiently knowledgeable about the culture so that he is capable of behaving in a manner minimally acceptable to its members. Again, this does not mean that he does everything they do, since the ethnographer's purpose is to observe rather than perform. But no matter what the actual circumstances, he is usually thrown into continual face-to-face interaction with the people, and this he strives to accomplish in the best possible form.

The greatest advantages of participant observation derive from the extended period of time spent in the field, as well as from the intimacy that can be developed with certain members of the community. The time factor is significant not only in that it allows ethnographers to assimilate the customary patterns of behavior, but also because it permits them to view the people "with their hair down." This is important because in many societies there are things people do not want outsiders to know, or they try to give them a special impression of what they are. And in every society there are certain rules of behavior that a majority of the people recognize as good and appropriate, and that they believe they should live up to. These may be general ideals about honesty, "a man's word is his bond"; or the people may place a high value on premarital female chastity; or there are stated rules about who "wears the pants" in the family—and hundreds of general notions of this kind. It usually turns out in practice, however, that there is wide variation in the degree to which people actually achieve these ideals of appropriate conduct: some people live up to them remarkably well, others hardly at all.

Nevertheless, when an outside observer comes into the community there is frequently an attempt to convince him that the ideals are very generally, or even universally, practiced. And if the observer does not stay long and comes armed only with a few quick interviews and questionnaires, it may not be difficult to convince him that what people say they do is what they actually do. Contrary evidence can temporarily be swept under the rug. But this is not so easily done if the observer is an anthropologist who remains on the scene for a year or more. It is simply too difficult to maintain a false facade for that length of time. Thus the fieldworker is inevitably witness to examples of behavior that do not conform to the ideal: a woman who has sworn she would never lift a hand against her children suddenly beats one unmercifully directly below the ethnographer's window; and in a community where people declare that alcohol is no problem, the fieldworker eventually identifies fifteen families in which the head of the household is hopelessly drunk most of the time. Participant observation is thus an indispensable tool for penetrating beyond what people say—and often believe—about their own culture.

Informants

Up to this point fieldwork has been presented as if it were a matter of a lone individual observing another society, almost as an ethologist (a specialist on animal behavior) might observe a troop of wild baboons. That is far from the case, however, since anthropologists, unlike ethologists, almost always gain the active collaboration of members of the societies they study. In fact, most of the information collected by anthropologists does not originate in their own empirical observations, but is rather supplied by *informants*, people who agree to collaborate with the fieldworker in his effort to understand their culture. It can even be said that the relationship an anthropologist establishes with informants is the crucial element in fieldwork. Whereas it is perfectly feasible to write a study of a culture without any on-the-spot observation, and has in fact been done many times, it would be difficult to write a comprehensive study of a society without information volunteered by members of that society.

From the moment an ethnographer enters the field situation, he is intent upon building personal relationships. Indeed, so much rides on the ability to successfully establish friendly relations that most ethnographers do not leave the matter to chance. They try to establish some sort of personal ties in the community before beginning work there. This can be accomplished by carrying letters of introduction, or friends might accompany ethnographers to their (the friends') native village, or an anthropological colleague places them in touch with his or her own erstwhile informants, and there are many other possibilities. But relationships created in this way usually serve only as starters, as initial contacts that the fieldworker can build upon to create enduring and fruitful relationships.

The ethnographer's aim is to find individuals who can supply accurate and trustworthy information about those aspects of the culture that he is most interested in. "Trustworthy" is the important word here, since the anthropologist usually knows very little about the culture in the initial stages and it is difficult for him to judge the quality of information provided. The anthropological literature contains many instances in which fieldworkers were given false and deliberately misleading data by unscrupulous informants. The Yanomamo Indians once perpetrated an elaborate hoax that had an ethnographer recording false information for five months before he discovered the deception (Chagnon 1968: 10–12).

To avoid this, the fieldworker tries to establish relationships of friendship and trust with those he is most dependent upon. In many societies this is accomplished by simply making friends. Virtually every ethnographer encounters a few individuals with whom friendly ties are more natural or more easily formed than with others, and these persons become his closest companions. In the ideal situation a bond of loyalty develops over time: the companions show a concern for the ethnographer's welfare, and he reciprocates in any way he can—by giving gifts, payments, rides, or advice, and sometimes a mere show of gratitude is sufficient. The friendship eventually becomes so close that, ideally, it is incompatible with deception. That this frequently does occur is evidenced by the fact that various anthropologists have had their informants "come clean" by admitting past misdeeds. In my own work in a Spanish village a friend made it a point to rectify "careless" information that he had supplied earlier, before our relationship had developed into one of mutual trust. And Liebow tells how his best friend among the black streetcorner men he studied confessed that he had previously lied to him, saying, "I didn't think nothing of it at first but then you and me started going around together and when we started getting real tight, my conscience started whomping me" (Liebow 1967: 249).

There are certain situations, however, in which it may be very difficult to form any ties of intimacy at all. This can be because members of a particular society tend to hold all outsiders at arm's length, or there may exist a wall of hatred between the ethnographer's society and that of the observed; and it may even be that the ethnographer is temperamentally incapable of becoming a trusted friend to anybody. One writer has remarked of Radcliffe-Brown (one of the world's most renowned anthropologists) that, because of his general aloofness, it would be difficult to imagine that he established close personal ties with any of the natives where he worked (Powdermaker 1966: 42). In situations such as these, the matter of informant trust becomes critical. Mutually acceptable forms of reciprocity must be worked out, usually implying that informants are paid or otherwise reimbursed for the time they spend with the ethnographer. He in turn must continually cross-check the information, asking the same questions of different informants to test for general reliability. It should be noted, however, that even in situations in which the informant relationship is based on friendship, the ethnographer must be careful to reciprocate in such fashion that informants do not come to believe that they are being imposed upon or exploited.

The rationale behind the use of informants is a simple one: every individual who has been socialized, and has hence learned the customs, rules, and behavioral norms of the society, possesses a store of knowledge that the fieldworker can profitably tap into, provided, of course, that he can formulate appropriate questions and the individual can supply sensible responses. The latter is an important proviso, since every fieldworker discovers that there is enormous variation in the abilities of different individuals to behave as informants. Some have excellent memories and others poor ones; some pay attention to minute cultural details and are sticklers for accuracy, while others can only converse in facile generalities and half-truths. Then there is also the matter of differential knowledge: certain individuals, due to their age, status, or occupation, have more complete or specialized information on specific cultural topics than do others. A priest may be the best informant on religious questions, women are generally superior to men in discussing child-rearing, and a few elderly men and women may be the last repositories of a waning cultural tradition. Depending on the problem they hope to study, fieldworkers attempt to develop working relationships with those who possess the requisite information.

There is another distinction among potential informants that is worth mentioning: the degree to which individuals are capable of analyzing and reflecting upon their own culture. In almost every society there are certain individuals who spend more time than others contemplating their social surroundings. Persons of this sort are particularly in evidence when anthropologists undertake fieldwork in complex societies. In countries like India, Japan, Brazil, or Spain, one frequently encounters on the local scene native intellectuals or scholar-historians who have spent a lifetime studying various aspects of regional society and history. Such individuals can be of tremendous help as suppliers of information and as guides to the local scene. Here is how Edward Norbeck described Minoru, his best informant in a Japanese fishing village (1970: 252–53):

> As time passed, I became well acquainted with one of the intellectuals of the community, a widow of forty-five years of age. . . . [who had an] uncommonly objective understanding of the whys and wherefores of life on Takashi-

ma. . . . As a member of her society, Minoru was in a real sense marginal, and had a rich measure of the detachment that comes with self-chosen marginality. But she was also a highly respected member of the community who actively participated in community affairs. These attributes added to high intelligence, keen interest in my work, friendliness, and a great store of knowledge of the local culture made Minoru my most valuable informant.

But persons of this kind—who shall be referred to as "analytical" informants—are by no means restricted to complex societies. Even in simple tribal cultures there may be individuals who are capable of standing back and gaining some perspective on their own society. Paul Radin once wrote a book (1927) on the "philosophers" frequently found in preliterate societies, and Douglas Oliver has remarked about the Siuai (a tribal people of Bougainville Island in the South Pacific) that (1955: ix)

Some of them, like Peuru of Mi'kahna, came to see and describe their institutions with clarity and objectivity. Others were too deeply immersed [in the society] for such perspective and served rather as unwitting bearers of the culture's norms and modes.

The vast majority of anthropological informants certainly fall into the "immersed" category, in the sense that they are so much a part of their societies that they are incapable of assuming, even for a moment, the stance of an outside observer. The anthropologist learns from them because their every word, belief, and act manifest the behavior and norms prevalent in that society. Individuals of this kind are indispensable if the anthropologist hopes to come to grips with the meaning that cultural forms have for the members of any society. Indeed, there are certain anthropologists (Spradley and McCurdy 1972: 47–8) who maintain that fieldworkers should *only* utilize immersed informants, and that individuals of an analytical disposition are to be avoided. This, they argue, is because marginal intellectuals are apt to impose their own, atypical constructions on the culture and thus distort it, whereas immersed informants are more likely to present attitudes and beliefs in unadulterated form, free of extraneous concepts and categories. This is strictly a minority view, however, since most anthropologists find that the advantages of utilizing detached and intellectually gifted natives far outweigh the disadvantages, especially when the information they supply is conjoined with that provided by others.

But the possibility of distortion is ever-present when working with informants. All individuals have specific interests and points of view that they communicate to the fieldworker, many of which do not accurately reflect the culture at large. This may be because the individuals themselves are atypical. A paranoiac, for example, might convince the anthropologist that an outwardly peaceful community is really shot through with all manner of crime and violence; and a misogynist could impart a decidedly slanted view of male-female relations. But distortion can also creep in because individuals fill different roles in the social order and they tend to reflect views consistent with their social positions. Even in a small peasant community the divergence of opinion on almost any matter between the Catholic priest, anarchist blacksmith, and village prostitute might be so great as to constitute radically different interpretations of local society. It would be simplistic in the extreme if the anthropologist were merely to adopt one of these perspectives as the "correct" one, since each is likely to be biased in a particular fashion. He will instead view each as part of the multifaceted reality that he must struggle to interpret.

Nothing could be more mistaken, therefore, than to believe that the anthropologist merely sits down with his informants and is "told what the culture is." This would be quite impossible, since all informants—even the most detached and analytical—can only give *their* version of their culture. A priest is disposed to emphasize certain aspects of the society and a prostitute, or a drunk, will emphasize quite different aspects. But it is precisely here that the anthropologist has an advantage: because he is not a member of the local society he can view it with some detachment; no socially conditioned role predisposes him to emphasize one reality at the expense of another. An additional advantage is that he works with many members of the community and gains specialized knowledge and a particular point of view from each. By so doing he hopes to attain a more comprehensive perspective on the culture than is typically available to any single member of that society. In fact, the ultimate goal for every fieldworker should be to develop a point of view that transcends that of any of his informants. As one writer has expressed it (Williams 1967: 28–29):

> At the completion of a general study an anthropologist, having systematically observed and interviewed key persons in a community, should ideally be possessed of more knowledge of the culture than any one person in the group. The observer should come to know the aspects of culture experienced by the hunter and the potter, ritual leaders, village herdsmen, children, the aged, the adolescent, the blind, the crippled, and the alcoholic. The anthropologist must make an effort to know both the widely shared aspects of the culture and those known only to a few persons.

As this comment makes clear, getting data from informants is but an initial step. The more difficult tasks of "putting it all together" and then interpreting the data in meaningful scientific terms are the ongoing responsibilities of the anthropologist, and his alone. And it might be added that these problems of synthesis and interpretation are likely to engage the ethnographer's attention for months, and even years, after the field project is completed.

Recording Information: What the Fieldworker Observes

A considerable portion of every ethnographer's day is devoted to recording information, either on film, taperecorder, or, most commonly, by writing in his notebooks. In fact if the fieldworker is not eating, sleeping, or otherwise engaged in practical activities, he is usually taking down information.

The almost obsessive concern with notetaking begins on the first day of entering the community and normally continues until well after the ethnographer has departed for home.

The question I want to ask here is, how does the field-worker decide what he will record and what to ignore? This is always a problem simply because it is a physical impossibility to write up everything. Nobody can pay equal attention to child rearing practices, kinship, pottery making, medical and botanical lore, woodcarving, dance, cosmology, ritual, and the hundreds of other divisions of the cultural world that are encountered in every ongoing society. It may be possible to note something of interest about each, but to explore any one of these realms in depth would require an independent project. Whole volumes have been devoted to most of these topics as found in particular tribal societies. It must be obvious, then, that the fieldworker is constantly *ignoring* certain things while assiduously recording information about others. What are the criteria by which the selection is made?

The answer relates to what was said near the beginning of this chapter about a "theoretical problem" that each investigator brings to the research situation. As noted, even prior to setting out for the field he has delimited a certain area, or relationship, within the society that is of special interest. It may be the association between child rearing practices and adult personality; or the contribution of food scarcity to aggressiveness; perhaps the analysis of cultural symbols as manifested in dance, or any of a hundred other questions of this kind. But whatever the problem, it automatically restricts the focus of study. Fieldworkers primarily interested in child rearing are not likely to spend a great deal of time investigating canoe-building, crop yields, or shamanistic curing. They concentrate instead on those aspects of the culture that are most likely to shed light on whatever it is that they have resolved to study. Having a problem gives ethnographers the advantages of specialization and economy of effort; they do not have to analyze everything because not everything is relevant.

Possession of a theoretical problem bestows another important benefit: it provides not only some inkling of the nature of the problem, but also ideas about its possible solution. That is, fieldworkers normally formulate certain hypotheses that are based on the theoretical literature, or on what other investigators have found in similar circumstances, regarding what they are likely to find. If they encounter condition X, then they can reasonably expect to find situation Y, and so forth. Certain associations that have been found together in the past are assumed to have some significant relationship. The theory, then, tells them both where to look and what they can expect to find. Of course their expectations need not be confirmed; they may encounter a situation that defies all theoretical logic. This occurs frequently and such situations are valuable since they disprove erroneous notions and may give rise to fresh theoretical insights.

But regardless of what is found in any particular case, the point is that a theoretical perspective enables anthropologists to perceive things that the layman would never take note of. The layman does not know what to look for, or, having found something, how to gauge its relevance. It is analogous to the situation of a biologist who takes her seven-year-old daughter into the laboratory where the mother is engaged in scientific research. The biologist looks through the microscope and "sees" the outcome of an experiment that may have considerable scientific significance. Her untutored daughter then looks through the same microscope but "sees" only splotches of color and light; the image can have none of the significance for her that it has for her mother, since the child lacks the training to permit her to interpret it. It is similar for a tourist, even a very perceptive one, in an unfamiliar society. He may witness the same events that an anthropologist does, and may even be able to record them with some fidelity. It is unlikely, however, that his observations will add up to anything of scientific value. The advantage that the anthropologist has is not that he is more perceptive or more sensitive than the tourist, and he may in fact be neither. It is rather that he has a problem and a theoretical background that enable him to place the discrete events that he observes in a scientifically meaningful framework.

In this effort to describe problem-oriented research, I have perhaps given an impression of greater rigor, or rigidity, than normally exists in practice. It would be incorrect, for example, to imagine that most fieldworkers have from the beginning such a well-defined problem that they bring with them a series of hypotheses to be tested in the field. Some fieldworkers do indeed proceed in this fashion, but they are the exceptions rather than the rule. Anthropological proposals tend to be on the order of general statements of purpose rather than specific designs for research; the ethnographer delimits an area of inquiry and then specifies some of the factors that are expected to have some relevance.

There are various reasons for this lack of precision. In the first place, fieldworkers often know little in advance about the societies they intend to study. This was especially true some decades ago when most anthropologists did research among societies that were poorly known to the outside world. Prior to going there, how could one say anything concrete about a people in the Solomon Islands or in the Amazon Basin who spoke unrecorded languages and had previously only been contacted by missionaries? Even today this continues to be a problem, since in their initial research anthropologists generally embark on studies of societies that they have read about but never previously visited. This means that they cannot be certain of the circumstances they will actually encounter. Many have written elaborate proposals only to find that local realities make the study difficult or impossible to carry out.

The anthropologist Jean Briggs intended to investigate Eskimo shamans (ritual specialists and curers) but discovered upon arrival in the Arctic that the Christianized natives were so ashamed of their pagan past that they would not admit that they had ever entertained such beliefs. The whole topic was taboo, and Briggs' proposal wound up on the scrap heap. While it is certainly unusual to have to discard an entire project, it is not at all uncommon for fieldworkers to discover that aspects of their research problems are impossible to implement: some matters are sensitive, certain procedures are too time-consuming or too costly, or the fieldworker finds that what can be accomplished under primitive field conditions is only a fraction of what he had thought possible in the comfort of his study.

There is in addition the question of relevance. In an unfamiliar society it is difficult to specify in advance what aspects of the culture may be relevant to any particular problem. In our own society pig production, warfare, and the timing of great religious ceremonies have no obvious relationship. Yet an anthropologist (Rappaport 1968) has shown these to be intimately connected aspects of culture in a small society in New Guinea. Unexpected relationships of this kind must be discovered in the ongoing process of fieldwork. They are not obvious to the outside observer and might never come to light if he adhered too closely to a plan of research in which "relevant" variables were specified in advance.

This need for flexibility, then, is the principal reason that anthropological proposals tend to be general rather than specific. Fieldwork is first and foremost a process of discovery. The ethnographer only learns the full ramifications of the problem as he becomes involved in the research. From the very beginning he entertains certain assumptions about the community and makes preliminary interpretations. But during all stages of the field experience there is a constant feedback between hypotheses and data. The more the investigator learns, the more capable he becomes of formulating penetrating questions that elicit new information. This information in turn causes him to modify or reject the hypotheses and interpretations thought plausible in the beginning. Thus the fieldworker is able to continually reformulate the problem as he proceeds (Dean et al. 1967: 277).

Then there is also the matter of serendipity. An incident or chance conversation opens up unexpected areas of inquiry, eventually disclosing realms of culture that had not previously been considered relevant. As the anthropologist follows these various leads, his research often takes directions that could not have been foreseen at the outset. Theoretical flexibility therefore serves important functions: it gives the investigator latitude to explore unfamiliar aspects of the culture, and it permits him to pursue his interests along avenues that open up while the investigation is in progress.

Some Disadvantages of Fieldwork

The previous sections of this chapter have shown that fieldwork is a valuable and even indispensable means by which
anthropologists develop understanding of other societies. This
section qualifies the endorsement somewhat by pointing out
that both in practical terms and as a mode of scientific
description and explanation, fieldwork has certain significant drawbacks. Indeed, if it did not have disadvantages it
would be difficult to explain why sociologists, political scientists, and other academics do not make as much use of
fieldwork as do cultural anthropologists.

The most important practical difficulty is that fieldwork
places great demands on both the time and convenience of
the investigator. Going into the field frequently requires considerable sacrifice; individuals must accept disruption in their
personal and family lives, and they normally exchange the
comforts of their accustomed routines for months of living
under trying and sometimes oppressive circumstances. And
while it is true that fieldwork offers rewards, it is also a
challenging and stressful period for most individuals.

It is also wasteful of time. As anthropologists become
burdened with teaching and other professional responsibilities, it becomes increasingly difficult to allocate the time
for lengthy periods of fieldwork. To require a busy professional to devote a year to traveling with a band of Gypsies
or to living in a Nepalese hamlet is to ask a great deal. It is
due to these reasons that for many anthropologists their first
field project—accomplished while they were still graduate
students—remains the lengthiest and most intensive they
ever undertake. There is in addition the question of how well
time is spent while in the field. There are some periods, such
as the early stages before any genuine rapport has been established, when there may be very little to do. However, when
the work proceeds as it should there is generally more to be
done than the fieldworker has time for. The obligations of
visiting, interviewing, and observing various activities, and
then of writing up the notes at the end of the day, can consume enormous amounts of time. It is not unusual for a
fieldworker to devote fifteen hours a day to these various

tasks for months on end! Fieldwork, like labor-intensive agriculture, produces abundantly, but only at the cost of enormous investment of time and effort.

The purely scientific limitations of fieldwork are also widely recognized. These are, first, that it is relatively *unsystematic*, making the findings difficult to substantiate in rigorous fashion. And second, it is susceptible to various kinds of *observer bias*.

The unsystematic nature of fieldwork stems from the unavoidably haphazard way in which much information is assimilated. Fieldworkers learn certain things about the society at an almost subliminal level. A gesture, a raised eyebrow, a nervous glance from an informant—these cues all "teach" them certain things, yet they may never be recorded in their notebooks. Much of the learning is also highly personal: they pattern their behavior on that of others and are rewarded if they behave properly and sanctioned if they do not. From each of these experiences they gain cultural sophistication, not very differently from the way children absorb the rudiments of their own culture. Ethnographers have, of course, other means of acquiring knowledge that are far more systematic: counting, sampling, interviewing, and carrying out structured observations. Nevertheless, the cumulative weight of *un*systematic learning bulks very large under any circumstances of participant observation.

This is not a weakness in terms of assimilation of knowledge; indeed, one might argue that what fieldworkers learn by personal experience is learned more thoroughly and indelibly than by any other means. It is a definite weakness, however, when anthropologists attempt to demonstrate their knowledge in scientific publications. Personal experiences cannot readily be quantified and rarely lend themselves to statistical treatment. Thus when anthropologists attempt to demonstrate an aspect of behavior learned through personal experience or by casual observation, they must frequently resort to an anecdote or to recounting a particular incident that was witnessed. They may be quite certain that the anecdote typifies a whole range of behavior, but if there is no confirming evidence of its generality, except for the assertion that this is so by the anthropologist, the reader may remain justifiably unconvinced. Of course every fieldworker would like to be able to buttress all personal observations with various independent measures. But this is not always possible, either because there is insufficient time for the observations, or the fieldworker does not consider them important at the time, or the information is hard to come by. The truth is that every ethnographer leaves the field with a great deal of intuitive knowledge and scores of hunches about the society that require additional substantiation before anybody else can be convinced of their validity.

A closely related problem is that of observer bias. Since fieldwork generally consists of one individual living with another people and attempting to describe aspects of their way of life, how can the reader be certain that the descriptions and interpretations are valid? Has the fieldworker observed and recorded the data faithfully? How do we know that he does not have a particular bias that has led him merely to find what he is looking for? And is it not possible for an ethnographer to become heavily dependent upon particular informants who present a distorted image of their own culture?

It must be admitted that these are real possibilities, and it is even quite certain that distortions of this kind have been incorporated into various ethnographies in the past. In one notable example, an anthropologist did a re-study of a community in Mexico that had been investigated years earlier by another anthropologist. The portrayal of the people in the second account was so remarkably different from the first that it led one of the ethnographers to remark that "the two books describe what might almost seem to be two different peoples occupying the same town" (Redfield 1960: 134). In another instance, two anthropologists independently studied the kinship system of a tiny community on a Pacific island and offered conflicting interpretations based on virtually the same census data (Goodenough 1956: 24). Examples of this kind are by no means rare.* One need only look at the

---

*As this book goes to press, a controversy rages over the very different interpretations of Samoan society presented by anthropologists Margaret Mead and Derek Freeman. See D. Freeman, *Margaret Mead and Samoa: The Making and Unmaking of an Anthropological Myth*. Cambridge: Harvard University Press, 1983.

voluminous literature by anthropologists and sociologists on black family and community life in American cities to be convinced that different observers are capable of looking at essentially the same reality and of interpreting it in significantly different ways (see Valentine 1968 for a review of some of this literature).

What are we to make of these facts? Various anthropologists have been sufficiently concerned over the reliability of fieldwork data that they have advocated specialized modes of inquiry by which data collection can be made more rigorous and precise. Many insist that more attention must be paid to quantification and sampling, and that greater care should be taken to describe the specific research operations employed in any investigation (Pelto and Pelto 1978). Others utilize techniques of systematic observation by which fieldworkers observe small groups of people and record, in standardized ways, the various types of behavior displayed. By this means the incidence of specific behavioral forms (aggression, nurturance, dominance, etc.) can be expressed quantitatively, reducing the possibility of careless generalization from one or two examples that the fieldworker has witnessed, but that may be essentially unrepresentative. Still others have advocated a kind of ethnography known as *ethnoscience*, which is an attempt to record the natives' perception of aspects of their own culture by working through native linguistic terms and modes of thought. Proponents of the technique claim that by operating through native categories, and by reducing the chance that fieldworkers will impose their own—or their culture's—implicit meanings on the society, ethnoscience can enhance the reliability of ethnographic reporting. And there are many other specialized methods available (questionnaires, structured interviews, projective tests), all of which systematize data collection and reduce the possibility of observer bias.

In spite of the growing reliance on these more systematic methods, it is unlikely that fieldwork will attain a degree of rigor that even approximates that of laboratory experimentation; nor is it likely to achieve the goal that some set for it of becoming "replicable." (That is, certain anthropologists argue that an important criterion of scientific performance is that the results are repeatable: an investigator who follows the same operations as an earlier researcher should be able to duplicate the earlier conclusions. They therefore argue that any two properly trained fieldworkers who study the same society ought to come up with very similar findings.)

As reasonable as the desire for replicability may seem, there are many reasons why it may not work out in practice. One of them has to do with the enormous complexity of a fieldworker's relationship to the community studied. The rapport and friendship established with certain informants sometimes makes it difficult to work with others. The web of intrigue and hostility bred of village factionalism, jealousy, or class antagonism, frequently binds the fieldworker more closely to one group than another, despite all efforts to remain neutral. The "sampling" of community sentiment is therefore biased by forces beyond the fieldworker's control. Anyone who reads Gerald Berreman's marvellous account (*Behind Many Masks*) of his fieldwork in a Hindu village will be made aware of these possibilities. Berreman shows how the two interpreters he used at different phases of his research affected the kind and quality of information obtained. Low-caste villagers were unwilling to voice the resentments they felt at their treatment by members of the upper castes as long as Berreman utilized a high-caste interpreter. When that interpreter departed and was replaced by a Muslim (a man with no place in the caste system), an entirely different climate of sentiment and opinion emerged. This example is extreme, but the problem is not unusual.

Every fieldworker must carve out a particular social niche within the community, a niche that is rarely precisely what the fieldworker wants but is simply the best that can be managed under the circumstances. Unfortunately, the social relations by which an individual surrounds himself act as subtle filters of the information received and even influence what is observed. If there is any real diversity in the community, this filtering can have considerable impact on the final product. It is less than realistic to imagine that any two fieldworkers would make the same adjustment to any complex community and therefore sample opinion and outlooks in the same way. For example, the peasant community that

I studied in Spain is small, with only a thousand inhabitants, and not terribly complex. Yet I am convinced that there is more than one reality to be discovered there. It is perfectly conceivable that another anthropologist—say a woman working mainly with female informants—might uncover aspects of the community that are unknown to me and that would even contradict notions that my work has fostered.

Another important reason why two accounts of the same society might not agree is that different researchers often approach the study from different theoretical angles. The variance, for example, between the way that functionalists and Marxian scholars interpret a single society can be very great indeed. The functionalist, predisposed to determine the various functions of social institutions, tends to focus on the cohesive elements in society, stressing the harmonious adjustment of parts, social solidarity, and the like. The Marxian, on the other hand, with a theory that emphasizes the elements of contradiction and conflict in modern society, tends to find evidence of coercion, exploitation, and class antagonism. And since elements of both cohesion and divisiveness are characteristic of every known society, it is perfectly legitimate for a researcher to concentrate on one of these elements at the expense of the other, the choice being determined by what he or she endeavors to explain. The resulting portrait will necessarily differ from one that is produced by a researcher who begins with different assumptions and looks in different directions.

None of the foregoing remarks about observer bias and lack of scientific rigor discredit the value of fieldwork. Virtually all cultural anthropologists believe that participant observation is unsurpassed as a means of attaining sympathetic understanding of other societies. Questionnaires, opinion surveys, and scheduled interviews yield more systematic and codifiable data, but they can never achieve the depth and quality of information attainable by a sensitive investigator who accommodates himself to another way of life in order to understand it. The wonderfully rich body of knowledge that has accumulated on almost all living societies in the last half-century could not have been collected except through firsthand fieldwork.

Finally, let us return to the matter alluded to at the beginning of this chapter: the impact of fieldwork on the anthropologist. There are probably very few members of the discipline who would not be willing to affirm that their field experiences have greatly enriched their lives personally as well as professionally. Anthropologists tend to learn a great deal about themselves while they are in the field, and it has been remarked that fieldwork is as much like rebirth as any adult experience can be (Richardson 1970: xi). They also learn a great deal from the societies they study. Here is what one anthropologist believes he has gained from his many years of fieldwork in Japan (Norbeck 1970: 265–66):

> And now I shall be wholly subjective in saying how I think my experiences in Japan have affected my views of man and the universe. My visits to Japan have made me . . . see with greater clarity that there are many ways of doing things and that no single set of ways is necessarily always superior to other ways. . . . I believe that my Japanese experiences have never been personally harmful and that they have brought me important benefits. The Japanese appreciation of aesthetics, for example, is both richer and more refined than that of my fellows in the United States. My own appreciation of aesthetics has been enlarged, refined, and made more rewarding as a result of my experiences in Japan. . . . I have, of course, seen ugly emotions among the Japanese—anger, greed, selfishness, and terrible jealousy. But I have also seen truly remarkable—and, I am sure, self-rewarding—denial of the self for the benefit of others. I have seen, too, the remarkable strength and importance of the value placed in Japan upon the control of all emotions that might be disturbing to others, a value that is at the same time a quest for a feeling of harmony with other human beings and the entire universe. I think that I have learned something about patience and something about the obligations and rewards of association with one's fellow men. I think also that I have thereby gained some measure of inner peace. If these ideas are illusions, they seem none the less valuable.

Suggested Readings

Berreman, Gerald, *Behind Many Masks: Ethnography and Impression Management in a Himalayan Village*. Ithaca, N.Y.: Society for Applied Anthropology, Monograph No. 4, 1962.

Berreman gives some insight into the complexity of fieldwork in a highly stratified community in India. The anthropologist must penetrate beyond the cultural facade that is displayed for outsiders. To do so requires patience, skill, and the arts of impression management.

Bowen, Elenore S., *Return to Laughter*. New York: Doubleday, 1954.

This is a fictionalized account of fieldwork by a professional anthropologist among a people of West Africa. No anthropologist who reads it, however, can consider it mere fiction. These are very real, and frequently humorous, accounts of what it is like to do fieldwork.

Geertz, Clifford, Thick Description, in Clifford Geertz, *The Interpretation of Cultures*. New York: Basic Books, 1973.

An engaging essay that reveals some of the complexity involved in ethnographic description and interpretation. Geertz gives short shrift to the view that anthropology is an experimental science in search of lawful regularities. Rather, he argues, it is an interpretative science in search of meaning.

Malinowski, Bronislaw, Introduction, in *Argonauts of the Western Pacific*. New York: Dutton, 1922.

Malinowski offered this prescription for fieldwork more than fifty years ago. Though written in an antiquated style and terminology, much of the advice is valid today. Notice particularly the three kinds of data anthropologists are advised to collect; and the ultimate aim of fieldwork, "to realize [the native's] vision of his world."

Pelto, Pertti J., and Gretel H. Pelto, *Anthropological Research: The Structure of Inquiry*. 2nd ed., Cambridge: Cambridge University Press, 1978.

The authors are concerned with what they consider the low level of methodological rigor in anthropological research. They believe that if anthropologists can be made to quantify, sample properly, specify variables, and generally "be more scientific," anthropology will make strides forward. Compare this message with the very different one implicit in Clifford Geertz's "Thick Description."

Powdermaker, Hortense, *Stranger and Friend: The Way of an Anthropologist*. New York: W.W. Norton, 1966.

A charming and lively anthropological autobiography. We learn something of Powdermaker's early life and the circumstances that led her into anthropology. She then describes how she conducted fieldwork in four different societies: among Melanesians of the South Pacific; in a segregated town in Mississippi in the 1930s; in the culture of Hollywood's filmland; and finally in Africa. An excellent book.

Chapter 3

The Meaning of Culture

The previous chapter described how cultural anthropologists go about their investigations; this chapter, and succeeding ones, will concentrate on the question of what it is that they try to explain. This might appear to be a tall order, since there is extraordinary diversity in the interests and outlooks of different anthropologists. One might concentrate on the symbolic meaning of art motifs, another measure the level of protein in the diet of some remote tribe, another analyze the network of social relationships in an African town, and the list can be indefinitely extended. In fact, if it concerns an activity in which various human beings are regularly engaged, it is likely that some anthropologist has studied it, or will do so in the future. This diversity of subject matter often makes it difficult for outsiders to grasp what the "core" of the discipline is, and they may even wonder if there is any central focus at all.

There is a central focus, though it is admittedly a very broad one. Cultural anthropologists like to say that they concentrate on human beings as social and cultural animals, and that they study the various patterns of behavior, customs, and beliefs that humans acquire as members of society. While this delineation of subject matter casts a large net, it also excludes a great deal. Anthropologists are generally not interested in purely individual action or in behavior that can be termed idiosyncratic, but rather in how the behavior of individuals is influenced by the social and cultural milieu.

Culture and Human Life

One of the outstanding characteristics of human behavior, and one that contrasts sharply with that of all other animals, is the degree to which humans live in a world of symbols and conventional understandings that anthropologists term *culture*. I will define culture here as the body of learned beliefs, traditions, and guides for behavior that are shared among members of any human society. The key word is *learned*. The customary behavior that distinguishes one human society from another is behavior that the members have acquired by observation, by imitation, or by instruction at the hands of other members of that group.

The process begins at birth, as infants are molded to conform to the standards of the family and society into which they are born. Babies may be strapped to a cradle board, allowed to crawl, toilet trained early or late, and taught to speak English, Russian, Arunta, or Navajo, depending on the customs of that particular society. Obviously, children have virtually no say in the matter: if they are taught to speak Japanese, to eat with chopsticks, to sleep on mats on the floor, and to bow as a sign of greeting, they will accept these practices as a matter of course. Moreover, they are likely to conform to them for the rest of their lives.

The child is also heir to a tradition that has been transmitted socially for countless generations. The hunting and survival lore that an Eskimo father teaches his son is not knowledge that the father has himself discovered or invented (though a tiny fraction of it may be), but rather a body of techniques and practices acquired from many previous generations. The techniques for building a kayak (seal skin boat) or an igloo, or for making a ball and socket joint for a harpoon, are cultural practices that have been developed and refined by thousands of minds in the past—in much the same fashion as modern chemistry or trigonometry are the cumulative products of generations of scientists and mathematicians. The same applies to language, the concepts of time and space, and the mores and etiquette that the child acquires early in life. They are all products of a cultural heritage for which the individual becomes a temporary receptacle, ready in turn to pass them on, with only slight modifications, to the next generation.

The great sociologist Émile Durkheim was one of the first to recognize the enormous power that human society exercises over every individual. As he expressed it (1895: 6):

> . . . it becomes immediately evident that all education is a continuous effort to impose on the child ways of seeing, feeling, and acting which he could not have arrived at spontaneously. From the very first hours of life, we compel him to eat, drink, and sleep at regular hours; we constrain him to cleanliness, calmness, and obedience; later we exert pressure upon him in order that he may learn proper consideration for others, respect for customs and conventions, the need for work, etc. If, in time, this constraint ceases to be felt, it is because it gradually gives rise to habits and to internal tendencies that render constraint unnecessary.

The constraint that Durkheim refers to is apparent if we observe child rearing practices in any society. Infants do not like to be weaned, to be toilet trained, to wait to be fed, or to be fit into schedules that are designed for the convenience of adults. When these conditions are first imposed they reject them by disobeying, wailing, throwing tantrums, and the like. But the pressure is unremitting: infants are permitted to cry for long periods, left alone, spanked, or otherwise punished for "unruly" behavior. They gradually learn that there is no recourse, that the world is united against them and that they must submit to adult pressure; the wailing and tantrums become less frequent, or cease altogether, as children acquiesce in the imposition of an ever-increasing number of cultural forms. By the time children are two or three years old they are already products of a specific cultural tradition: they speak a particular language, have definite food preferences, have learned stereotyped gestures and salutations, and have begun to classify and categorize parts of the environment in ways that are peculiar to that society. Plastic individuals are thus shaped to a cultural mold.

It is important to emphasize that these practices are not "programmed" in the individual, nor are they even in any sense individual products. In the above statement Durkheim remarks that cultural instruction is an attempt to impose ways of behaving that the child "could not have arrived at spontaneously." What is meant, of course, is that specific cultural practices are not "natural" to the human organism, and that if left alone individuals would not develop them. How would the individual decide to refer to a horse as "horse" rather than as *caballo* or to decide that such-and-such a day is a Thursday rather than a Monday, or to show respect by standing stiffly erect rather than by bowing? None of these concepts or acts are any more natural from a physical or biological standpoint than are others. In fact they are wholly arbitrary, a series of agreed-upon conventions established in a particular cultural tradition.

This is, in fact, one of the outstanding features of human society, this ability to bestow arbitrary meaning on things or acts that the individuals of that society then abide by— or are constrained by—just as if the meanings were a part of the "real" world. This bestowal of meaning is so all-encompassing that we are frequently unaware of it; it extends to our modes of social interaction, to particular sounds, and even to time and space.

For example, a trout or a beaver presumably perceives no difference between one day and the next, except that it may rain on one and the sun shines on another. But in certain human societies one day is a "Sunday" and the next is a "Monday"; and while there are clearly no physical characteristics that regularly distinguish the two, once they have been classified there is a world of difference between them. On a Sunday one may arise late, worship the Lord, mow the lawn, and watch the Dallas Cowboys on television; on a Monday the same person is perhaps awakened by an alarm, goes to the office, anticipates coffee breaks, and battles the traffic home.

A similarly conventional order is imposed on space: humans divide it into inches, meters, furlongs, marathons, and a thousand other purely arbitrary distances and measures. It can even be converted into sacred space, as when enclosed by a church, or become profane when bounded by a discotheque; and any individual who fails to recognize the difference is likely to cause a considerable ruckus.

All human languages are also elaborate systems of symbolic meanings in which particular sounds are made to stand for the things and concepts represented. For adult Americans the words "gladiator," "Watergate," "Gettysburg," "Nazi" conjure up a world of associations that cannot even remotely be communicated to the most intelligent chimpanzee, porpoise, or duck.

In all these respects, therefore, human beings are set apart from all other animals. The enormous plasticity and variety that is manifest in human behavior around the world is attributable to the fact that learning—what individuals are taught —is the basis for most human customs. There is no other animal that displays even approximately the range and variety of behavior as does *homo sapiens*, and the reason, of course, is that animals learn so much less. This statement is true despite the many studies in recent years, particularly of primates in the wild, that have shown these animals capable of considerable imitative learning that can become the basis for alternate practices in different groups.

Among certain monkeys, for example, observers have found that an innovation by one individual, such as washing food in a brook, can be imitated by others until the practice spreads throughout the troop and becomes part of their "customary" behavior. Moreover, the practice may remain entirely foreign to a neighboring troop of monkeys in which the innovation has never taken place. Studies of chimpanzees in their native habitats have demonstrated that they also learn from each other and pass on a considerable variety of skills. They have been observed to fashion simple tools from twigs, branches, or blades of grass and to use them to fish termites (which they eat) from their nests; they use rocks to break open fruits and nuts, and some have been observed to use

leaf sponges for collecting rainwater. All of these tasks depend
on imitation for their transmission; the young animals observe
adults in these activities and try the skills themselves until
they develop proficiency.

These various studies of animal learning have convinced
many anthropologists that the distinction that used to be
made between human and animal behavior, considering the
former to be based on learning and the latter to be based
overwhelmingly in biology, is a generalization that obscures
more than it clarifies. If our definition of culture consists of
learned traditions that are socially, as opposed to biologically, transmitted, then certain animal species can be said to
possess a rudimentary form of culture as well. Another significant development in recent years has been the new interest in sociobiology (the study of the biological basis of social
behavior), from which investigators are discovering that there
are biological correlates to specific features of human behavior that were formerly unsuspected. Both of these developments have tended to upset the culture/biology dichotomy
and have made anthropologists rather more cautious in
specifying the underlying factors that distinguish human from
animal behavior.

Yet such caution may not be necessary. Even if animals
are capable of learning a great deal and of transmitting certain traits to other individuals, the degree to which they do
so certainly pales in significance when compared to the extent
of learning that transpires in any human society. A major
reason for the gross difference is that human learning is
cumulative and that of animals is not. Among humans each
generation adds to the cultural store of knowledge, beliefs,
and techniques. An innovation in one generation is passed
on and reworked until it becomes the basis for another innovation in a subsequent generation. The same is not true of
animals; their learned traits are not cumulative. As Marx
expressed it, animal behavior is "endlessly repetitive": each
generation repeats, within certain limits, the behavior of
previous generations. Thus if it were possible to transport
ourselves back in time 2 million years, we would probably
find chimpanzees using twigs to fish for termites, and primitive men (or hominids) using simple sticks, clubs, and stone

tools. But 2 million years later we find the chimps "endlessly repeating" the same or nearly the same behavior, whereas the sticks, clubs, and stone tools of our primitive men have evolved into nuclear reactors, rocket ships, and electronic brains.

Another means of illustrating this vast difference is by contrasting the degree of human dependence on learned traditions with the relative lack of animal dependence on theirs. If domesticated animals such as puppies, kittens, or goslings are removed from the litter immediately after birth, and provided nourishment, but kept from all contact with their own kind, they tend to develop into fairly normal adult animals. Dogs or cats might not hunt or defend territory as effectively as would be the case if they had been able to observe adult animals engaged in these activities, but there is probably very little else that would not appear typically "doglike" or "catlike" about them.

The matter is more complex if we conduct a similar experiment with monkeys or chimpanzees, since it has been shown that infant monkeys reared in isolation from their mothers tend to develop symptoms of psychological distress: they become asocial, are sexually impotent, and suffer various forms of emotional pathology. But if the same monkeys, still isolated from their mothers, are reared with companions of the same age—that is in infant peer groups—they tend to develop normally (Harlow and Harlow 1962: 146). In other words, the necessary ingredient appears to be social contact in the early stages of development, rather than anything specific that individuals learn from their mothers. Intimate contact with other animals apparently triggers responses that facilitate personal and social development.

Unfortunately for science, no such experiments can be conducted with human beings. We obviously cannot remove infants from adult care, or place them in the sole company of infant peers, merely to discover what will become of them. Nonetheless, it is not difficult to hazard the guess that a child reared in the absence of adult contact would not develop normally; nor would infant peer groups be able to do the job. Human beings must learn highly specific things from members of a previously enculturated generation if they are to become viable members of any society. Infants housed together, but whose biological needs were met, would not even be able to teach each other to walk; they would learn nothing of language, the use of tools, or how to make fire; nor could they learn anything about ethics, art, religion, philosophy, or any of the other characteristics that mark off the distinctive realm of human culture.

There is, in fact, abundant evidence to suggest that infants left in this state would not merely be deficient in learning, in the sense that they would lack specific knowledge, but would become wholly dysfunctional mental defectives. There are a few fairly well attested cases in which infants have been shut away, locked in closets, and raised by uncaring parents; their biological requirements were met but they were provided virtually no instruction, socialization, or meaningful human communication. These children are an awesome spectacle. They have no speech, cannot walk normally, have dulled senses, show little facial expression, and have a mental development far inferior to their chronological age. The following is a newspaper account of one such child discovered in 1973 in Los Angeles, California.

GIRL, 13, CAPTIVE IN OWN
HOME SINCE INFANCY

LOS ANGELES (UPI)—A 70-year-old man and his wife were arrested Monday on suspicion of keeping their 13-year-old daughter imprisoned in their home most of her life.

Susan Wiley is deformed, unable to talk, wears diapers, has retarded muscle development and has the mental capacity of a 12-to-18 month-old infant, a spokesman for the sheriff's office said. . . . Sgt. Bill Culbertson said Susan lived in almost total confinement in her room for the past 13 years and had almost no contact with the outside world. Her plight was discovered by a social worker who visited the home.

Susan was admitted to Children's Hospital, where a spokesman said she had a chance to become a normal teenager. Corrective therapy was expected to take two years. . . . Neighbors told investigators that on occasion they noticed Susan seated on the front porch of her house or in the back yard but they never saw her leave the house. Authorities said her posture is stooped, and she shuffles instead of walking.

Children's Hospital said her abnormalities appeared to be caused by her environment and there seemed to be no medical reason for her retardation.

A similar child, of five years of age, was discovered in Pennsylvania in the 1930s and was observed on various occasions by the sociologist Kingsley Davis (1940: 564– 65). The child was severely retarded when discovered, though she had apparently been normal at birth and until about the age six to ten months, when the period of pronounced parental neglect ensued. Davis concluded, therefore, that the child's motor and mental retardation was due to the absence of social stimuli and communicative symbols during the first few years of her life.

What these and other cases suggest is that the human organism requires a great deal of stimulation and continuous learning—of language and of other symbolic systems—to maintain even normal functioning. Humans, like almost all primates, require social contact; but unlike other primates, they require in addition a more or less continuous input of meaningful symbolic communication if normal mental functions are to be aroused. As Clifford Geertz has written (1973: 68, 49):

> . . . man's nervous system does not merely enable him to acquire culture, it positively demands that he so so if it is going to function at all. . . .
>
> Man without culture would not be . . . instrinsically talented apes who had somehow failed to find themselves. They would be unworkable monstrosities with very few useful instincts, fewer recognizable sentiments, and no intellect; mental basket cases. As our central nervous system—and most particularly its crowning curse and glory, the neocortex—grew up in great part in interaction with culture, it is incapable of directing our behavior or organizing our experience without the guidance provided by systems of significant symbols. . . . Without men, no culture, certainly; but equally, and more significantly, without culture, no men.

These facts clearly indicate that cultural learning is a necessary ingredient in the development of any normal human being. An implication of this viewpoint is that "natural men"— that is, individuals who reveal basic human nature uninflu-

enced by culture—can never be found, since the very process
of becoming human demands the assimilation and use of
cultural knowledge. Only in mental hospitals, in wards that
house the most severely deranged patients, do we encounter
individuals who lack all sense of cultural order and awareness. Yet it is precisely these individuals who we are *least*
disposed to consider exemplary of anything characteristically human.

Cultural Channeling of Behavior

When anthropologists employ the term *culture* in the specific
sense to refer to Eskimo, Cheyenne, Fulani, Japanese, or
any other society, they refer to the shared systems of meaning that serve as principles and as guides for behavior, or as
one anthropologist (Kluckhohn 1949: 21) has expressed it,
as a "blueprint for all of life's activities" in each of these
societies. An individual who has grown up and has been
socialized in one of these traditions can be thought of as
having learned a complex set of rules, norms, and principles
that serve as generalized guides for action. This knowledge
makes it possible for people to interact more or less pre-
dictably with other members of the society; they know what
to expect of each other most of the time.

The importance of predictability, and how it is affected
by rules, can be illustrated if we think for a moment of a
system of automobile traffic. When we drive our cars on city
streets we feel secure only if we can assume that other motorists will observe approximately the same rules as we do: that
they will stop at red lights, slow down at yellow ones, not
wander across double lines, signal before turning, and so
on. Without such regulations, and the expectation that others
will observe them, the system would not be reliable. We
would not dare, for example, to pass through an intersection
at 40 miles per hour if we were not assured that other drivers
will heed the opposing red light. The mutual adherence to
rules, therefore, makes a complex system of traffic possible.

There are certain rare occasions, however, when people
do drive in the absence of rules, and such occasions are
instructive. Many of us have had the experience of driving

into a large shopping center late at night. Since the parking areas are usually deserted at these hours it is tempting to proceed diagonally across the lot directly to one's destination. It can happen, however, that another driver decides to do the same, in the opposite direction, and both motorists are suddenly confronted by headlights coming directly at them. It is a frightening experience. In the absence of discrete lanes or other highway markings, neither driver can predict what the other will do. The wisest choice is to come to a complete stop, or to change course markedly so the other car is given very wide berth. Once back on the street the problem disappears. There, cars speed by us at distances of only a few feet without causing alarm. This is because of the traffic rules that make it possible to anticipate the actions of other motorists. Their actions are channeled, as are ours.

A social system is similar to this. We know in a general way how others in our society will behave because we assume that they acknowledge most of the same rules that we do. We are so accustomed to the rules, in fact, and to the predictability that they afford, that when certain rules are not upheld we feel imperiled.

Take the example of a woman who walks along a city street and suddenly notices that the fellow in front of her is gesticulating and carrying on an animated conversation with himself. The woman may slow her pace to avoid passing the man, or she may even walk to the other side of the street. Her discomfiture is due to the fact that the fellow is not obeying a fundamental rule, i.e., that one should not talk to oneself in public. And if he fails to observe that rule, it makes us wonder if he is constrained by any rules at all. Can he be trusted not to curse, threaten, or lash out? Thus much the same that applies in the traffic example applies here: actions that are not bound to rules are unpredictable, and as such are potentially hazardous.

The real significance of rules, therefore, is that they channel behavior and lend pattern and predictability to social action. In no society do people behave randomly, or even, most of the time, in terms of what might be called individual choice, but rather they behave in accordance with prescribed rules and norms established in their social system. Once we know something about the system of cultural norms in any society, it is not difficult to anticipate much of the conduct that takes place. As one anthropologist has commented (Kluckhohn 1949: 21):

> A good deal of human behavior can be understood and indeed predicted, if we know a people's design for living. . . . Even those of us who pride ourselves on our individualism follow most of the time a pattern not of our own making. We brush our teeth on arising. We put on pants— not a loincloth or a grass skirt. We eat three meals a day— not four or five or two. We sleep in a bed—not in a hammock or on a sheep pelt. I do not have to know the individual and his life history to be able to predict these and countless other regularities, including many in the thinking process, of all Americans who are not incarcerated in jails or hospitals for the insane.

Individuals of a society embrace their cultural norms because they have been habituated to them through their education and upbringing, in the process that anthropologists term *enculturation*. As we have seen, from the moment of birth infants are subjected to a barrage of cultural influences that are designed to make them think, act, and feel like the adult members of that society. Some of these influences are direct and explicit, as when children are taught particular skills, rules of etiquette, or religious beliefs.

But along with this learning there is also another of a far more elusive kind. This is the learning that takes place by means of unconscious imitation, through the subtle transmission of cues from one individual to the next, or from the symbols expressed in myth, art, literature, and ritual. Each individual can be thought of as a receptor of a constant flow of impalpable cultural signals from these various sources, all of which combine to form attitudes, values, and conceptions about the surrounding world. In any particular society these signals tend to be repetitive and to form definite patterns, so that even without conscious awareness the individuals of a community are disposed to think and to act in similar ways. American sexual behavior is an example of this kind of patterned regularity, despite the fact that very little is explicitly taught about it. One writer has remarked (Downs 1975: 47):

> Many Americans were profoundly shocked and many others were just as profoundly relieved to learn from Dr. Kinsey that sexual behavior was generally similar throughout American society. . . . In our own society, until recently, sex was not freely discussed and it is still not clear how one generation conveyed to another the "proper" position for sexual intercourse—and conveyed it so impressively that severe mental and emotional distress can result from deviation.

As with sexual behavior, so it is with hundreds of other aspects of our culture. We learn about them by the transmission of cues so subtle that they operate like the "hidden persuaders" sometimes used in advertising or the subliminal messages that can be beamed over television: the conscious mind may be unaware that a message is being sent, yet the individual can be powerfully motivated by the appeal.

The end result of these various processes of learning is that individuals of a particular society inevitably assimilate a complex cultural code—a kind of mental map of their culture—that serves as a recipe or program for behavior in a large variety of circumstances. This cultural code is very similar to the linguistic codes that guide human speech. When a child learns his native language he unconsciously assimilates a general body of rules for forming meaningful sentences. By reference to these rules, the child is able to generate grammatically correct phrases of discourse that he has never previously encountered. Moreover, the child accomplishes this without being conscious of the rules that he systematically employs. Nor are most adults able to articulate even a fraction of the grammatical principles that guide their speech, though they may use them flawlessly.

The cultural code is very similar in its operation. It is composed of prescriptions, rules, and norms that the actors can bring to bear in appropriate situations. The enculturated individual has a socially appropriate response (a handshake, a bow, a solemn voice, righteous indignation) for almost every occasion. Moreover, he is so habituated to these responses, and performs them so unthinkingly, that they have the appearance of reflex actions rather than of behavior that conforms to specific rules. Indeed, the individual is rarely aware of behaving according to cultural type. When asked why a particular act is performed he is likely to justify it in terms of individual choice: he "felt like" doing it or it was the only "reasonable" response under the circumstances. But in reality, to bow from the waist is no more reasonable a form of greeting than is a handshake, nor is uncontrolled wailing at funerals any more reasonable than to endure them in solemn dignity. Certain societies encourage one kind of behavior and others encourage another. The individuals "feel" like acting in a certain way because their culture has taught them that a particular response is appropriate under certain conditions.

This point of view runs counter to many of the cherished ideals of our own society, particularly those concerning rugged individualism or the value that we place on the independent hero who triumphs over social convention. It is nevertheless a fact, and one that any anthropologist or sociologist will attest to, that the behavior of most individuals most of the time—and including that of persons we consider exceptional—falls within the rather narrow range permitted by their culture. This is true not only in our own society but in every society on earth. And the reason that individuals are not normally aware of this, or that they do not constantly feel the burden of their culture upon them, is because cultural conditioning is so much a part of their existence that it is inseparable from their individual being.

Some of these notions can be illustrated by looking at particular case examples. Many years ago Ruth Bunzel undertook a study of the creative process among Pueblo Indian potters of Arizona and New Mexico. Bunzel interviewed the women as they worked in an attempt to understand how they conceived of the artistic process. Bunzel was struck by the fact that despite the consistent repetition of particular artistic motifs in the designs the women painted, there was a great deal of mental effort and artistic agonizing in the origination of these designs. All of the women claimed to invest a great deal of thought in each pattern; they spoke of sleepless nights and sometimes even of having concepts for designs appear to them in dreams. It was clear, therefore, that each woman thought of her designs as individual creations, as products of her own mind; yet Bunzel pointed out that there were obviously other factors at work (Bunzel 1929: 53):

A woman in all sincerity reproduces a familiar type of ornament, believing it to be something derived from her own consciousness. The decorative content and treatment are long since familiar to the ethnologist; he can analyze the whole pattern into definite well known motives which regularly appear together. . . . An analysis of the material with the potter is illuminating. She is puzzled and somewhat chagrinned to have it pointed out that she has used three designs on the jar, although she has frequently expressed a decided preference for four designs. She can offer but one explanation: "We always use three when we make this design." They always *do* use three in this particular design, but of this fact, so striking to the ethnologist, she has never before thought. She is also much interested to have pointed out to her that the particular rim design chosen is invariably used with this body design and one other of similar character, but is never used in association with the very different deer and sunflower design. "Yes, that is right. We always do it that way, but I never thought about it before." As a matter of fact, however much she may rationalize, she has probably never thought about the design, its structure, or its elements, at all. She has experienced it unanalytically as a configuration, just as she has experienced the forms of her vessels.

Here we have a particularly vivid instance of cultural suggestibility. The artistic tradition is so much a part of the consciousness of these women that their creations inevitably assume the logic of that tradition, despite the fact that they are unaware of obeying guidelines or "rules" in the creation of their artifacts. They in fact think of themselves as enjoy-

ing considerable personal autonomy in this regard; yet Bunzel's analysis demonstrates that the element of free expression is far more circumscribed than any of the women imagine.

What is true of the Pueblo Indians is equally characteristic
of our own Western society: ideas, concepts, or acts that we
associate with certain creative individuals can be shown to
owe as much to cultural insinuation as to individual imagination. The anthropologist Alfred Kroeber pointed out years
ago (1917) that many of the great inventions and discoveries
of Western civilization have occurred simultaneously: two
or more individuals hit upon a revolutionary innovation at
virtually the same time. This has occurred with the invention
of calculus; the discoveries of oxygen and the cellular basis
of life; the inventions of the telescope, steamboat, telegraph,
telephone, and photography; the reduction of aluminum; the
discovery of anesthetics; the formulation of the theory of
natural selection in evolution; and the discovery of the principles of genetics—and there are certainly hundreds of other
instances of this kind (Ogburn 1922; and White 1949). Ideas
and inventions that have remained inaccessible to humanity
from time immemorial are suddenly discovered by two or
three individuals at once.

These facts clearly indicate the importance of cultural
suggestibility; once a certain type of knowledge or technology becomes available, it points the way—almost inevitably—to new potentialities. Scientists who operate within the
same tradition of research, or artists who share a particular
art style, are likely to make parallel discoveries or innovations simply because the logic, or unfolding of potential, in
that research tradition, or art style, encourages certain possibilities and discourages others. In his book *The Structure
of Scientific Revolutions*, Thomas Kuhn has shown how scientists, once they operate under a common paradigm (a theoretical model for research), come to share the same set of
assumptions about the world: they begin to think in similar
ways and to investigate a similar range of problems. It is no
wonder, therefore, that they frequently discover many of the
same things, since their thought is channelized in particular
directions by identical models. Most of the time, Kuhn con-

tends, scientists see what they are trained to see, and, what is more, they systematically ignore aspects of nature that fail to conform to prior expectations (see Kuhn 1962, particularly Chapter 10).

Another, but very different, way in which to illustrate the dependence of individuals on their sociocultural milieu is by looking at the enormous number of rules and obligations that guide social interaction in any society, and to which individuals must conform if they are to be approved and accepted by their fellows. Many of these rules are in the nature of etiquette relations. The sociologist Erving Goffman has in a number of publications analyzed various of the obligations that are associated with face-to-face interaction in our own Anglo-American society. He has even argued that social interaction can be likened to theatrical performance because of the extent to which individuals find it necessary to "act" in the sense of projecting idealized images of themselves whenever they come into the presence of other human beings. He points out that individuals do not present their naked or "true" selves to others in social interaction, but rather project better-than-real images that they think others will respect.

This can be illustrated in most basic terms if we take the example, say, of a Robinson Crusoe on an uninhabited island. As long as he lives in solitude he is free to act without inhibition. He can talk to himself, cut wind as violently and frequently as he pleases, stroll about naked, and even smear food on his face and beard without concern. He can, in effect, act just as "naturally" as he pleases. But let another human being (a Man Friday, say) come into his presence and this behavior is abruptly regulated. Our Robinson Crusoe then projects an image of himself as a certain kind of person, with a certain dignity, and definitely as one who maintains control over his bodily impulses. Having a human audience is sufficient to lend his behavior the quality of a "performance."

Goffman's work also makes us aware of the large number of rules that people obey even in the most casual circumstances of their everyday lives. Even the very loose social gatherings that occur in airports, on trains, or on public streets have certain situational proprieties associated with them that are very widely observed. In American public places, for example, people take considerable care not to intrude on the "personal space" of other individuals. Personal space can be defined as the immediate space surrounding every person which is thought to be his "own" and should not be transgressed by others. Americans constantly observe these boundaries by maintaining a respectful distance. If an accidental intrusion (by passing too close, bumping elbows, etc.) occurs, it is typically acknowledged by an apologetic "I'm sorry" or "pardon me." These rules seem so natural that Americans become uncomfortable when they must deal with people who do not share the same spatial definitions. Latin Americans, for example, tend to establish a normal conversational distance that is much closer than the North American custom. Two social scientists describe a typical incident (Hall and White 1960: 9–10):

As soon as a Latin American moves close enough for him to feel comfortable, we [North Americans] feel uncomfortable and edge back. We once observed a conversation between a Latin and a North American which began at one end of a forty-foot hall. At intervals we noticed them again, finally at the other end of the hall. This rather amusing displacement had been accomplished by an almost continual series of small backward steps on the part of the American, trying unconsciously to reach a comfortable talking distance, and an equal closing of the gap by the Latin American as he attempted to reach his accustomed conversational space.

Similar rules are followed regarding the amount of visual attention that we are permitted to allocate to other persons in public arenas. In American society it is customary to accord strangers what Goffman calls "civil inattention." This is the practice of conceding them a civil look or glance, but then quickly withdrawing the attention so that it is clear to the individual that he is not being stared at or being subjected to visual scrutiny. As Goffman writes (1963: 84, 87):

In performing this courtesy the eyes of the looker may pass over the eyes of the other, but no "recognition" is typically allowed. Where the courtesy is performed between two persons passing on the street, civil inattention may take the special form of eying the other up to approximately eight feet . . . and then casting the eyes down as the other passes—a kind of dimming of lights. . . .

Perhaps the clearest illustration both of civil inattention and of the infraction of this ruling occurs when a person takes advantage of another's not looking to look at him, and then finds that the object of his gaze has suddenly turned and caught the illicit looker looking. The individual caught out may then shift his gaze, often with embarrassment and a little shame, or he may carefully act is if he had merely been seen in the moment of observation that is permissible.

Virtually all Americans can recognize their behavior in these examples. Conformity to these rules is so widespread in our society that only small children and mental incompetents ordinarily ignore them. Indeed, as Goffman points out, it is precisely the failure of certain individuals to observe these practices that arouses our suspicion that they are abnormal. A reaction to a person who fails to accord others civil inattention is typically: "Look how that man stares at us. There must be something wrong with him." And mental hospitals are full of patients who disregard the proprieties that preserve the sanctity of personal boundaries (Goffman 1956: 484):

Thus on Ward B [of a mental hospital], male staff members were plagued by such statements as "Why did you cut yourself shaving like that," "Why do you always wear the same pants, I'm getting sick of them," "Look at all the dandruff you've got." If seated by one of the patients, a male staff member might have to edge continuously away so as to keep a seemly safe distance between himself and the patient.

The Cultural Code and Individual Action

The previous illustrations are meant to reinforce the idea, stated earlier, that cultural norms have an enormous influence over the kinds of behavior that will be found in any society. Indeed, the predictability of behavior is partially a result of the fact that individuals share similar cultural conditioning. It is important at this point, however, to interject a note of caution: to say that cultural norms exert a "powerful influence" is not the same as saying that behavior is utterly "determined" by those norms, or to suggest that individuals are robot-like creatures of their culture. If the latter were the case we would expect greater uniformity of behavior than is found. But all societies exhibit diversity: there are in all of them individuals who adhere closely to the rules of proper conduct, just as there are those who defy, evade, or ignore rules that others accept as binding. Conformity as well as deviance are aspects of every known society.

There are many reasons why this is the case. The most obvious is that culture is just one, among many, guides for individual conduct (Freilich 1972: 283). Individuals are subject to various extracultural pressures as well, such as their unique biology or the sway of individual biography and temperament, and even the physical circumstances that members of the same society confront will differ and influence choices they make.

It is not hard to imagine, for example, that hyperactive children will experience greater difficulty fitting into pre-school routines than will normal ones. And a person who is viciously attacked by a dog in childhood may develop a neurosis that conditions lifelong attitudes and behavior toward animals. Physicians and psychologists have collected volumes on biologically and psychologically induced regularities, or irregularities, of this sort. Culture, per se, does not have a great deal to do with them.

There are many explanations for diversity within societies, however, that *are* culturally related. First, not all individuals are socialized in exactly the same manner. Even in very small-scale societies there are variations in what children are taught in different families or in what they learn from their peer groups. Nor are all individuals exposed to identical agents of socialization throughout life. In a tribal society the son of a chief will have different role models and different expectations placed on him than will the son of a poor widow of the same village. And in our own society a young girl who attends parochial schools run by Catholic nuns will be exposed to different influences than will one who attends the coeducational public schools.

An even more important reason for behavioral diversity is that socialization is a very imprecise instrument. What the individual actually absorbs in socialization is a general "program" for behavior, a series of ideal norms and guidelines for action. But how these general principles should apply in any set of concrete circumstances is difficult or impossible to specify. To return to an earlier example, it is of course true that any adult American recognizes the circumstances in which it is socially appropriate to shake hands, and there is a certain moral force behind the custom that accounts for its generality. But the moral force also makes it possible for the individual to use the custom for his own ends. By openly *refusing* to shake hands, a man can deliver a cutting insult to another who has, say, behaved indiscreetly with the first man's wife. Dress codes are another example: certain occasions require that special clothing be worn. But there may be circumstances in which individuals will want to dress *in*appropriately as a means of expressing contempt for the occasion, as when defendants are brought to trial in cases that they believe are flagrantly unjust. As these examples suggest, individuals always have a degree of leeway in the application of cultural principles to specific circumstances. They must interpret particular situations and choose among available alternatives.

It is also worth noting that social rules rarely receive total compliance. This is especially the case when the norms impose some degree of sacrifice on the part of individuals. In such cases there is always a tendency to evade or stretch the meaning of the rules or to otherwise minimize their consequences. We see this in our own society in regard to traffic laws, income tax obligations, and norms that discourage premarital sex. Almost nobody complies entirely, and it is the same in virtually every society. It is for this reason that anthropologists make a careful distinction between "ideal" behavior (behavior that is socially prescribed) and "real" behavior (what people actually do). This deviance between theory and practice was a theme consistently reiterated in the work of anthropologist Bronislaw Malinowski in the early part of this century. On the basis of his studies of the Trobriand Islanders of the South Pacific, he criticized the anthropologists of his day who had suggested that primitives were slaves to custom or that they were passively obedient to social norms (1926: 30):

> Whenever the native can evade his obligations without the loss of prestige, or without the prospective loss of gain, he does so, exactly as a civilized business man would do . . . . Take the real savage, keen on evading his duties, swaggering and boastful when he has fulfilled them, and compare him with the anthropologist's dummy who slavishly follows custom and automatically obeys every regulation. There is not the remotest resemblance between the teachings of anthropology on this subject and the reality of native life.

This chapter has defined the anthropological meaning of culture and illustrated the pervasive influence that cultural norms exert in channeling and directing behavior in any human society. But in doing so, a far-fetched cultural determinism that would deny individual autonomy or motivations of self-interest has been avoided. Most of us, most of the time, do in fact behave like Bunzel's Pueblo potters: we act according to cultural guidelines even when we are least aware of doing so. But we are also capable, in certain circumstances, of acting like a Malinowskian native: we seek to manipulate the system for selfish ends, and by so doing we achieve some freedom from its control.

Suggested Readings

Geertz, Clifford, The Impact of the Concept of Culture on the Concept of Man, in Clifford Geertz, *The Interpretation of Cultures*. New York: Basic Books, 1973.

A thoughtful essay on the meaning of culture and its importance for understanding the nature of human life. Geertz argues that without exposure to systems of significant symbols, infants cannot be transformed into human beings.

Goffman, Erving, *The Presentation of Self in Everyday Life*. New York: Doubleday, 1959.

Goffman writes about our own Anglo-American society and heightens our awareness of the vast number of rules that are obeyed, often unconsciously, in everyday life. Here he describes how we project better-than-real images of our selves to others.

Goodenough, Ward H., *Culture, Language, and Society*. 2nd ed., Menlo Park, Calif.: Benjamin/Cummings, 1981.

The view of culture as "guides for behavior" that is developed in this chapter owes much to Goodenough. This little book provides an excellent discussion of the relationship between culture and the individual.

Kluckhohn, Clyde, Queer Customs, in Clyde Kluckhohn, *Mirror for Man*. New York: Premier Books, 1949.

This treatment of the culture concept is still one of the best available, despite the fact that it was written over thirty years ago.

White, Leslie A., The Symbol: The Origin and Basis of Human Behavior, in Leslie A. White, *The Science of Culture: A Study of Man and Civilization*. New York: Grove Press, 1949.

When scholars try to assess the crucial abilities that separate humans from all other animals, they inevitably focus on the human capacity for construction and use of symbols. Here Leslie White argues the case persuasively.

Chapter 4

The Question of Utility

Whenever an anthropologist studies another culture, he attempts in some fashion to "make sense" out of the customs and practices observed; this is to say that he tries to place the behavior of the people in a frame of reference that renders their actions intelligible or meaningful. He must not only accomplish this for himself, in the sense of achieving personal understanding, but also must translate the behavior into terms that are in some manner comprehensible to an audience back home.

This task of translation can be complicated since many of the customs that anthropologists describe strike outsiders as senseless and bizarre—like the practice of cutting fingers from the hands of Dani women mentioned in the first chapter. Nevertheless, it is the anthropologist's intention to place even such customs as these in an intelligible frame. Other writers might refer to foreign peoples as "mysterious," "inscrutable," "enigmatic," or "weird"; but anthropologists rarely permit themselves the luxury of such terms, since to do so is tantamount to an admission of failure in the anthropological enterprise. It is the anthropologist's task precisely to *de*mystify: to show how customs make sense, that they are reasonable or logical once we understand the set of cultural meanings in which they are embedded. "Understanding a people's culture," as one author has expressed it, "exposes their normalness without reducing their particularity. . . . It renders them accessible: setting them in the frame of their own banalities, it dissolves their opacity" (Geertz 1973: 14).

The Issue of Cultural Utility

Almost from the beginning of anthropology as a scientific discipline there have been those who have attempted to make sense out of cultural forms by demonstrating that there is some practical utility to the customs described. Those who adopt this position argue that customs or institutions are not simply random practices, but rather they respond to genuine needs in the life of that society. This is most frequently expressed by saying that cultural practices have "functions" or, alternatively, that they are part of a society's "adaptation" to its environmental circumstances. The following statement, taken from a textbook, represents this point of view (Harris 1971: 141):

> . . . culture is man's primary mode of achieving reproductive success. Hence particular sociocultural systems are arrangements of patterned behavior, thought, and feeling that contribute to the survival and reproduction of particular social groups. Traits contributing to the maintenance of a system may be said to have a *positive function* with respect to that system. Viable systems may be regarded as consisting largely of positive-functioned traits, since the contrary assumption would lead us to expect the system's extinction.

And another (Ember and Ember 1981: 32):

> . . . customs which diminish the survival chances of a society are not likely to persist. . . . Those customs of a society that enhance survival chances are *adaptive* and are likely to persist. Hence we assume that, if a society has

survived to be described in the annals of anthropology, much if not most of its cultural repertoire is adaptive, or was at one time.

The suggestion of both of these quotations is that culture is to a large extent utilitarian, and that the task of interpreting a custom consists of searching for the function the practice serves within the society or of deciphering the role it plays in adjusting the society to its environment. From the first perspective even witchcraft beliefs can be shown to serve important purposes. In the tribal societies where witch beliefs are most prevalent, there are frequently no codified laws, police, courts, or other agents of institutionalized authority. The problem therefore arises of how potential deviants can be made to observe the norms of appropriate conduct. Belief in witchcraft can serve the ends of social control in various ways. Since the individuals most commonly accused of practicing witchcraft—a most dangerous accusation—are those who stand out as "different" from others and also are those who tend to make numerous enemies, there is pressure on the individual to conform to general rules of conduct and to avoid giving offense to many people. Also, in a society in which it is believed that anyone may secretly practice witchcraft, an offended individual might be capable of exacting revenge in the most dastardly way. It is not difficult to see, therefore, how belief in witchcraft, by restraining deviance, can be interpreted as fulfilling definite social functions, and it is this aspect that has been emphasized by those who interpret customs in utilitarian terms.

Anthropologists are by no means in agreement, however, that all or even most cultural practices can be shown to have functional utility. There is also a long tradition in the discipline of those who maintain that many customs do not respond to a utilitarian calculus, and that certain practices are maintained not because they are the best or the most efficient ones, but simply because their users become so attached to them that alternatives are never considered. This was the point of view taken by the anthropologist Franz Boas and by many of his followers. Ruth Benedict, for example, delighted in describing how customs or culture traits could be elaborated to obsessive extremes in any particular society, far beyond social utility. She once remarked (Benedict in Calverton 1931: 813):

> . . . anthropologists have made up their minds. . . .
> [that] it is usually beside the point to argue, from its im-
> portant place in behavior, the social usefulness of a cus-
> tom. Man can get by with a mammoth load of useless lum-
> ber, and he has a passion for extremes. . . . After all, man
> has a fairly wide margin of safety, and he will not be
> forced to the wall even with a pitiful handicap. Our own
> civilization carries its burden of warfare, of the dissatisfac-
> tion and frustration of wage-earners, of the overdevelop-
> ment of acquisitiveness. It will continue to bear them.

What Benedict says, then, is that it is futile to explain customs in terms of utility, simply because any culture may incorporate a large number of inefficient and disadvantageous customs. Much the same point has been argued by the various critics of "functionalist" studies in anthropology. The authors of an article entitled "The Dismal Science of Functionalism" write (Gregg and Williams 1948: 602):

> Surely most students of society agree that the persistence of
> habit and tradition is such that there is no guarantee that
> only positive and "neutral" cultural elements survive, or
> that "if an element actively interferes with efficiency" it
> will be eliminated. . . . History, as Veblen knew, records
> numerous instances of the triumph of imbecile institutions
> over life and culture.

There is a wide difference, therefore, between anthropologists who believe that cultures consist mainly of "positive-functioned" traits, and those who speak of "imbecile institutions" and of customs elaborated to "fantastic extremes."

Which side of the controversy is correct? Unfortunately, this is one of those issues in social science that is not resolvable by declaring one point of view unequivocally superior to the other. Like the "nature-nurture" polemics in psychology, or the debate over the role of ideas versus material forces in history, there does not appear to be a definitive solution. Each side is capable of marshalling certain kinds of evidence that support its own position and that appear to belie that of its opponents.

A perpetual argument of this kind is possible simply because human cultures everywhere betray two quite opposed tendencies. There is, first of all, in every culture a dynamic element, one of practical adjustment to circumstances. Members of all societies must face the problems of obtaining food, shelter, and livelihood from their environments. They must possess an adequate technology and be able to form the necessary economic and institutional arrangements that provide for the survival and continuity of the population. What in the last chapter we called culture—the norms, knowledge, and beliefs that serve as guidelines for behavior—must always be minimally appropriate to a particular environmental context. Eskimo culture must, for example, provide the knowledge and techniques necessary for survival in an arctic setting, or the population could not continue. This is necessarily a dynamic element simply because the circumstances to which a society must adjust are never entirely stable. The environment undergoes change, new technology arises, the population increases, or whole groups migrate to new areas. Whatever the specific sources of change, individuals discover that their acquired culture is never fully appropriate in the altered circumstances; practices that were adequate for the parental generation are less appropriate for their offspring. There is a perpetual need, therefore, for innovative behavior as individuals are forced to modify the acquired culture to cope with changing circumstances. This, then, is what is commonly referred to as the adaptive dimension of human culture.

There is a second dimension, however, that is virtually the opposite of the adaptive mode. This is the tendency, also found everywhere, to conserve and defend established cultural practices. In no society does change occur entirely without opposition, and it is fair to say that resistance to change is just as ubiquitous a feature of human culture as is change itself. One important reason for this is that in every society norms and customs are imbued with emotional significance. Once a pattern of behavior becomes established it takes on a quality of appropriateness: it ceases to be a neutral act and becomes a "proper" one. Moreover, this investiture of feeling is nonrational in the sense that the custom is adhered to not because it is reasonable but because it is customary. People get used to performing an act in a specific way and it appears "natural" to them; hence deviations appear *un*natural and therefore wrong.

The example of table manners is illustrative. If we are forced to eat with individuals for whom it is customary to slurp, belch, or spit during the meal we experience discomfort, just as a Moslem might be revolted by our use of the left hand to convey food to the mouth. The feelings of disgust arise, not because there is anything intrinsically wrong with the foreign customs, but simply because they infract our own norms of appropriate conduct.

This emotional attachment to customs is more pronounced in certain areas of culture than in others. The sphere of religious belief provides examples of fantastic adherence to traditional behavior. In seventeenth century Russia the attempt to institute even minor religious reforms—the use of three fingers instead of two in making the sign of the cross, changing the spelling of the name Jesus, and insisting that the exclamation *alleluia* should be repeated two rather than three times—produced a fanatical resistance in which as many as 20,000 dissenters burned themselves alive in barns and churches rather than accept the innovations (Florinsky 1969: 152–54). While this example is extreme, it is not different in kind from the unthinking adherence to custom that is encountered in almost every realm of cultural behavior.

It should be emphasized that the emotional resistance to change is only one source of cultural conservatism, and that there are others. Before dealing with this general topic, however, let us return to the perspective of cultural adaptation, both to elucidate the approach and to show why many anthropologists find it one of the most appealing keys to the understanding of human behavior.

Culture as Adaptation

Many years ago Ruth Benedict wrote a famous book, *Patterns of Culture*, in which she attempted to illustrate the enormous diversity and range that is to be found among human cultures. She was particularly intrigued by the fact that the dominant concerns, or foci, of cultural attention are so varied from one culture to the next. In one society an enormous amount of energy is invested in a particular line of behavior, whereas a neighboring people might ignore that whole pattern of conduct (1934: 35):

> One culture hardly recognizes monetary values; another has made them fundamental in every field of behavior. In one society technology is unbelievably slighted even in those aspects of life which seem necessary to ensure survival; in another, equally simple, technological achievements are complex and fitted with admirable nicety to the situation. One builds an enormous cultural superstructure upon adolescence, one upon death, one upon after-life.

Benedict followed these observations by drawing a famous contrast between the Pueblo Indians of New Mexico and the Indians of the Great Plains. Borrowing terms that had earlier been employed in the analysis of Greek drama, she said the dominant tendency in Pueblo culture could be characterized as "Apollonian," whereas the neighboring Plains Indians were "Dionysian." In describing the Pueblos as Apollonian, she meant that there was a marked distrust of individualism in the culture, and that proper behavior in all spheres of life required the submergence of the individual within the group. Thus the ideal Zuni or Hopi Indian does not stand out from his society; he is not an innovator or a charismatic figure, but rather one who conforms to tradition and keeps to the middle of the road. The individual avoids ecstatic religious experience, the use of drugs or self-torture, or anything that would take him beyond the bounds of moderation.

In marked contrast to the Apollonian Pueblos are the Dionysian Indians of the Plains. Benedict used the latter term to describe the various forms of immoderate behavior that were sanctioned in Plains culture and the relatively free hand given to individual initiative. Where the Pueblos valued restraint and moderation, the Plains Indians craved all forms of violent experience. Benedict describes how Plains warriors sought visions as a means of attaining supernatural power (1934: 81):

> On the western plains men sought these visions with hideous tortures. They cut strips from the skin of their arms, they struck off fingers, they swung themselves from tall poles by straps inserted under the muscles of their shoulders. They went without food and water for extreme periods. They sought in every way to achieve an order of experience set apart from daily living.

Moreover, men usually went alone on the vision quest, since seeking power was a matter left to individual ambition.

Plains institutions fostered self-reliance in other ways as well. Their warfare could almost be described as a system of free enterprise. Any man who wanted to achieve status and honor could get together a war party to raid the camps of their enemies; and a successful male career depended on the number of valorous deeds accomplished in war. These were acts of individual glory such as touching an enemy's body in battle, stealing horses from an adversary camp, or wrenching a weapon from a foe in hand-to-hand combat. The successful warrior was thereafter encouraged to boast publicly of these exploits, and if he was to attain chiefly rank or even to marry well, he had to accumulate many of these honors. Thus at every point the individual male was disposed to parade his successes and to outdo his fellows in competition for prestige.

This, in essence, is the contrast that Benedict drew between the two cultures: the one emphasized conformity and moderation, the other extravagance and individual display. In the years since Benedict made this characterization, various critics have pointed up inaccuracies in her account and others have considered that many of the generalizations were far too sweeping. Nevertheless, it is also widely agreed that there was more than a germ of truth in the description and that she depicted a genuine difference in cultural orientation.

What is most surprising about Benedict's account, however—or at least surprising from the point of view of contemporary anthropology—is that she made almost no attempt to *explain* the contrast: that is, *why* the Pueblos were Apollonian and the Plains Indians Dionysian. This was apparently a matter of little importance to Benedict, since she did not think it was possible to specify why particular cultures developed as they did. She believed that once a culture evolved certain dominant values, such as self-effacement among the Pueblos, all the institutions of that society and all its future development were somehow molded in accordance with those primary values.

To most present-day anthropologists this has an almost mystical ring. Virtually none would go as far as Benedict in the belief that values in themselves exert such determining influence on cultural development; nor would most agree with her assumption that societies evolve in virtual independence of their environmental contexts. Today, if one were to ask why such a contrast existed between the Pueblo and Plains Indians, the matter would be thought of as largely a problem in cultural adaptation. As mentioned earlier, it is widely assumed that there must be some degree of fit between the productive-economic enterprises of any society and the customs, attitudes, and values that prevail among the population. If we therefore analyze the subsistence requirements of a particular society, we can generally understand something about its cultural norms as well. The case at hand can be used to illustrate this relationship.

Since the Pueblos were agriculturists who depended on cultivated crops, and the Plains Indians were nomadic hunters, we might expect important differences to stem from this contrast. The successful cultivation of crops would seem to demand different skills, and perhaps even different personality characteristics, than would buffalo hunting and predatory warfare. Anthropologists have frequently pointed out that agricultural societies tend to place greater stress on various forms of disciplined behavior than do hunting and gathering societies. In a well-known study (Barry, Child, and Bacon 1959) that compared child training practices in various agricultural groups with those that prevail in hunting and gathering societies, it was found that the former tended to place a much higher premium on obedience, responsibility, and conformity to social rules. The authors reasoned that since survival in agricultural societies depends on the successful planting, harvest, and storage of produce, members must accustom themselves to frequent and monotonous labor, and they must respond to the recurrent agricultural tasks whenever the situation demands. Any delay in attending a harvest could mean loss of the entire crop. As the authors write (1959: 52):

> [In agricultural societies] carelessness in performance of routine duties leads to a threat of hunger, not for the day of carelessness itself but for many months to come. Individual initiative in attempts to improve techniques may be feared because no one can tell immediately whether the changes will lead to a greater harvest or to disastrous failure. Under these conditions, there might well be a premium on obedience to the older and wiser, and on responsibility in faithful performance of routine laid down by custom for one's economic role.

Similar reasoning, incidentally, could help account for the oft-noted conservatism of peasant populations the world over.

In hunting and gathering societies, on the other hand, where food supply depends on daily foraging, there is a more immediate relationship between the effort and skill expended on any one day and the resulting success. Individual hunters are often encouraged to develop personal abilities and initiative. Here is how one writer (Miller 1955: 286) describes the skills required in the hunting economy of the Fox Indians:

> Success in hunting expeditions required that individuals spend long periods in complete solitude, traverse many miles of difficult wilderness, undergo extended hardships and deprivation, and exercise considerable initiative and ingenuity to contend with animal quarry. . . . Such a sub-

sistence system put a premium on qualities of individual
initiative, self-dependence, forbearance, and the capacity to
size up a situation and act on one's estimate. . . . Fox
child-rearing practices produced and encouraged such
qualities.

Other reasons that innovative and experimental behavior is
not discouraged among hunters is that lack of success on
one day can be made up the next, and furthermore, the food
supply of the entire group is rarely at stake.

If this reasoning is correct, and if it explains some of the
broad differences between these two types of societies, then
much of the contrast that Benedict described between Apollonian Pueblos and Dionysian Plains Indians can be understood as the social consequences of fundamentally different
ecological adaptations. Of course, not all of the variation is
explained, nor should we expect it to be. But this seems at
least a reasonable way to approach the problem, and it is
certainly better than arguing that the contrast is merely
attributable to different values.

The above example points up one of the main characteristics of the adaptational approach, namely, that it directs
attention to the way that societies adjust to, or cope with,
their environing circumstances. Those who utilize the
approach argue, therefore, that if we hope to come to terms
with the causes or underlying determinants of cultural phenomena, we must attend to the crucial relationship between
cultures and their environments. The significance of this
relationship has been demonstrated time and again by eco-
logically oriented anthropologists who have analyzed situations of social change, particularly ones in which societies
are forced to adjust to new habitats or to radically altered
external circumstances. Under such conditions it is not unusual to find that a fundamental restructuring of the social
system takes place as the group begins to cope successfully
with the new circumstances. One of the classic examples of
such a transformation is that which occurred on the Great
Plains of North America as a result of the introduction of
the horse from Europe in the seventeenth century A.D. Some

of the consequences of that historic event present an impressive example of cultural adaptation, and the account of it here has the added advantage of permitting elaboration of features of Plains Indian societies that were only hinted at in the preceding account.

Adaptation on the Great Plains

The reason that the Plains area provides such a remarkable example of cultural adaptation is that it was the end point of a significant migration of Indian tribes between the seventeenth and nineteenth centuries. Before that period the Great Plains were very sparsely occupied. The poor water resources, the unvariegated flora and fauna, and the lack of sheltered areas made the open grasslands an inhospitable environment for tribes with simple technology. The severe conditions in winter must have been particularly difficult to overcome. For these reasons, prior to the introduction of the horse most of the human population of the area was located on the forested margins rather than on the Plains proper. And while many of the peripheral tribes sent seasonal hunting parties onto the Plains, virtually none remained the year-round.

This entire situation began to change in the mid-seventeenth century with the introduction of the horse from Spanish settlements in the Southwest. The first Indians to take up a mounted way of life were probably the Apache, who lived close to the Spanish frontier and had access to horses. Once they acquired them, the use of the animals spread rapidly to tribes to the north and east. The speed of diffusion was due in part to the tremendous military advantage that mounted warriors had over pedestrian peoples. The Apache began raiding neighboring tribes to drive them out of coveted areas and to acquire captives which they then sold as slaves to Spanish settlements in exchange for more horses (Secoy 1953: 23). These raids impelled neighboring peoples such as the Caddoans, Ute, and Comanche to obtain horses and develop similar patterns of mounted warfare in self defense. Thus a kind of chain reaction took place that led to almost universal

utilization of the horse on the Great Plains by about 1750
A.D. (Kroeber 1939: 87).

The military advantage was of course only one motive for
taking up an equestrian way of life; another was that men
on horseback could achieve far greater success as Plains
buffalo hunters than could men on foot. Not only could they
obtain more game, but by using the horse as a pack animal
it was possible to carry greater amounts of equipment and
supplies, such as pole-supported tepees, that made life comfortable and secure on the Plains even in winter. Once these
possibilities opened, newly mounted peoples converged from
all directions to stake out territories on the Plains and to
center subsistence activities on the remarkably abundant bison.
By the nineteenth century, almost thirty autonomous societies were competing for living space on the Great Plains.

It is important to note that very different kinds of peoples
were caught up in this process. The tribes that made up the
nineteenth century Plains culture came from widely different
areas, spoke mutually unintelligible languages, and originally had very dissimilar customs. There was even an important difference in subsistence type. The groups that had lived
previously in the Rocky Mountain region or to the west of
the mountains, such as the Comanche, Ute, and Plains
Shoshoni, had been hunters and gatherers before migrating
onto the Plains. Many of the tribes that converged from the
east, on the other hand, like the Cheyennes, Sioux, and
Arapaho, had earlier maintained some form of agricultural
existence.

What was remarkable, however, and what has most
intrigued anthropologists about the Plains example, is the
degree to which many of the former differences were over-
ridden in the common environment of the Plains. No matter
what their previous cultural traditions had been, all Plains
tribes came to share a common set of customs, institutions,
and technology. They became so much alike, in fact, that
anthropologists have considered the Plains culture area as
one of relative cultural homogeneity. The set of common
traits and practices included equestrian hunting of buffalo,
which was the major item in the diet of all Plains groups.
The social organization of each tribe was characterized by a

summer phase during which the main body of the tribe camped together; this was followed by a winter phase when the society would break up into smaller units. Social status for males was based on a system of war exploits and bravery, and the men of each tribe were organized into various military societies that conducted raids on enemies and acted as occasional tribal police. A particular ceremony, the Sun Dance, became the most important religious rite in the annual cycle. Even artwork conformed to a common pattern, being almost everywhere based on principles of geometric design. There were in addition numerous details of dress, food preference, horse culture, weapons, and equipment that were generally similar among all Plains tribes.

This combination of elements had not characterized any of the groups before migrating onto the Plains, and some tribes had manifested virtually none of the traits previously. In fact, many tribes changed so extensively in the course of the migration that it has been difficult to find any cultural similarities, except language, between them and the groups from which they derived. An authority on the Cheyennes has remarked that their transformation from a village-dwelling Algonquian group to what they became as Plains nomads was so great that it seemed "impossible of belief but for the connected documentary proof of fact" (Mooney in Gladwin 1957: 113). Much the same can be said for certain Shoshonean societies. While still living in the arid Great Basin prior to acquisition of the horse, we must suppose that the ancestors of the Comanche lived much like the Basin hunting and gathering groups that have been described by Steward (1938). Warfare among those societies was almost unknown, and they have been depicted as remarkably timorous and shy. A nineteenth-century observer described the Basin peoples as (DeSmet in Steward 1938: 219)

. . . so timid, that it is difficult to get near them; the appearance of a stranger alarms them; and the conventional signs quickly spread the news amongst them. Every one, thereupon hides himself in a hole; and in an instant this miserable people disappear and vanish like a shadow.

and Steward (1938: 242) remarks that

> Explorers' journals are . . . full of accounts wherein men
> fled ingloriously at the arrival of strangers, leaving their
> women to the latters' mercy.

Yet once certain of these groups acquired horses and entered upon a Plains career, they became some of the most formidable and dauntless warriors in all of North America. The military prowess of the mounted Comanche was such that they were dreaded by Apaches, Spaniards, and Texans alike. One author (Farnham in Hoebel and Wallace 1952: 3–4) wrote:

> . . . their incomparable horsemanship, their terrible
> charge . . . and their insatiable hatred make the enmity
> of these Indians more dreadful than that of any other tribe
> of aborigines.

How are transformations of such magnitude to be explained? And why was it that the various tribes, originally so different, developed such remarkable similarities once they became Plains nomads? The answers seem to lie in a combination of factors. First, the adoption of equestrian hunting in a new and highly competitive environment demanded flexibility and resourcefulness. Customs and practices that were inappropriate in the new situation were rapidly discarded or replaced by more practical expedients. Also, each tribe was forced to conform to the same general environmental conditions. The exigencies of mounted buffalo hunting and the requirements of self-defense in a situation of rampant warfare led to common solutions to common problems. Once a group worked out successful means of coping with the various obstacles, their responses were imitated or borrowed by neighboring societies. In the following account, examples are chosen that illustrate how processes of ecological adaptation led to similar institutions and practices among the different tribes. It should be kept in mind, however, that processes of borrowing and imitation were also at work.

One of the problems that all Plains societies had to contend with was that of devising efficient means for hunting the buffalo. This animal played such a crucial role in the Plains economy, providing not only food but clothing and equipment as well, that without it the Plains Indians could not have existed. An intimate association grew up, therefore, between the herds of buffalo and the societies that depended upon them.

A characteristic of Plains buffalo is that they maintained a distinct yearly cycle. The huge congregations of animals that are so much a part of western folklore came about only during the mating season, a period lasting from midsummer through fall. Throughout the rest of the year the herd was broken into small clusters, and the animals were dispersed across vast stretches of prairie.

This cycle had important consequences for the Indians. Since the most successful hunting occurred when large numbers of animals could be taken at once—that is, when the herd was fully congregated—this was the time when each tribe came together for large communal hunts. Winter, on the other hand, forced a dispersion of the Indians. Oliver (1962: 17) explains:

> [Each tribe] had to be dispersed in winter and concentrated in the summer. The buffalo were too scattered in the winter months to permit large numbers of people to band together, and the opportunities provided by the dense herds in the summer months were too good to miss, since food was stored at this time for the rest of the year. Moreover, the compact summer herds drew the Indians together for the simple reason that large parts of the buffalo range were without buffalo at this time.

We can see, therefore, that there were sound ecological reasons for the distinct summer and winter phases of each tribe, the phases representing adjustments to the seasonal habits of the buffalo. Even had members of the tribe wished to camp as a single unit during the winter months, they could have done so only with difficulty because of the low density of game in any particular region. According to their own traditions, the Cheyennes once tried to remain together as a tribe throughout the year; many nearly died of starvation that winter and they never made the attempt again (Eggan 1966: 54).

Another distinctive feature of Plains life, also understandable in adaptational terms, was a peculiar institution known as the camp or buffalo police. This organization was common to all Plains tribes except the Comanche. In each tribe the police were composed of members of a single military fraternity that was charged that year with responsibility for organizing the tribal ceremonies and for policing the great communal hunts. Their mandate applied only to the time of tribal congregation and did not carry over to the periods when the individual bands camped alone.

The most striking feature of these police was that they held coercive authority over other adult members of the tribe and often meted out severe and summary punishments for breaches of tribal regulations. This degree of authority was remarkable because it contrasts with the highly individualistic and egalitarian nature of Plains societies generally. In all Plains tribes the adult male was regarded as an autonomous individual who was subordinate to no external authority. Even men who qualified as chiefs actually held very little power, and none was capable of compelling others to do their bidding. An observer (Parkman 1856: 118) of the Oglala (Sioux) has written that a chief

. . . knows [only] too well on how frail a tenure he holds his station. He must conciliate his uncertain subjects. . . . Does he fail in gaining their favor, they will set his authority at naught, and may desert him at any moment; for the usages of his people have provided no sanctions by which he may enforce his authority.

And the same author adds (118) that

. . . very few Oglala chiefs could venture without instant jeopardy of their lives to strike or lay hands upon the meanest of their people.

This democratic and proud spirit pervaded all aspects of Plains life, with no man willing to concede the authority of any other over him. Yet the power of the camp police was a striking exception; not only did they hold extraordinary disciplinary powers, but all reports indicate that the rough and ready justice that they administered was accepted with almost lamblike obedience.

The explanation for this seeming paradox resides in the fact that the powers of the camp police were restricted to very special occasions, the most important of these being the period of cooperative buffalo hunting carried out in summer. As noted above, this was the time when the most efficient hunting took place; the congregated nature of the herds meant that a successful hunt sometimes yielded enough food to last many months. Success, however, depended on the united effort of a large number of men. Working in concert, they attempted first to surround a herd and then to stampede it in controlled fashion so that mounted hunters could ride alongside and fell the animals almost at will. Individual hunting, which would nullify this advantage by alarming and dispersing the herd, was strictly prohibited. Hoebel (1960: 53) describes the situation for the Cheyennes:

From the time of the performance of the great ceremonies to the splitting up of the tribe at the end of summer, no man or private group of men may hunt alone. . . . A single hunter can stampede thousands of bison and spoil the hunt for the whole tribe. To prevent this, the rules are clear, activity is rigidly policed, and violations are summarily and vigorously punished.

It seems clear, therefore, that such rules were invoked as a matter of economic obligation. The individualistic ethic of Plains culture came into conflict, on certain occasions, with the opportunity to provide food for the tribe as a whole. At these times the normally unfettered individual became strictly subordinate to agents representing the communal will. The emphasis on obedience in this case is therefore not unlike that described earlier for the Pueblo Indians. In both cases the effect was to harness and restrain individuals to better protect the food supply. The difference, of course, is that the restraint in Pueblo society was constant, due to the unremitting nature of agricultural activites, whereas in Plains societies it was exceptional, invoked to meet the needs of a temporary situation.

Finally, one of the outstanding and most widely noted characteristics of Plains life was the remarkable military complex that developed. As previously noted, in all these societies the men competed for status and honor by accomplishing courageous deeds in warfare. From the time of infancy the individual male was prepared for battle and steeped in its legends, and he came to think of fighting and military glory as primary goals of existence. As Wallace and Hoebel (1952: 245–46) write of the Comanche, so it was among all Plains societies:

> The life of the male came to be centered around warfare and raiding. . . . War was regarded as the noblest of pursuits, one which every man should follow; and from earliest youth boys were taught to excel in it. They were taught that success in war brought in its train the respect and admiration of the men, women, and children of the tribe, and that the most worthy virtue for a man was bravery. They were taught that death in battle, aside from being glorious, protected one from all the miseries which threatened later life and were inevitable to old age.

As mentioned earlier, some of the tribes could hardly be described as warlike before migrating onto the Plains, yet all developed the same military obsession once they became Plains nomads.

There were various reasons why such a transformation was inevitable. We should remember, first of all, that the origins of Plains culture coincided with the period of the advancing American frontier. As the settlers moved westward they uprooted the Indians in their path and forced them farther west. These in turn came into conflict with the tribes already there. The invaders usually had the advantage since they possessed weapons—steel knives, axes, and firearms— acquired from contact with whites. A vast series of conflicts were thus initiated as Indian tribes vied with one another for the constantly diminishing western territory. As one writer (Newcomb 1950: 323) has commented:

> These were not boyish raids for adventure or glory; they constituted serious warfare, fought by men defending their homes and families against invaders seeking to escape from their own ravaged and overrun homes to the east.

At the same time, the availability of the horse was making the Great Plains an attractive environment, with the result that many of the displaced tribes sought new homelands there. Such a large number of tribes converged on the Plains that competition was intense, and any tribe that remained did so only by virtue of aggressive defense of its position. The histories of many tribes record a series of movements as they either advanced or were forced to retreat in the face of powerful enemies.

All of these conflicts were aggravated by possession of the horse. Every group had to possess the animals, since none could hunt effectively or defend themselves without them. Yet the distribution of horses was far from uniform; some groups were in perpetual need while others were fairly well supplied. But even the latter societies suffered periodic shortages that made them desperate to acquire more. Trade was always a possibility, but a more immediate means of obtaining them was by raiding the camps of neighboring tribes. This expedient was resorted to on a large scale, and a pattern of almost continual horsestealing developed, followed by revenge expeditions that often mushroomed into bitter warfare. The horse also exacerbated conflict by enormously increasing the mobility and potential range of each society, so that the various tribes continually encroached on territory claimed by others (Newcomb 1950: 321).

Once we are aware of this background, it is not difficult to understand the enormous emphasis placed on military virtue. The Indians of the Plains were engaged in a life-or-death struggle for living space and hunting grounds. Losers in the struggle faced annihilation, as actually occurred in the case of certain Caddoan groups; or tribes could be driven

entirely off the Plains as happened to the Southern Ute and
the Apache in the face of relentless Comanche aggression.
Under such circumstances it was absolutely essential to produce the type of men who could bear up under danger and
would unflinchingly meet any threat to the tribe from without. The society was best served, therefore, by men who not
only did not fear combat, but who relished it. Much of the
socialization of the Plains warrior—the toughening of the
body, the search for supernatural power, the horrendous self-
torture—can be understood as means of steeling individuals
for the inevitable battles they must wage in defense of their
way of life.

Conclusion

Nobody who is familiar with the Plains example can deny
the significance of adaptive or coping behavior in such
instances. Here are societies that underwent such a degree
of transformation that they came to bear little resemblance
to the societies from which they had sprung only two or
three generations earlier. Mooney (1907: 361) says of the
Cheyennes that they experienced "such entire change of habit
and ceremony that the old life is remembered only in sacred
tradition." And a commentator (Kardiner 1945: 47) on the
Comanche writes that "many features of their original culture were completely forgotten, and . . . they tended to accept
constant changes in their ways of living."

The reason for these changes, of course, is that members
of each tribe were forced to adjust their behavior to constantly shifting circumstances. These circumstances were so
novel and unprecedented that the older generation could not
serve as adequate models for the young, nor could they pass
on much of the traditional culture, since most of it was simply irrelevant in the new context. In this dynamic period,
then, members of each generation had to create their own
patterns of behavior; they had to learn from the school of
everyday life and experience—from failure and trauma—
and thus continually modified the ancestral culture. It was a
situation, therefore, in which coping behavior, or new adap-

tive strategies, were perhaps as important in contributing to the cultural outcome as were customs acquired from the past. And this, to generalize broadly, is probably true of most situations in which there are extensive changes in a way of life.

The aim of this chapter has been to demonstrate the significance of the adaptational perspective, and the cases presented are ones that place the approach in a favorable light. The reader might well conclude from these examples that culture is basically a utilitarian instrument, and that as human beings cope with their surroundings they create the norms, values, and institutions most appropriate to those conditions. Such conclusions would be premature. While it is certainly true that there is an adaptive-utilitarian dimension to culture, culture is clearly not *only* that. There are many reasons why human societies do not always cope effectively with their circumstances. The question of why this is so is the subject of the next chapter.

Suggested Readings

Harris, Marvin, *Cows, Pigs, Wars and Witches: The Riddles of Culture*. New York: Vintage Books, 1974.

Marvin Harris is anthropology's most forceful exponent of the view that culture and customs make practical sense. In a number of publications he has tried to show that customs which on the surface appear wasteful or extravagant, actually contribute to the long-term advantage of the people possessing them. Here he looks at cow love in India, the Jewish taboo on pork, and other matters.

Hoebel, E. A., *The Cheyennes: Indians of the Great Plains*. New York: Holt, Rinehart and Winston, 1960.

A short but excellent treatment of one of the important Plains tribes. It is written in a framework that assesses the relationship between culture and the individual personality, and therefore gives a good sense of what Plains life must have been for those who experienced it.

Oliver, Symmes C., Ecology and Cultural Continuity as Contributing Factors in the Social Organization of the Plains Indians, *University of California Publications in American Archeology and Ethnology*, Vol. 48, No. 1, 1962.

A fine paper on the significance of ecological adaptations in the origin and spread of Plains Indian institutions. Oliver tries also to gauge the importance of forces of historical continuity.

Secoy, Frank R., *Changing Military Patterns on the Great Plains*. Monographs of the American Ethnological Society, Vol. 21. New York: J. J. Augustin, 1953.
This is a historical study of the shifting patterns of warfare and military hegemony on the Plains from the seventeenth to the early nineteenth centuries. Secoy analyzes the repercussions of various items of military technology that entered the Plains area in this fateful period.

Steward, Julian H., *Theory of Culture Change*. Urbana: University of Illinois Press, 1938.
The adaptive framework that is developed in this chapter owes a great deal to the writings of Julian Steward. This book is a collection of some of his most influential papers on the approach that he termed "cultural ecology."

Wilkinson, Richard G., *Poverty and Progress: An Ecological Perspective on Economic Development*. New York: Praeger, 1973.
An anthropologist draws on ecological theory, as it has developed in anthropology, and applies the logic to problems of economic development. Wilkinson is as interested in the forces that favor stability as in those that stimulate change. An interesting and thought-provoking book.

Chapter 5

Cultural Persistence

At the beginning of the last chapter it was noted that once cultural practices become established, there is a general tendency to conserve them. Wholesale and sudden transformations in a way of life, like that described for the Plains Indians, are rare in human history. People do not, except under special circumstances, discard customs or cultural preferences easily, even when viable alternatives are available. We are all familiar with those ethnic enclaves in American cities in which the people continue to eat—at considerable expense—the foods they learned to like as children, and reject the more accessible and cheaper foods around them. The same occurs with language, elements of dress, and recreational and religious preferences. These are frequently clung to so tenaciously that any attempt at forcible change can provoke spirited resistance. What is characteristic of our own society is true the world over: most individuals, most of the time, are deeply committed to their own customs.

One of the reasons for such commitment is that human beings are not infinitely flexible. Despite the fact that any normal infant has the potential to learn all varieties of human culture, this capability is never realized. As one anthropologist has remarked: "One of the most significant facts about us [human beings] may finally be that we all begin with the natural equipment to live a thousand kinds of life but end in the end having lived only one." (Geertz 1973: 45).

We live only one partly for the reason that learning our first cultural responses impairs our ability to learn or appreciate others. The language that we acquire as infants, and that becomes our native tongue, generally remains our most fluent form of communication. Ability in languages encountered later in life is always influenced to some degree by what linguists term "language interference." Our first language interferes with the second, so that we speak the latter with an accent and make syntactical errors that native speakers would never commit. The same occurs with perceptions of beauty: becoming accustomed to one pattern limits appreciation of others. The little West African girl who is familiar only with the facial features and hair styles in her black African community will react with shock and displeasure on her first encounter with a blonde European and is likely to consider the European incomparably ugly. The same is true of motor skills: once established they are unlikely to change. Alfred Kroeber (1948: 348) gives the example of the carpenter's plane:

The Japanese carpenter pulls the plane toward himself, centripetally. The Western workman pushes it away from his body, centrifugally. Probably one method is as good as the other in most cases. But once a certain skill has become established in connection with pushing, it is impossible for a given individual to be equally skillful when he substitutes the pulling motion. He may attain such skill by deliberately trying to learn a new habit, but meanwhile his work is that of a novice. As there is usually no reward for a change, and likely to be an obvious penalty, because of temporarily decreased quality of performance, the change is not made, and the individual remains a lifelong addict to the particular set of habits that first became established in him.

The term "lifelong addict" is more than a metaphor. Cultural proclivities have the same addictive quality as do tobacco or drugs. The latter change the chemical balance of the body to create an enhanced need, just as cultural usages influence our perceptions and shift muscular patterns so that each individual becomes not only a user of his culture but also a product of it. The consequence, of course, is that one's own customs appear "natural," since both body and mind have been molded to accommodate those forms, whereas different usages appear "unnatural" and even perverse. This, by the way, is one of the foundations of the widespread phenomenon known as *ethnocentrism*, the high valuation placed on one's own culture and the correlative disparagement of foreign customs.

This addictive quality of culture should make clear, therefore, that cultural choices are never made in a vacuum. Individuals are inevitably influenced by prior exposure and early commitments. And since each generation strives to pass these preferences on to its offspring, it is not surprising that we encounter instances of remarkable cultural persistence that are attributable to habit and to the dead weight of custom rather than to any practical advantages. How otherwise can we explain the American aversion to garden snails and the Spanish-French culinary esteem of the same fare? The following is a Los Angeles Times-Washington Post news dispatch (January, 1980).

SANTA ROSA, Calif. — Don't poison the snails. Eat them! That's the advice from Frenchman François Picart, 32, a recent immigrant to California from Perigueux, France, who thinks it is criminal the way Californians poison snails. "Snails are low in calories, high in protein, rich in minerals," insists Picart. "Would you poison the cows? Of course not. Yet . . . Californians spend millions each year poisoning the snails instead of enjoying the *escargots* . . . as the *piece de resistance* of any meal."

Picart describes California as a snail paradise. "There are billions of snails crawling all over California — billions of the same snails that are like caviar to my countrymen," Picart says.

After discovering that nobody in the United States was exploiting them commercially, he established a snail farm in California and currently endeavors to sell them to specialty shops in the western states.

Another, equally striking, example of perpetuation of cultural bias is the clam-eating tradition on one side of the Atlantic Ocean and the preference for mussels on the other. Americans on the Atlantic coast are avid clam-eaters, but make almost no use of the mussel; whereas Europeans prefer the mussel and pay far less attention to the clam. And since the same species of mussel occurs abundantly in both areas, the difference is largely a matter of conditioned preference (Kroeber 1948: 351). This example, like the others, illustrates a simple point; namely, once cultural propensities become established they can effectively exclude alternatives, even ones that appear equally viable from a practical point of view.

The Limitations of Prior Accomplishment

But what do such cases tell us about the utilitarian or non-utilitarian nature of culture? After all, it could be pointed out, one manner of planing wood is as good as another; and any combination of foods will suffice as long as they guarantee the caloric and nutritional minimum.

The matter would be different, however, if it could be established that there are instances of cultural persistence that not only exclude alternatives, but that also appear to actively impede the efficient operation of social institutions. Human culture is in fact replete with examples of this kind. One of the important sources for this viewpoint is the work of the radical economist Thorstein Veblen. And since many of Veblen's most fruitful ideas have been amplified and disseminated through anthropology by Elman Service (1960: 93–112), the account that follows is also deeply indebted to the latter's insights.

In his book *Imperial Germany and the Industrial Revolution*, Veblen dealt with the intriguing question of why societies that borrow technological or institutional devices are often able to make more efficient use of them than the countries in which the innovations arose. Veblen stated the question as follows (1915: 23–24):

Why do the borrowed elements lend themselves with greater facility and effect to their intrinsic use in the hands of the borrower people than in the hands of the people to whose initiative they are due? Why are borrowed elements of culture more efficiently employed than home-grown innovations? . . . It would of course be quite bootless to claim that such is always or necessarily the case, but it is likewise not to be denied that, as a matter of history, technological innovations and creations of an institutional nature have in many cases reached their fullest serviceability only at the hands of other communities and other peoples than those to whom these cultural elements owed their origin and initial success.

The particular question he tried to answer was why Imperial Germany (1871–1918), a borrower nation and a latecomer to industrial development, was able to create a manufacturing economy of such efficiency that by the early part of the twentieth century she had outstripped England, the country from which much of the machine technology was borrowed. Veblen's answer was complex. He noted, first of all, that any country that pioneered in technological innovation was apt to suffer a "penalty" for taking the lead. Thus the early lead that Britain established in industrial development, from about 1770 to 1830, meant that her factories and equipment were closely adjusted to conditions—of markets, energy sources, technical knowledge—that prevailed in the early part of the nineteenth century. But as the century wore on, and as the so-called second industrial revolution occurred (based on greater automatization, mass production, and the widespread resort to electrification), English productivity lagged appreciably behind that of both Germany and the United States.

The reason, as Veblen pointed out, was that England had become committed to an earlier stage and scale of industrial operations. Her railways, for example, were constructed with a very narrow gauge so that tunnels, stations, and the width of cars all limited loads that could be handled. This was of no great consequence in the early stages of industrialization, but as the scale of operations and competition from other countries increased, it became a serious defect. Likewise, the early commitment of British industry to steam power considerably slowed the pace of conversion to electricity, and to utilization of the internal combustion engine. As early as 1867 many observers thought that the English iron and steel industry was not keeping pace with world competition; by the 1880s it was abundantly clear that the industry suffered a severe case of "hardening of the arteries." Many of the significant advances in steelmaking technique (such as the basic steel process, and continuous rolling) were English inventions, yet they made little headway in Britain, while at the same time they laid the basis for vastly more efficient steel production in Germany and in the United States (Levine 1967: 39–42).

Concerned Englishmen were aware that failure to adopt the new methods permitted other countries to surpass them. Yet the explanation that steelmen typically gave for rejecting the new methods was that they were "unsuited to English conditions" (Burn 1940: 58, 63–64, 183–218). What they meant, of course, was that incorporation of the innovations would have entailed too great a restructuring of the industry as constituted, at too great an expense, to make them advantageous. As one economist explains (Frankel 1955: 301):

> As a firm, industry or country develops and its technology becomes more intricate, interconnections proliferate which limit sharply the range of new methods it can assimilate. Not all new techniques can be utilized, but only those which can, in some sense, conform to the past. Unlike the young enterprise or newly industrializing country which is, technologically, a *tabula rasa* without any system whose contours demand conformity, modernization for the established enterprise or country is limited by the extent to which the necessary changes can be made to "fit" the existing system.

Thus it was not practicable for the British to build larger ships for their merchant marine unless they were also willing to build larger docks, to deepen harbors, and to widen canals. Or, returning again to the railway example, introducing up-to-date freight cars would have entailed changing the tracks, terminal facilities, shunting devices, and every other railway contrivance that was adjusted to the older cars (Veblen 1915: 130).

Veblen did not, therefore, accuse the British of stupidity, or of shortsightedness, or of having "sinned against the canons of technology." Their decline relative to other countries was, in a certain sense, inevitable; being due, as he expressed it, to the "restraining dead hand of their past achievement" (1915: 132). In other words, the case provides an example of a people so committed to previously established ways of doing things that they were unable, or unwilling, to initiate changes that would in the long run have led to enhanced efficiency. In the jargon of contemporary anthropology, the English did not "adapt" in a wholly effective way.

Integration as an Impediment to Change

It is important to note the extent to which the preceding argument hinges on the notion of social or economic inter-relatedness, or what anthropologists commonly refer to as *integration*. Virtually all students of society, whether economists, sociologists, or anthropologists, recognize a tendency for the various elements in a social system to cohere or "fit together" in some fashion. The instance noted above — that there was a size relationship between British ships and the country's harbors, docks, and canals — is typical; and similar linkages can be demonstrated in every realm of cultural behavior. The fact that the Japanese eat with chopsticks rather than with silverware obliges them to serve their meals as morsels, precut in the kitchen; and the soup bowls are designed like cups, to be drunk from. Such relationships abound in every society, and some are so evident that they hardly require comment.

But many such linkages are not obvious, and it is only by means of careful analysis that one can discern the multifarious and frequently unexpected connections that exist in a particular social system. The *functionalist school* in anthropology has been especially active in demonstrating such interdependence; their studies have shown time and again how a change in one element, due to its linkages to various others, can have wide repercussions throughout a society.

An aspect of integration that has received far less attention, however, and should be stressed here, is the extent to which it can exercise a restraining influence on social change. Since, as has been noted, there is a tendency for the parts of a social system to become adjusted to one another, it should be evident that the effort to reform or change a particular practice will have inescapable consequences for other institutions. In many cases this is not a significant impediment to reform: either the perceived benefits of the change are thought to outweigh the disadvantages, or, more frequently, the potential social costs are not even remotely anticipated.

It frequently happens, however, that through the process of integration a custom or practice becomes so firmly embedded in a cultural matrix—so inextricably bound to everything else—that it cannot be altered without adversely affecting other, cherished, institutions. In such circumstances there is generallly great resistance to innovation and change. Even practices that if judged on their intrinsic merits would be considered hopelessly retrograde and inefficient, can be maintained indefinitely simply because to change them would threaten the balance of the social whole.

History provides some striking examples of this kind of conservatism. The instances cited below all betray a single tendency: they are examples of how customs, once integrated into a cultural framework, endure for long periods in spite of their apparent inefficiency.

A pertinent instance cited by Service (1960: 103–04) is that of the evolution and diffusion of writing in the ancient Near East. It is now generally accepted that the alphabetical system of writing that is employed in most areas of the world today is the product of three distinguishable stages in the evolution of writing. The earliest stage was marked by the appearance of pictures, known as pictograms or ideograms, used to represent objects and ideas. In this phase there was no connection between the thing represented and the spoken language. Thus in Egyptian hieroglyphic writing the sun was portrayed as a circle with a dot in the center, and the idea "to weep" was conveyed by a picture of an eye with lines extending below.

In the next stage, the development of *rebus* writing, a crucial link was forged between writing and the spoken language. The rebus principle makes use of the fact that pictures can be used for the sounds that they suggest rather than only for what they portray. A simple example would be if we were to use a picture of an eye to stand for the pronoun "I." Employing such a system for the English phrase "I saw Aunt Rochelle," we could draw the picture sequence of an eye, a saw, an insect, a man rowing, and a sea shell. Use of this convention led eventually to the third or purely phonetic stage of writing. In this development conventionalized signs, or letters, were used to represent the basic sounds of speech, which is of course the principle upon which an alphabet is constructed. With this accomplishment any phrase that could be spoken could also readily be written (Kroeber 1948: 371–72).

It appears that this entire sequence of development, from pictograms to true letters, occurred in the writing system of ancient Egypt. By the end of the fourth millenium B.C. there already existed twenty-four letter signs that could easily have become the basis for an Egyptian alphabet. Yet the Egyptians never took advantage of the alphabetical principle to reform their writing. They continued instead, for thousands of years, to employ a cumbersome system that utilized pictograms, ideograms, rebus writing, and true letter signs all mixed together.

It is not the Egyptians, therefore, who are credited with the invention of the alphabet; this distinction goes to one of their Semitic neighbors, most likely the Phoenicians. The "invention" was of course little more than an act of intelligent borrowing. A Semitic people who had no previous means of writing became acquainted with Egyptian script; they perceived the usefulness of the phonetic principle and constructed an entire system on that basis. Their freedom to innovate was due to the fact that they possessed no writing at all; and since writing had no "place" in their culture— no linkage to other institutions—they were able to devise a system based solely on efficiency and economy of effort.

The reasons that the Egyptians never took a similar step must remain a matter of conjecture. But it is likely that reform was unattractive because of the potentially unsettling effects on other aspects of Egyptian culture. We can surmise that the hieroglyphs played a prominent role in religious ideology, and in certain instances may even have been considered sacred. The care and delicacy with which they were inscribed suggests also that they had great aesthetic appeal. Moreover, any major change would have entailed a painful process of relearning, with the disquieting prospect that subsequent generations would be unable to read the sacred monuments and texts.

If we are forced to speculate in relation to ancient Egypt, however, we need not do the same for modern China and Japan. These countries even today employ a mixed syllabic and ideographic (or logographic, or word sign) script. Indeed Sino-Japanese writing is the only major system in the world that has not been displaced by the greater simplicity and efficiency of the alphabet. Movements urging alphabetical reform have arisen at various times in both countries, but so far none has succeeded.

The advantages of reform are clear: in an era of electronic communications logographic writing is especially awkward. Simple typewriters as they are known in the West cannot be employed, since even an elementary rendering of the language requires machines capable of printing between two and three thousand distinct characters. Both typesetting and telegraphy are made extremely complicated and expensive. Use of dictionaries, indexing of books, and teaching children the written language—all could be enormously facilitated by adoption of a phonetic alphabet. Nor would such a step be difficult from a purely technical standpoint. Efficient phonetic scripts have been devised for both Chinese and Japanese. Indeed, Japanese can be written simply and economically using only seventeen letters of the Roman alphabet, supplemented by two diacritical marks (Reischauer and Fairbank 1958: 515).

Rather than implement such a reform, however, the Japanese prefer to perpetuate a system of writing that has been called the "least efficient in wide use anywhere in the world"

(Reischauer and Fairbank 1958: 515). The orientalist George Sansom, referring to the Japanese use of "sidewriting" (*furigana*)—which is a syllabic script written alongside ambiguous characters to clarify their meanings—has remarked (1928: 44):

> One hesitates for an epithet to describe a system of writing which is so complex that it needs the aid of another system to explain it. There is no doubt that it provides for some a fascinating field of study, but as a practical instrument it is surely without inferiors.

Japan may in fact be the only country in the world where the blind have advantages in learning over those with sight. Since blind students learn to read and write by means of a simple phonetic braille, they do not have to invest the enormous amount of time that other Japanese students must in memorizing thousands of characters (*kanji*) (Hall 1949: 315–16):

> . . . interesting evidence of the waste in learning time in acquiring the traditional system of writing with *kanji* is given by schools for the blind. The Tokyo Government School for the Blind, for example, teaches the same material to blind students as the regular national elementary schools teach normal seeing students. Blind secondary school students take the standard secondary school course . . . in four years instead of the five normally required for students who can see, and who must memorize *kanji*.

If, then, Sino-Japanese writing has all of these disadvantages, why is it being perpetuated? The answer lies in the close association between writing and other aspects of Japanese and Chinese culture. An alphabetical reform would unavoidably entail a significant cultural loss, since persons taught the new writing would be unable to read the older script. The younger generation would thus find itself cut off from a large portion of its literary heritage. Of course, transliteration of the most significant books, magazines, and journals would be undertaken; but it would be an extremely costly process and it is unlikely that more than a small portion of the existing literature would ever be rewritten. This is because most works of the past have a primarily historical or scholarly interest; their small readership would not warrant the effort and expense of transliteration.

There is also an important aesthetic issue. Certain types of Chinese and Japanese poetry, verse, and calligraphy are so intimately bound up with Chinese characters that they would not carry their full range of meanings apart from them. In fact, what are defects of logographic writing from a practical standpoint—the ambiguity and complexity of meaning—may lend additional suggestive power to poetic expression.

Another consideration, and one that is common to all fundamental reform, is that the inconvenience of the change-over would have to be borne primarily by the generation that institutes the change. Its substantial investment in memorizing the old characters would be jeopardized, and its members would also have to learn to read and write over again in adult life. The benefits of the reform, on the other hand, would accrue mainly to future generations. As Kroeber (1948: 409–10) has remarked, "people in the mass don't come as altruistic as that."

Finally, there are important reasons of a nationalistic kind. In both China and Japan the systems of writing have become closely tied to their conceptions of themselves as distinct peoples; they have become, in a sense, symbols of national identity. Both peoples are therefore loath to exchange what they consider their birthright for a "foreign" system. This purely emotional or symbolical attachment is very powerful, and it lies behind many of the arguments and rationalizations that spokesmen occasionally adduce for retention of the ancient characters.

But for the persistence of inefficient customs we need not resort to ancient Egypt or to the Orient. Anglo-American society exhibits some remarkable instances of virtually the same kind. The metric controversy in the United States is a prime example. For almost two hundred years various groups of Americans have urged their countrymen to abandon the chaotic English system of weights and measures (ounces, pounds, inches, feet, yards) and adopt instead the more systematic and decimal-based metric system. Since its inception in France in 1790 the metric system has spread from country to country throughout the world and has now achieved almost universal acceptance. The United States remains the only industrialized nation that has neither adopted the metric standard nor become officially committed to metric conversion; it is, in fact, one of only about ten countries in the entire world that are nonmetric. And while there can be no doubt that metrics are gradually gaining ground even in the United States, there is still opposition to full conversion (see, for example, the GAO *Report to the Congress*, 1978).

During the nineteenth century American resistance to metrication was not unlike the opposition that developed in all countries where such a change was proposed. The problem was always one of interrelatedness: since weights and measures are linked to almost every activity and occupation, opponents complained of the difficulty of inducing people to give up ingrained habits, of having to retrain employees, and especially of the disruption and chaos that would result from the changeover. As might be expected, there were also nationalistic overtones, since Americans were asked to substitute a foreign system for customary usage. The anti-metric song "A Pint's a Pound the World Around," popular in the 1880s, betrays some of these feelings (Treat 1971: 90):

> They bid us change the ancient "names,"
>   The "seasons" and the "times";
> And for our measures go abroad
>   To strange and distant climes.
> But we'll abide by things long clear
>   And cling to things of yore,
> For the Anglo-Saxon race shall rule
>   The earth from shore to shore.
>
> Then down with every "metric" scheme
>   Taught by the foreign school,
> We'll worship still our Father's God!
>   And keep our Father's "rule"!
> A perfect inch, a perfect pint,

The Anglo's honest pound,
Shall hold their place upon the earth,
Till Time's last trump shall sound!

Prometric forces almost overcame these objections on a number of occasions in the nineteenth century, but never quite mustered the necessary congressional majority. In a sense they missed a golden opportunity, since the change to metrics then would have been a far simpler proposition than it was later to become. For when the metric debate reopened in the 1920s the country was then well on its way to becoming an industrialized society. The techniques of mass production required not only complex machinery but also standardized and interchangeable parts, and this standardization came to be based almost entirely on the English system of weights and measures. American manufacturers thus invested billions of dollars in machinery geared to nonmetric dimensions; to suddenly revise the basis of measurement would have occasioned them enormous expense. As one authority (Perry 1955: 87) writes:

Industries that had favored the change to metric measures in 1902, or hadn't cared, or didn't then exist, were now appalled by the idea of converting. In the early years, it might have made excellent sense. But now they had spent their money on tools, machines, inventories, drawings, and other items in inch measure, and their personnel was accustomed to inch measure. Were the change to be made now, they feared, the cost would be staggering and the period of transition one of prolonged confusion. They sent word to their Congressmen that metric legislation simply must be stopped.

Industrialization had the obvious effect, therefore, of binding the United States even more firmly to its outmoded system of measurement. As the above passage indicates, there are many individuals who, although they oppose metric reform, readily concede that it is an excellent system of measurement, far superior to the one in present use. Their opposition stems entirely from the fact that the country appears hopelessly committed to the established system. This argument recalls a comment made during congressional hearings on the metric question in 1902. In response to an antimetric witness, a Congressman retorted: "According to your theory, if a nation adopts a system of some kind, no matter how bad it is, it is better to keep it than go to a new" (Treat 1971: 127).

That societies sometimes do follow such logic helps us understand what Veblen meant when he spoke of the restraining "dead hand" of past achievement, or when he implied that societies are often held back by the debris of their own history.

The Critical Role of the Social Past

It will be helpful at this point to reiterate the main thread of the argument and to draw out some of its implications. These various instances of inefficient customs and practices have been brought forth to contend that human culture cannot be thought of as only a utilitarian instrument for coping with external circumstances. Every human society is also a historical growth, and as the preceding examples clearly show, past commitments exert a powerful influence on the way that societies respond to current circumstances. It is because of this historical influence, and because of the complex web of interrelationships that obtain as a result, that societies usually do not adapt to new conditions optimally. Adaptation is rarely a matter of choosing the most efficient alternatives. New adjustments, or adaptations, are almost always compromises between the limitations imposed by the preexisting culture and the opportunities offered by new conditions. "To adapt then," as Marshall Sahlins (1964: 137) has expressed it, "is not to do so perfectly from some objective standpoint, or even necessarily to improve performance: it is to do as well as possible under the circumstances."

This is also why it was noted earlier that sudden and revolutionary social transformations are comparatively rare. It is far more common to find societies making piecemeal or makeshift adjustments that allow them, at one and the same time, to preserve familiar institutions and to take advantage of new opportunities. Thus the Japanese refuse to discard their inefficient writing; this does not mean, however, that they do not compensate in other ways. There are numerous occupations in Japan, from copyists to skilled typists, as well as ingenious technological devices, that make it possible to apply their writing to a modern, industrial society (Miller 1977: 56). It is of course costly in terms of time and effort, but it works.

Americans do much the same. While no generalized metric reform has taken place, metrication has been accepted in many spheres of the economy: in scientific work, medicine, the pharmaceutical industry, the military, and many other areas. This kind of adjustment, by means of which societies "change just enough so that they do not have to change" is extremely prevalent; it enables us to eat our cultural cake and to have it too.

What emerges clearly from this discussion, therefore, is the fact that no society entirely escapes its past. There are always elements that persist from prior conditions and that inevitably set limits to future flexibility. Even the example of the Plains Indians is not a significant exception to this generalization.

As described in the last chapter, all of the Plains tribes developed remarkably similar institutions as they abandoned earlier ways of life for equestrian nomadism on the Plains. Nevertheless, anthropologists who have studied the situation have shown that despite the enormous changes, none of the societies entirely remade themselves; in every tribe there were examples of the persistence of earlier institutions. Thus Oliver has noted that formerly agricultural groups like the Crow tended to maintain a semblance of their earlier clan organization, despite the fact that it was almost certainly inefficient under the new circumstances. He has also shown that the different patterns of leadership that obtained in different tribes were attributable to the past histories of each. Groups that had formerly existed as simple hunting societies maintained very loose and informal systems of leadership on the Plains. Their chiefs or headmen held no formal offices and were simply those who proved themselves more capable, or more valiant, than others. The situation among the formerly agricultural tribes was very different: chiefs were sometimes elected to specific terms of office, and they served in formalized tribal councils that constituted important decision-making and judicial bodies. Oliver (1962: 58) sums up:

> The conclusion seems inescapable that the *differences* in leadership patterns among the True Plains tribes reflect differences in the types of leadership that they had when they first moved onto the Plains. They certainly had to adapt to the new Plains situation, but they did this by modifying existing institutions.

Another anthropologist, Thomas Gladwin, essentially agrees. He has contended that even if the Plains tribes did develop common practices, this does not imply that all basic differences were eradicated. To this end he made a careful comparison between Cheyennes and Comanche and was able to point to remarkable differences in basic personality and in the quality of interpersonal relations. Whereas Cheyenne socialization aimed at creating a sexually repressed, controlled adult, the Comanche emphasized uninhibited sexuality and personal freedom. Thus a young Cheyenne woman was constantly supervised in order to protect her virginity. Chastity was strictly defined, so that an unmarried woman was defiled not only by intercourse, but also if a man "touched her genitals, or even her breasts" (Gladwin 1957: 116).

Contrast this with the nonchalant Comanche, who did not object to sexual play between children and were unconcerned with virginity. Comanche youths routinely crept into the family tepees of their girlfriends to have sexual intercourse. When a man decided to marry a woman he would simply sleep late in the morning and allow her father to discover them in bed. The father would then "make the boy a brief and friendly speech . . . and invite him to breakfast" (Linton, quoted in Gladwin 1957: 119).

Another notable difference was the amount of in-group aggression tolerated. The Cheyennes strongly discouraged aggression within the tribe, and the killing of a member of the tribe was regarded with utmost seriousness: it was an offense against society and against the supernatural. A Cheyenne murderer was expelled from the community, and if he was ever allowed to return he was treated as a pariah for the rest of his life.

Especially were Cheyenne chiefs expected to exercise restraint. When affronted, a laudable chiefly reaction was to feign indifference and to remark that the affront had no more importance than if a dog had urinated on his tipi (Hoebel 1960: 38). The Comanche, on the other hand, tolerated considerable in-group hostility. Even within-tribe murder did not rouse the community to action, and the active pursuit of revenge was the appropriate response to any serious affront (Gladwin 1957: 121).

Gladwin thus argues that striking differences persisted despite the facade of common institutions. He argues in addition that the differences existed because each society adjusted to the Plains environment by building upon pre-existing organizations rather than by adapting *ex nihilo* to the new situation. This is of course consistent with our main contention: that adaptation is almost inescapably a form of compromise between past history and current realities.

The Perpetuation of Cultural Patterns

What has been presented in the chapter to this point are some of the causes of the phenomenon often referred to as *cultural inertia*. Anthropologists have frequently observed that once cultural patterns come into being they tend to endure, or, as it is sometimes expressed, they can "take on a life of their own."

It should be obvious, though, that inertia is an inadequate characterization, since *vested interests* are just as frequently responsible for maintaining a system in being as are ingrained habits or mere complacency. Sociocultural systems are in this respect not fundamentally different from economic or technological systems. Earlier we saw how the problem of interrelatedness caused the British industrial economy to mature along the "same old grooves after the early start" (Levine 1967: 148); and an expert on the development of British railways remarks how they "set into a mould very early," had difficulty changing what had once become established, and thus perpetuated their original form (Simmons 1978: 263). Societies betray some of the same characteristics: they also tend to develop along pre-established grooves and to conserve a distinct character over time. And while this character does change, it can prove remarkably resistant to external influences.

Anthropologist George Foster has even coined a term for this rigidity of form: *cultural crystallization* (1960: 227–34). Some years ago he conducted an investigation of the technology and customs transmitted to Latin America from Spain after the Spanish conquest in the sixteenth century. He was intrigued by the fact that a very large portion of the Hispanic cultural traits that are now disseminated throughout Latin America had their origins in southern Spanish prototypes. Thus many Latin American technological items such as agricultural and fishing implements, as well as regional costumes, popular religious festivals, and even dialectical forms of Spanish—all reflect the customs of Andalusia and Extremadura more faithfully than they reflect the customs of the more northerly regions of Spain. Yet Foster was able to show that there were as many, or more, emigrants from central and northern Spain throughout the colonial period than from the two southern regions. Why then were the northern emigrants not able to transmit and establish their customs in America as effectively as the men and women from the south?

Foster's reply is that the crucial difference was not the *number* of emigrants who proceeded from each region, but the *sequence* in which they arrived. It is clear that a disproportionately large number of the first soldiers and colonists to come to the New World were in fact from the southern regions. These were the individuals who were on the scene during what Foster calls the "fluid period" when colonial culture was first taking shape. This was a time when solutions had to be found to the most pressing problems, crucial decisions were made, and an institutional structure was hammered out by means of which Spaniards and Indians were able to regulate their conduct. In working out solutions to these various problems, it was natural that the settlers drew upon precedents with which they were most familiar, namely, those from their native regions of southern Spain.

This fluid or formative period, characterized by innovation and expediency, did not last for more than a few decades. Once a viable institutional framework came into being, and once the various parts of the culture became comparatively well integrated, the structure grew far more rigid and resistant to innovation. Indeed, the institutions that were established in this relatively brief formative period provided the basic framework for Latin American colonial societies for the next two hundred years (Foster 1960: 232–33).

Thus when toward the end of the sixteenth century patterns of emigration from Spain changed, and more colonists from the north and central parts of the country came to the New World, they encountered a culture already in being, and one that had "crystallized" into a definite pattern. These colonists found that they had to adjust to the forms already established. The customs and practices that they brought with them did not readily take hold, simply because they came too late: functional equivalents already existed. Nor could their customs compete on an equal footing with those previously established, since the latter had the advantage of a nearly perfect "fit" with the system as constituted. Thus it was not a matter of the greater suitability of one set of customs over the other; Foster believes that the culture of the latecomers would have served just as adequately as responses to New World conditions as did that of the early arrivals. It was simply a matter of which practices came into use before the system hardened into a mold.

Though Foster applied his argument only to colonial Latin America, it would appear that the ideas have far broader relevance. For crystallization suggests that once a pattern becomes established, it then tends to resist elements that would alter the original contours. A clear implication is that many elements of Latin American culture prevailed not because they were the "best" or most appropriate in relation to environmental conditions, but simply because once they became part of an integrated pattern they were difficult to dislodge.

If this reasoning can be applied to other social contexts, it brings up an important question: how often do customs persist simply because they harmonize with an entrenched social pattern rather than because they are congruent with the external circumstances in which a society is situated? Or, stated in different terms, is it common to find enduring sociocultural traits whose persistence has almost nothing to do with adaptation—in the sense of adjustment to environmental conditions—but has very much to do with their "place" in a constituted social pattern?

The answer is that it is probably very common. We have only to look at the contrasting civilizations established in the New World by Englishmen, Spanish-Portuguese, and French to recognize that the original cultural endowment was crucial in each case. The European countries implanted institutions that have set their various American descendants apart for three hundred years. Indeed, in the Canadian case the English-French dichotomy still threatens to divide the country into two separate nations. And the contrasts that are manifest between North Americans and Latin Americans in legal-political institutions, in relationships between the sexes, in matters of hierarchy and social class, in attitudes toward work and leisure, in the different valuations of rural and urban life—all can be traced to the very foundations of the two American civilizations. Each began with different institutional starting points that imposed distinct developmental imperatives. Adaptations to New World conditions have done remarkably little to erase the differences.

For a simple example, consider the pan-Mediterranean appreciation for city life that Spaniards and Portuguese transmitted to the New World. The following is a description of attitudes in contemporary Spain (Foster 1960: 35):

> The love of crowded and busy streets, noisy markets, and cool coffee houses with their opportunities for endless conversation is ingrained in the Spaniard. To him the urban way of life, however simple its form may be, is a basic value without which life would be difficult.

Virtually the same complex of attitudes can be found throughout Latin America; in the desert towns of Mexico, in tropical forest regions, and, as the following passage indicates, in tiny communities scattered throughout the interior of Brazil (Harris 1956: 32):

> The people of Minas Velhas [of the eastern Brazilian highlands] . . . are passionately fond of the quality of life called *movimento*. At the fair or a religious *festa*, the *movimento* is at its best—a combination of shuffling feet, voices in debate, church bells ringing, a band playing, firecrackers going off, and people milling about in their best clothes. The average level of *movimento* is the factor which most distinguishes the city from the country and a good city from a mediocre one in the eyes of the people.

In the United States, as in England, the dominant sentiment is reversed. Quiet suburbs and treelined lanes are idealized; if one must live in a city, it should be one with many parks and bucolic recreation areas that provide welcome relief from life in the streets. Cities are frequently conceived to be dehumanizing, oppressive, noisy, and unhealthy (Eames and Goode 1977: 55). This is the common viewpoint unless, of course, it concerns one of America's Mediterranean-derived ethnic groups. Here is a sociologist's characterization of attitudes in an Italian-American neighborhood (called West End) in Boston, Massachusetts (Gans 1962: 22–23):

> West Enders avoid "the country," by which they mean not only rural and vacation areas, but also the lower density suburban towns. They do not like its isolation and, even at vacation time, they go to the densely populated resort areas where the crowds and entertainment facilities of the city prevail. . . . I was told by one social worker of an experiment some years back to expose West End children to nature by taking them on a trip to Cape Cod. The experiment failed, for the young West Enders found no pleasure in the loneliness of natural surroundings and wanted to get back to the West End as quickly as possible. They were incredulous that anyone could live without people around him.

What this example of urban attitudes demonstrates is that once a particular type of community is established it carries with it certain principles of organization, outlooks, and values. It also demonstrates that environment is occasionally an insignificant factor, since in this case the same "Mediterranean" urban complex can be found in virtually every natural region of Latin America, and even in some North American cities where Latins have formed their own communities. Much the same could be said about male-female relations and about attitudes toward physical labor: these are generally similar throughout Latin America and are consistent with forms still encountered in Spain, but differ strikingly from prevailing patterns in the United States.

There are those who would answer this argument, however, by maintaining that the contrast is largely a question of development: that once Latin American countries achieve the same level of industrial maturity as the United States their institutional structure will change accordingly. And to a certain extent this is likely to happen. But differences, even important ones, will always remain. The lessons of Japanese industrialization should convince anyone that modernization does not necessarily eliminate national singularity. The Japanese transformation is in fact an excellent example of some of the very processes discussed in this chapter: of the pervasive influence of the past, of the tendency to make compromise adjustments and to build upon pre-existing institutions. Latin American countries can be expected to do the same and are also likely to perpetuate distinctive styles of cultural growth.

Conclusion

The emphasis that has been placed on conservatism and stability in this chapter is not intended to disavow anything that was said about the adaptational perspective in the last chapter. It is rather to stress that there are always *two* features of human society and culture that must be considered in any set of concrete circumstances: *adaptive modification* and the tendency to *preserve what exists*. This opposition is manifested by a perpetual tension in society between efficiency and stability: efficiency because humans prefer to accomplish their ends with economy of effort; and stability because as soon as social practices come into existence they become encrusted with vested interests of various kinds.

Another reason the forces of persistence have been accentuated is that they are so often overlooked. The historian Crane Brinton puzzled over this fact in his famous account of western revolutionary history in *The Anatomy of Revolution*. In a summary statement he noted that even the greatest revolutions do not succeed in carrying out more than a fraction of the social reforms advocated by the revolutionary enthusiasts. In what Brinton calls the "crisis stage" of revolution, the committed radicals attempt to institute sweeping reforms. They often want to alter the structure of the family, change the personal habits of individual citizens, abolish all sources of inequality and usher in a brotherhood of man on earth. These great designs fail. Or if some are achieved the victory is only temporary. When the revolutionary dust settles there is always a period of convalescence that witnesses a return of much of the structure of the old society. Brinton concluded, therefore, that the everyday behavior and habits of individuals are modified only with great difficulty, and this is because there are always forces operating against change. He says (1952: 260–61):

> . . . if we adopt the very plausible concept of social equilibrium, we must expect to find certain forces pulling in the opposite direction [against revolutionary change], in the direction of stability. These forces are not as a rule articulate. They do not seem to interest intellectuals as much as do forces making for change. They are perhaps a bit undignified, and certainly undramatic. Insofar as they do get themselves translated into language, they appear in a variety of logical disguises difficult to penetrate. But they are there, and as we have seen, they set a definite limit to what the reformer or revolutionist can do.

This chapter has specified what some of these inarticulate and undramatic forces are and has pointed to their significance.

Suggested Readings

Gladwin, Thomas, Personality Structure in the Plains, *Anthropological Quarterly*, Vol. 30, pp. 111–24, 1957.
Gladwin compares the typical personality traits of Cheyenne and Comanche Indians to show that there was considerable continuity with the cultural past in each case.

Sahlins, Marshall D., Culture and Environment: The Study of Cultural Ecology, in Sol Tax, ed., *Horizons of Anthropology*, Chicago: Aldine, 1964.
An excellent essay on the relationship between culture and environment. This represents one step in Sahlins's developing concern about the validity of an ecological viewpoint. For his more recent stance see his *Culture and Practical Reason*.

Sahlins, Marshall D., and Elman R. Service, *Evolution and Culture*. Ann Arbor: University of Michigan Press, 1960.
The authors explore the process of cultural evolution by examining some of the similarities between biological and cultural evolution. The section that bears most directly on the question of persistence is the final chapter, "The Law of Evolutionary Potential."

Sharp, Lauriston, Steel Axes for Stone-age Australians, *Human Organization*, Vol. 11, No. 1, 1952.
This study exemplifies with remarkable clarity the functionalist dictum that societies are composed of mutually interrelated parts, and that if one part is affected there are ramifications throughout the whole. Sharp shows how the introduction of European technology to an aboriginal tribe undermined social roles, upset their totemic cosmology, and led to rapid cultural disintegration.

Veblen, Thorstein, *Imperial Germany and the Industrial Revolution*. Ann Arbor: University of Michigan Press, 1915.
This little classic should be required reading for anyone interested in the relationship between economic forces and social change. Veblen is as capable of showing how economic forces can give rise to social institutions as he is of analyzing the social forces that can harness and constrain economies.

Chapter 6

The Native's Rationale and Symbolic Meaning

If the reader has drawn the appropriate implications from the previous discussion, it will be evident why anthropologists cannot always view customs as sane, practical wisdom or as the "best" way of doing things: there is simply too much in human behavior and culture that cannot be explained in such terms. How then does this accord with what was said in Chapter Four about the anthropologist's task of making sense out of all manner of customs, and the effort to demonstrate the essential "reasonableness" of these customs once the environing context is understood? The argument concerning integration is a partial answer to this question, since there it was demonstrated that customs have not only an external context (climate, physical landscape, other societies), but also an internal one: they fit into, or have a place within, a sociocultural system. Practices that therefore make no sense in terms of the external environment, and in fact may be inefficient and even maladaptive from that perspective, frequently make excellent sense once we perceive their linkages to other parts of the social whole.

Interpreting Behavior: The Native's Rationale

But there is another and equally important respect in which customs can be understood *in*ternally, and this is by viewing them as part of the logical, meaningful order of the actors in any particular society. This is what was referred to in Chapter One as the subjective point of view, and it is a crucial component of anthropological understanding.

A subjective approach, or view from the inside, as it is sometimes called, is essential to the anthropologist simply because all human beings inhabit a cultural world of symbolic meanings and shared understandings. Like all animals, humans reside in a universe of physical, material things: of rocks, trees, mountains, air, and so forth. But unlike any other animal, they also inhabit a world entirely of their own making, a world of conventionalized meanings that may have only a tenuous relationship to the material realm. Moreover, this synthetic or manmade environment can exercise just as powerful an influence on their behavior as the world of everyday things. Some examples from Eskimo ethnography will illustrate.

Edward Weyer, a student of the Arctic, once described the marvellous resourcefulness that Eskimos display in dealing with their harsh environment. With very few resources, without metal (in former times), and with very little wood, they successfully hunted whales, the world's largest animals. They built ingenious snow houses to protect themselves from the cold, even fashioning translucent windows from sheets of ice. Weyer describes how their dog-drawn sledge could be constructed despite the unavailability of the normal materials (1932: 71):

> The height of ingenuity is displayed in the building of a
> sledge of frozen hide. Pieces of walrus skin or musk-ox
> skin are soaked in water, folded into the desired forms,
> and allowed to freeze solid. . . . The frozen hide is used
> chiefly for runners, the cross-pieces being commonly of
> bone. The Arvilingjuarmuit [an Eskimo group] . . . would
> roll up raw meat or fish in the hide that was to be frozen

for sledge runners. After thawing, the skins were fed to the dogs that had drawn the sledge, while the contents were eaten by their masters.

Eskimos know in meticulous detail the habits of the animals they hunt. On the open ice, hunters creep up on sun-basking seals by imitating their body movements and uttering their typical barks and sounds; by convincing the animal that he is just another seal, the hunter approaches so close that he is able to leap up and harpoon the beguiled animal.

Wolves are taken with "spring bait." This is accomplished by sharpening the ends of a small strip of whale bone. The springy material is then doubled by force and tied with sinew. It is next buried in a lump of fat and the whole is frozen. The sinew is then cut and the lump is thrown out onto the snow. During the night a wolf discovers the morsel and gulps it down. The warmth of his stomach melts the fat, releasing the whale bone spring, which rips the animal internally, killing it. Another manner of taking wolves is by burying a blood-smeared knife in the ground with only the sharp blade protruding. A hungry wolf is attracted by the blood, begins licking the knife, and cuts his mouth and tongue. "Excited by the taste and smell he gormandizes, literally whetting his own appetite. Finally he dies, bled to death and gorged with his own lifeblood" (Weyer 1932: 73).

These are striking examples of the Eskimo mastery of the environment. They have a technological solution to almost every problem, and display such ingenuity in overcoming subsistence dilemmas that they have been called "remarkable primitive engineers" (Balikci 1970: 3).

Such mastery, however, relates only to the physical environment. There is another world that Eskimos must contend with, and here their behavior stands in stark contrast to the foregoing characterization. Weyer writes (1932: 74):

> Aside from his physical environment, the Eskimo faces another set of life-conditions, his spirit world. As with all peoples . . . his imagination fills the world with ghosts, demons, and deities, to him just as exacting in their

requirements as the forces of the natural world. And in his responses to this supernatural environment, in contrast with his responses to the physical environment, he often displays what, on the surface at least, might seem to be inefficiency and lack of economy.

Weyer refers here to the elaborate supernatural measures taken to protect themselves from harm, since Eskimos believe that dangerous, unseen forces threaten them from all sides. Rasmussen (1931: 239) described people of the Netsilik tribe who lived in such fear of the half-human, half-animal spirits imagined to roam the nocturnal landscape that they were reluctant to venture out at night, even to urinate. Encounters with these spirits were a daily occurrence. The following incident is typical (Rasmussen 1931: 60). On a trip across King William's land, one of Rasmussen's Eskimo companions forgot his gunpowder at the morning camp. He therefore sent his wife back along the trail to retrieve it. Since it was a long distance back, she was reluctant about the mission and set off sullenly. She returned unexpectedly two hours later, distraught and crying. She blubbered that she had been chased and almost overtaken by an evil spirit, and so she had turned back. Her husband was deeply moved by her story, consoled her, and set out immediately to fetch the powder himself. Rasmussen comments: "It would never occur to him for a moment that the [wife's] tale of the spirit might be a pretext to relieve her of the long and fatiguing trudge."

Eskimos also surround themselves with numerous amulets and charms designed to ward off a particular calamity or to enhance a certain skill. The parents of one Netsilik boy, in order to protect him and to make him into a great hunter, had sewn eighty different amulets into his clothing, so many that he was restricted in his movements.

By far the most important means of warding off danger, however, is through the observance of taboos. A taboo is a prohibition against a certain act or type of behavior, and such prohibitions are a ubiquitous feature of Eskimo life. In virtually all spheres of activity there are various acts that are thought to be dangerous and are proscribed.

Take, for example, the observances that become necessary after a hunter has killed a seal and brings it back to
camp. Before dragging the carcass into a dwelling, the hunter
must lift a cup and gently pour drinking water over the dead
animal's snout. Then, before butchering the animal, there
are numerous things that should not be done (Rasmussen
1931: 167):

> In winter, while the sun is low in the sky, no woman may
> sew or do any other work as long as the seal brought into
> the house has not been cut up. Nor may men work in ordi-
> nary stone or soapstone, or in wood or iron. No footwear
> may be dried over the rack and no woman may comb her
> hair or wash her face.
>
> If it is cold outside and rime has covered the window
> pane, this rime must not be scraped off as is usually done,
> as long as unflensed seals lie on the floor. And if there
> is old blubber from last season's . . . [hunt] lying in the
> house, this must be taken out through the window—never
> through the doorway—before the seal is even brought in.

How are we to interpret all of this? It should be obvious
that behavior of this sort presents the anthropologist with
problems of greater complexity than does the purely instru-
mental conduct associated with making a living. In the case
of the spring bait trap, for example, the anthropologist's task
is merely one of observation: he watches as the spring mechanism is constructed and then sees its practical result, a dead
wolf. The intent of the operation is not difficult to comprehend, it is mere cause and effect.

But the custom of giving dead seals a drink, or the labo-
rious procedure of removing blubber through an airtight window instead of simply taking it out the door—how are these
acts to be understood? What practical outcome can we discern?

The answer, of course, is that there *is* no practical outcome, or at least none that can be directly observed. The
best resort of the anthropologist in such instances, therefore,
is to attempt to penetrate the mental world of the natives—
to ask them what they *think* they are accomplishing when
they do these apparently impractical things.

To pursue the example at hand, if we were to ask the Netsilik Eskimos why they observe the abovementioned conventions after a seal is killed, they would likely reply that they are observed "to please the seal's soul." Probing farther, we would discover that Eskimos not only believe that animals have souls, but that the soul is thought to return to the sea to be reincarnated as another seal. If the dead animal therefore considers that the hunter has treated his body with thoughtfulness and respect, the reincarnated seal will then be willing to become prey for that hunter again. If, on the other hand, in his treatment of the animal the hunter fails to observe certain proprieties—such as offering drinking water as if to an honored guest, and refraining from most ordinary activities until the flesh is properly disposed of—the animals will avoid that hunter in the future and he will be plagued by lack of success in the hunt.

This knowledge, then, helps to "explain" the Eskimos' behavior. Once we understand their beliefs regarding souls and animal reincarnation, the practice of giving dead animals a drink and the various ritual expressions of respect embodied in the system of taboos all follow logically: they are a means, we would say magical ones, that the hunters employ to ensure their future success.

A great deal of anthropological explanation is of just this kind: the investigator tries to disclose the context of meaning in which particular acts take place. Once the underlying premises are understood, the practices appear reasonable, at least from the native's point of view.

The Issue of Logical Behavior

Thus the attempt to understand a people by uncovering the thoughts that lie behind their actions can yield important insights. Since no people consider their own behavior either preposterous or bizarre, there is necessarily a logic to it that can be discovered by putting ourselves in their place. This approach depends, of course, on one important assumption: that ideas and behavior are indeed logical. There has been some controversy on this point, since anthropologists have occasionally encountered beliefs so exotic that they appear to defy explanation in rational terms. In fact, certain scholars at the turn of this century claimed that the patterns of thought of primitive peoples were "mystical" rather than logical, and that if we were to understand them we would have to follow a completely different set of mental processes from those familiar in our own society.

Yet close scrutiny of beliefs of tribal peoples has invariably shown that there is an impressive logical consistency to them once we grant the premises upon which they are based. Perhaps the most famous demonstration of this point was carried out years ago (1937) by Evans-Pritchard in his study of the Azande, a tribal people of central Africa.

The Azande are a people who are intensely preoccupied with witchcraft and magic, a set of beliefs that can be said to constitute a focal point of their culture. The major premise of this system of beliefs is that certain unidentified men and women, living among them, possess inherent powers to do others harm. By a mere act of will these witches are thought capable of sending a spirit entity called *mbisimo mangu* ("the soul of witchcraft") through the night to feed upon the organs and flesh of their intended victims, causing illness and death. Virtually all serious sickness and all deaths are attributed by the Azande to the evil machinations of witches. In their view of things there is virtually no concept of accidental death: people die because they have been murdered, either by witches or by the vengeance magic that people employ to retaliate against persons suspected of witchcraft.

Even the activities of daily living are thought to be menaced by witches. Thus if a potter discovers that some of his wares have cracked while in the kiln, he hints darkly of witchcraft; if a farmer's ground-nut crop is ruined it is due to witchcraft; if a child injures her toe on a root while walking through the village, she suspects witchcraft; if a man is gored by an elephant while out hunting, he says the injury was caused by witches. "If in fact," says Evans-Pritchard, "any failure or misfortune falls upon anyone at any time and in relation to any of the manifold activities of his life it may be due to witchcraft" (1937: 63–64).

Now this strikes us as a singular set of beliefs. How can a people fail to recognize that accidents occur? Are they so blind to natural causes that they cannot see that it is old age that eventually kills a person and not the actions of witchcraft?

Evans-Pritchard asked some of the same questions. He tells us that he frequently argued with his Azande hosts when they explained events in terms of witchcraft, events that appeared to him readily explicable by reference to natural causes. He soon discovered that Azande did not attempt to account for all phenomena mystically. They had in fact very clear notions about natural causation. Thus when a young boy injured his foot on a stump and attributed the injury to witchcraft, Evans-Pritchard protested that witchcraft had nothing to do with placing the stump in his path. The boy readily agreed, saying that it was nature that had placed the stump there. Nor did he argue that his cut was caused by witchcraft, for it was clearly the stump that had occasioned the injury. What he *did* explain by resort to witchcraft was the fact that, despite keeping his eyes open for stumps, he had knocked into this one, when on hundreds of other occasions this had not happened. In other words, the only aspect that he attempted to explain by witchcraft was a particular concatenation of events.

This boy, like all Azande, distinguished clearly between ultimate and secondary causes, witchcraft being the ultimate cause. Thus when a man of the village committed suicide it was generally believed that he had been killed by witchcraft even though everybody knew that the immediate cause of death was by hanging from a tree; and further, that the man had hanged himself in the first place because he was angry with his brothers. When Evans-Pritchard then asked why it was logical to say that death was attributable to witchcraft, his Azande friends reasoned that (1937: 71)

. . . only crazy people commit suicide, and that if everyone who was angry with his brothers committed suicide there would soon be no people left in the world, and that if this man had not been bewitched he would not have done what he did do.

To provide a final example, when an old granary collapsed and injured several people sitting beneath it, the Azande thought witchcraft was responsible. But they did not argue that witchcraft caused the granary to fall. They all knew perfectly well that termites had consumed the supports causing the wood to weaken and crumble. Neither did they say that witchcraft induced the people to go there at that time, for it was obviously the afternoon heat that led them to seek shelter under the granary, as Azande are accustomed to do on every hot day. But they *did* think that witchcraft brought these two chains of events together. Here Evans-Pritchard points up the slight difference between their reasoning and our own (1937: 70):

> We say that the granary collapsed because its supports were eaten away by termites. That is the cause that explains the collapse of the granary. We also say that people were sitting under it at the time because it was in the heat of the day and they thought that it would be a comfortable place to talk and work. This is the cause of people being under the granary at the time it collapsed. To our minds the only relationship between these two independently caused facts is their coincidence in time and space. We have no explanation of why the two chains of causation intersected at a certain time and in a certain place. . . .
>
> Zande philosophy can supply the missing link. . . . [They know] why these two events occurred at a precisely similar moment. . . . It was due to the action of witchcraft.

What the Azande explain by reference to witchcraft, then, are coincidental events that result in misfortune. In our own society a person who is suddenly injured, or catches a rare disease, or experiences some dreadfully bad luck often asks, "Why has this happened to me?" The Zande does not ask such a question because he knows the answer: some spiteful person wishes him harm, and has bewitched him.

Thus it is the logic of Azande notions that emerges from Evans-Pritchard's account. Once the mystical premise—that witches exist and that they do people harm—is granted, there is no difficulty in following their arguments, since they are coherent and logical. It is only the underlying premise that we disagree with. The Azande example is not fundamentally different, therefore, from that of a Western scientist who arrives at flawed conclusions not because his *reasoning* is faulty, but because the theory that he employs is unsound from the beginning.

Both of the preceding examples, of Eskimo and Azande, thus show the advantage of penetrating the subjective world of the natives. Once we understand native conceptions we are able to put ourselves in their place; their beliefs and behavior become patterns of thought and action that we ourselves might perform under the same circumstances. Evans-Pritchard has even remarked that while living among the Azande he found that it was easy to fall into their way of thinking: "I too," he tells us, "used to react to misfortune in the idiom of witchcraft, and it was often an effort to check this lapse into unreason" (1937: 99).

Finally, it is worth noting that the subjective approach that has been outlined here is virtually unique to the sciences that deal with humankind. A physical scientist, say a chemist or physicist, is concerned only with the objective properties of the phenomena investigated. He cannot inquire into the subjective attitudes, ideals, or motivations of gases or metals, because such phenomena possess nothing of the sort. Even the zoologist who studies a deme of lizards does not interpret their behavior in terms of lizard ideals or philosophy, because if these exist at all they do so at an extremely rudimentary level. But with humans it is very different. Like the Eskimo and Azande, all people create elaborate systems of shared meanings and then live to some extent in accordance with these manmade conceptions. As one anthropologist has expressed it, man is unique in that he is the only animal perpetually "suspended in webs of significance he himself has spun" (Geertz 1973: 5).

When the Individual Does Not Understand

Now that the significance of the actor's point of view has been sufficiently stressed, I hasten to add that it is not the end-all of anthropological research. The approach has, in fact, very significant limitations. As noted in Chapter Two, the interpretation of a society that an anthropologist obtains never derives entirely from the statements and beliefs of his informants. There are many things about a society, and about their own behavior in it, that most individuals simply do not understand. This is because many human actions are of a traditionalist, rote kind; they are engaged in because the individuals have been taught to perform them, and not because they know the specific reasons behind their actions. Thus it is conceivable that the anthropologist mentioned earlier who asked Eskimo hunters why they give dead seals a drink could receive in reply a shrug of the shoulders and nothing more enlightening than, "it is the way of our ancestors"; and it might happen that no member of the community could provide any more satisfying explanation.

Much the same occurs in our own society when we ask why men button their shirts on the right, but women button theirs on the left. The immediate answer, of course, is that we buy our clothes this way; but why they are designed to such a pattern is not readily apparent. Even women who sew their own clothing follow this design, and if questioned on the matter they say something like, "that's the way women's clothes are made" or "it's always done that way."

A great deal of culture is like this: customs are adhered to with very little thought given to them. This unanalyzed nature of culture is not as obvious as it might be, due to the propensity for individuals to offer folk explanations, or what Franz Boas called "secondary rationalizations," for various aspects of their own behavior. In contemporary America this is done frequently. I remember as a small boy asking my mother why our relatives always said "God bless you" or "Gesundheit" when I sneezed. My mother "explained": "They say your heart completely stops when you sneeze, and it's a dangerous moment. People bless you because of this danger."

There is probably no medical foundation to such an explanation. Yet a reflex custom like this, in pragmatic America, calls out for justification. The pseudomedical explanation makes it appear at least partly reasonable.

An explanation of similar nature is encountered in many American Jewish households when children ask why Jews are counseled not to eat pork or shellfish. In orthodox families the answer may simply be "tradition," with no additional attempt at explanation. But in households of nonpracticing Jews the children are sometimes told that these animals were originally considered unclean for good medical reasons. In olden times, the story goes, pork was a dangerous food because, if not properly prepared, one could contract a disease. The ban on shellfish was instituted for similar reasons: at certain times of the year mollusks were contaminated and therefore dangerous. Both prohibitions can be understood, therefore, in practical, hygienic terms.

Such explanations have a number of difficulties. Dangerous diseases have always been contracted from sheep and cattle, just as from pigs, yet there was no prohibition. And what about the flesh of many other animals prohibited by the Hebrews? Can all be explained in the same medical terms? Moreover, even if there were originally medical reasons for the prohibitions, why have they been maintained for centuries under conditions in which the original reasons no longer apply?

This is not, of course, the place for an extended discussion of food taboos. Let it suffice that anthropologists have not generally given much credence to these folk explanations (Douglas 1966: 41–72; Harris 1974: 28–38). They can be thought of as rationalizations: the ways that Americans explain to themselves customs that they essentially do not understand.

These examples demonstrate that there is a portion of any culture that remains covert, or at least that lies outside of the objective awareness of members of that society. When anthropologists deal with these aspects of culture they must perforce seek explanations for cultural practices that surpass the natives' understanding. This disparity between the natives' comprehension and that of the scientific observer becomes particularly apparent when anthropologists deal with what will be referred to as *symbolic meanings*.

Meaning and the Symbolic Realm

Ever since the work of Émile Durkheim early in this century, anthropologists have been aware that complex symbolical codes exist in every society. Durkheim made this point most forcefully in his analysis of the religious beliefs and rituals of the Australian aborigines (Durkheim 1912). He argued that their religious rites were most profitably viewed *not* in terms of the professed beliefs of the natives, but as a *wordless language of symbolical acts* that, taken together, expressed important truths about their society. He rejected, in other words, the notion that the avowed beliefs of a people are essential keys to understanding religious actions. Rather than concentrating on the beliefs, the more important task was to *decode the messages about society* that are expressed particularly in ritual (Skorupski 1976: 18).

An illustration will make this clear. Let us look for a moment at some of the religious rites that were widespread in China prior to the ascendancy of communism there in 1949. The rites in question were household rituals and were based on an elaborate cult of ancestor worship. In the main room of virtually every Chinese home there was an altar that contained spirit tablets commemorating the family's dead. All significant domestic ceremonies were conducted before this altar, the most important being funeral rites and periodic sacrificial rituals carried out to memorialize deceased members of the family.

In the funeral ceremonies the conscious attention of the bereaved was on a complex of notions regarding the dead person's soul. Various ritual acts were performed that aimed at ensuring the safe conduct of the spirit on its journey to the afterworld. To this end the corpse was dressed in elegant clothing, it was provisioned with the personal effects believed necessary for the afterlife journey, and the route of the funeral procession was littered with paper money to buy noninterference from evil spirits (Yang 1961: 29–33). The periodic sacrificial rites that were conducted in the home were also concerned with the souls of the departed; incense was burned for them and rice was placed before the altar to provide the spirits nourishment.

It is important to note, however, that the above rites were carried out in a carefully prescribed manner; each family member was required to kneel and to pray in turn. As a Chinese scholar has written (Yang 1961: 39):

The head of the family performed the rites first, and the other members followed in the order of their status in the family. In the case of sacrifice on the death anniversary of a departed member, full rites were not performed by a senior member to the spirit of a junior member, such as a living father to a dead child. As in the mortuary rites, the enactment of the status of each family member during a sacrifice was a rehearsal of the family organization. The family as a well-patterned unit of collective life was thus periodically impressed upon the members.

Ritual actions are here interpreted, therefore, as a symbolic expression and reaffirmation of crucial social values. In essence the ritual "says" something to each participant. It impresses upon them the principles of hierarchy, birth order, and prerogative—values that were of fundamental importance to the Chinese family and society. The ritual also suffused these principles with a sacred quality, making them seem an immutable part of the natural order.

Many participants may have been unaware of the specific messages embodied in this ritual. But the fact that they were unaware of them does not mean that messages were not received and that they did not have an impact on behavior. As early as the third century B.C. Confucian scholars extolled the purely social effects of sacrifice rites. The common people, it was admitted, thought that the rites were "a serving of the spirits"; but educated people recognized that they were to reinforce important social ideals (Yang 1961: 48). And in the *Book of Rites* we read that, "Rites . . . punishments, laws have one and the same end, to unite hearts and establish order" (quoted in Radcliffe-Brown 1952: 159).

But this entire question of individual comprehension remains a controversial one in anthropology, since various scholars have voiced suspicion of studies that deal with unverbalized symbols that the natives are supposedly unaware of (Kaplan and Manners 1972: 115–16). The noted anthropologist S. F. Nadel once remarked that if the participants in a society are not conscious of their own symbols, then the latter cannot have any significant effect on behavior.

He contended, therefore, that "uncomprehended symbols have no part in social enquiry" (Nadel 1954: 108).

An issue very similar to this has been debated at length in the field of literary criticism, with some commentators arguing that if readers are not cognizant of the particular symbols in a literary work, the symbolism cannot have meaning for them. Others have argued, however, that there are many different levels of awareness. A student of symbolist literature has accordingly written that even if a reader does not apprehend the particular analogy intended by a symbol he (Tindall 1967: 15)

> . . . may respond beneath the level of awareness and find himself surprised by an enrichment he cannot account for. Perhaps this is the commonest and best way to take symbolist writing. For critics, however, unawareness is a fault. Their response to symbolism . . . [is] far keener than that of most authors and readers.

The above writer thus contends that a reader may appreciate a symbolic relationship, and respond to it, without being able to articulate its meaning. Indeed the same can even be true of the author of a literary work. The following letter, written by Herman Melville to Mrs. Nathaniel Hawthorne, reveals how Melville became aware of some of the symbolic meaning in his own *Moby Dick* (quoted in Tindall 1967: 13):

> Your allusion for example to the "Spirit Spout" first showed me that there was a subtle significance in that thing —but I did not, in that case, *mean* it. I had some vague idea while writing it, that the whole book was susceptible of an allegoric [read symbolic] construction, and also that *parts* of it were—but the speciality of many of the particular subordinate allegories, were first revealed to me, after reading Mr. Hawthorne's letter, which, without citing any particular examples, yet intimated the part & parcel allegoricalness of the whole.

It comes as something of a surprise to learn that Melville was creating certain symbolic meanings without being consciously aware of doing so.

These examples of symbolism in literature are invoked here because of the obvious parallels that can be drawn with the study of culture. People in everyday life express themselves symbolically, just as writers and artists do, without necessarily understanding the full range of meanings of their expression.

A second parallel arises from the fact that enhanced awareness of symbolical meaning can emerge from detailed analysis. In the study of literature it is the perceptive critic who routinely attains this level of comprehension; by dissecting a literary work and examining the part-to-whole relationships, the critic renders explicit what remains merely implicit for others. This is similar to the advantage the anthropologist enjoys in the study of society. By assuming a broader perspective than that of any of the participants (see Chapter Two), and by discovering how one institution fits with another, anthropologists are able to perceive connections and meanings that are not obvious to members of that society.

Since this is a rather abstract discussion, some examples of symbolic expression in our own Western culture will be helpful. In each of the following examples there is an effort to show that symbolic expression is utilized by individuals as a matter of course, but that, like language, it is usually employed intuitively, so that individuals rarely comprehend the larger ramifications of its usage.

The Social Meaning of Body Symbolism

Various anthropologists have pointed out that the way we treat our own physical bodies—the care with which we adorn the body or leave it in a state of relative abandonment—is a powerful means of expressing our relationship to the social order (Hallpike 1969; Douglas 1973; Firth 1973: 262–98). In particular, it has been argued, this bodily symbolism is used to express either conformity or lack of conformity to the central norms of the society. Let us examine this proposition in detail.

If we observe the occupational structure of American society, it is readily apparent that people of different professions adhere to rather different codes of dress. Generally speaking, and of course admitting many exceptions, male members of professions that are charged with supporting the main morality of the society, or whose occupations are heavily dependent on enforcement of the legal code, such as judges, lawyers, accountants, stockbrokers, business executives, all tend to dress conservatively. Their apparel and bodily trim suggest a buttoned-down, controlled quality; suits and shirts tend not to be flamboyant, hair is worn short-to-medium in length (relative of course to the style of the day), and it is groomed; if they sport facial hair, it tends to be tidily trimmed rather than shaggy.

On the other hand, individuals who belong to professions that are associated with social criticism, or whose members think of themselves as alienated in some way from the mainstream of society—such as artists, writers, intellectuals, certain types of college professors—all tend to adopt a looser, less managed style of dress and bodily care. Their clothing tends toward the fanciful and frequently betrays a disorderly or careless quality. Hair is commonly worn longer and less restrained than the prevailing style; if beards and mustaches are grown, they are more likely to be shaggy than to be carefully cropped (Douglas 1973: 102).

These are, of course, broad generalizations; but in the main the characterization holds. It does so because members of different professions express, in bodily idiom, their degree of adherence to, or alienation from, the established society. Tightness of dress and rigid body control suggest obedience to the social order; looseness and unbridling of the body signify freedom from social control (Douglas 1973: 102).

But let us drive this proposition harder. If there is indeed a symbolic association between detachment from social norms and degree of bodily abandonment, we thus have a right to expect that when persons *want* to suggest that they stand outside of the moral order, or at least want to imply that social rules do not affect them, they will frequently express this by adopting bizarre conditions of bodily attention.

There are various types of individuals who, for diverse reasons, endeavor to express alienation from society; the most notable are religious devotees of various kinds, such as hermits, holy men, and prophets. But social revolutionaries and rebels also fit the mold, as do persons with certain kinds of mental disorders.

Religious prophets are individuals thought to be divinely inspired spokesmen for God. They are people with a message, and they generally denounce the evils of their society and proclaim a new morality. Their characteristic pose, therefore, is to stand apart from, and to condemn, society. Religious hermits are similar, but rather than attempting to deliver a message they entirely renounce the company of other people to live in isolation.

A most striking characteristic of both prophets and hermits is that they tend to be unkempt and bizarre in personal adornment. While we do not know a great deal about the appearance of the ancient Judaic prophets, what we do know is significant. We learn that Elijah wore his hair long enough to attract negative comment; Isaiah went, for a time, completely naked; Jeremiah paraded with a yoke around his neck; John the Baptist dressed in animal skins; and other prophets wore iron horns on their heads (Weber 1952: 286–87). Our picture of more recent, Christian, prophets is of course far richer in detail. The following is a characterization, taken from eyewitness accounts, of Antonio Conselheiro, a prophet who appeared in northern Brazil in the late nineteenth century (Da Cunha 1944: 127–28):

And so there appeared in Baía the somber anchorite with hair down to his shoulders, a long tangled beard, an emaciated face, and a piercing eye, a monstrous being clad in a blue canvas garment and learning on the classic staff. . . .

We are told that the man ate little, had no regard for bodily well-being, and was "filthy and battered in appearance" (Da Cunha 1944: 128–30).

Da Cunha's reference to the prophet as an "anchorite" is entirely fitting. The anchorites were Christian hermits who deliberately abandoned society in fourth century Egypt and Syria. They refused even the company of other monks, preferring to live in isolated huts or in desert caves. Their dress was wholly unconventional. Some went entirely naked, covering their bodies only with their unshorn hair; others dressed in animal skins; still others tried to imitate animals, even grazing in the fields like cattle. All of them treated their bodies with contempt. They hung heavy weights around their necks, did punishing exercises, and mutilated themselves. One of the most famous of these hermits, St. Simeon Stylites (ca. 389–459), is reported to have lived on top of a pillar for over thirty years, arriving at such a state of physical neglect that we hear of people gathering to worship "the worms that dropped from his body" (Burns 1980: 222).

What all of these religious enthusiasts have in common, and what they all apparently express, is that they obey a law that is higher than that of mere humans. Their disregard of appearances and bodily comfort, with its rejection of worldly vanity, suggests that the conventions of society have no bearing on them; they exist, in effect, outside of the common society, obedient only to God.

A second category of individuals who express distance from the larger society by undisciplined styles of dress are various types of social rebels. One needs only to recall the counterculture movement in the United States of the late 1960s and early 70s to be aware of the association between rebellion and bodily expression. The word "dropout" was coined for those who in various ways rejected life in conventional society. Their slack clothing, granny dresses, jeans with patches and holes in them, and particularly the long and unkempt hair became symbols of protest against what was referred to as the establishment. The dropouts, or hippies, labeled conventional people as "straight," "square," or "uptight"—words that aptly characterize the disciplined control over both dress and manners that is always the mark of the organization man. The words that they applied to themselves, on the other hand, were terms like "loose" or "laidback" that signified informality and relaxation of control.

A final group of persons who employ bodily laxness to symbolize alienation from society are certain kinds of mental patients, ones who deliberately violate social rules in order to express contempt for their surroundings. A convenient way for the patient to accomplish this is to disregard the many norms that exist in our society concerning personal appearance and bodily control. Thus patients may refuse to groom themselves, intentionally expose their genitals, cut wind and belch loudly, and in other ways refuse to exercise the control over the animal body that is demanded in all polite society. An observer of these transgressions remarks (Goffman 1963: 27):

> . . . the importance [for everyday social interaction] of a disciplined management of personal front is demonstrated in many ways by the mentally sick. A typical sign of an oncoming psychosis is the individual's "neglect" of his appearance and personal hygiene. The classic home for these improprieties is "regressed" wards in mental hospitals where those with a tendency in this direction are collected. . . . Similarly, when a mental patient starts "taking an interest in personal appearance," and makes an effort at personal grooming, he is often credited with having somehow given up his fight against society and having begun his way back to "reality."

Up to this point we have concentrated on symbols of alienation. As all of the preceding illustrations suggest, however, the symbolism operates in two directions. Thus if loose and untrammeled hair represents freedom from social control, the opposite, closely cropped or shorn hair, is often a sign of strict obedience or conformity (Hallpike 1969).

If we examine the situations in which heads are regularly shaved in our Western society, we find that it is a common practice in certain Catholic orders of monks and nuns, with military cadets and recruits, and with prison populations (though the practice with prisoners is less common now than in the recent past). In each of these situations the head is shorn, or a part of it is, upon entry into a highly disciplined and regimented organization. All of the entrants give up, or have taken away, a significant degree of personal choice in determining their own conduct, and must then abide by strict rules of behavior that emanate from the organization. The situation of convicts is unique only in that they do not enter as a matter of personal choice; the symbolism, however, is the same. Giving up the hair serves as a statement that the entrant, candidate, or novice is under strict discipline; and just as the organization has taken a part of his physical being, so does he also owe it a part of his moral being.

It is highly significant that all of the individuals who have their heads shorn also place their bodies, or have them placed, in uniforms. A uniform is perhaps the ultimate expression of the harnessed body; it is emblematic of regimented order and signifies the degree to which the individual wearing it is at the service of the organization. It is for this reason that we expect a certain, predictable kind of behavior from individuals in uniform; if the body is held in check in such a way, we assume that behavior is similarly constrained. This attitude even carries over into nonwork situations. It often happens that some public emergency arises when a postman or other uniformed individual is off duty; yet people often expect that individual to act in a more self-sacrificing manner than other, nonuniformed citizens who witness the same emergency.

The instances of hair cutting and rigid body control as emblems of social conformity might be extended to historical periods, though with diminished confidence. Is it coincidence, for example, that the 1950s in America, noted as as period of conformity, Republican administration, and campus quietism (Lipset 1972: 185–90), was also the era of the butch haircut, flattops, and the like? And can we expect the 1980s, almost certain to be an era of social and political conservatism, to witness the extinction of the hair styles and clothing of the past rebellious decade? And does the fact that women who go into business, or otherwise enter areas of the traditionally male domain, tend to shorten their hair have a significance beyond the fact that short hair is easy to manage? For it is also true that long hair in women may be a powerful symbol of feminine whimsicality and capriciousness (Hallpike 1969: 261), qualities most women do not want to be associated with in the earnest world of business and careers.

Interpretations: The Culture/Nature Contrast

It is certainly possible to find examples that do not conform to the above pattern, but the cases brought forth are sufficient to show that there is at least a general connection between bodily style and social commitment. The instances also demonstrate how anthropologists typically proceed when investigating symbolic meaning. By finding various contexts in which the same or similar behavior manifests itself, they are able to ask what is common to all the cases and are enabled to say what the behaviors appear to express.

The question that arises at this point, however, is why should the pattern exist at all? Why is existence outside of society so often symbolized by an unbridled body? And why does bodily restraint suggest social allegiance?

At the deepest level the answer probably lies in the contrast, recognized in all societies, between the ordered world of human culture and the untamed world of animals and nature. This culture/nature contrast is one of those basic distinctions, like that between right and left, high and low, day and night, that are probably encountered everywhere.

Let us look at some examples of these contrasting qualities and how they are typically expressed. The right/left distinction is one that occurs very widely. Our society, for example, like many others, has seized upon the obvious physiological difference between right and left hands and has generated an elaborate classification in which the right stands for superiority, nobility, and goodness, and the left is associated with inferiority, weakness, and evil (Hertz 1909).* This is expressed in various forms in everyday speech. When we say some-

---

*Handedness is almost certainly a pan-human trait based on genetics. Estimates of the incidence of right-hand dominance in all known human populations range from 80 to 95 percent (Porac and Coren 1981: 4).

thing is "right" we can mean either that it is correct or just, and words like "righteousness," "upright," and "rectitude" reflect this association. We swear oaths by the right hand, we use it in all greetings, and the right side of a political dignitary, or of one's host on a ceremonial occasion, is the side of greatest honor. Seating on the right was of even greater significance formerly than it is today; for we read that (Vanderbilt 1952: 690)

> In Victorian and earlier times any lady a man seated on his left was no lady. He so proclaimed the fact to prevent any passing male friend from introducing her to his wife.

Finally, rightest political parties originally were those that upheld legitimate power, the "devine right" of kings.

The left hand, on the contrary, comes in for incessant abuse. Many English terms that express impropriety or evil refer to lefthandedness. The word "sinister" derives from the Latin term for the left side. When we say that someone pays a lefthanded compliment we mean that it is awkwardly delivered or insincere. A person notably lacking in social graces is said to be "gauche," the French term for left. And those who hold political views that aim at changing or abolishing the constituted political authority are known as leftists. The right/left distinction surfaces frequently in art and literature. In paintings that portray the Last Judgment, for example, Christ is depicted with his right hand aloft, sending the righteous to paradise, while his left hand gestures downward, banishing sinners to hell.

This last analogy points up a closely related contrast, that between high and low. The former is made to stand for happiness, exaltation, and esteem, while the latter signifies gloom and belittlement. When we say that a person is "up," "high," or "on cloud nine," we mean that he is happy. One who is "low," "depressed," or "downcast," is sad. The aristocrat has high birth, while the peasant's is low. "Lofty" sentiments are good, "base" instincts are reprehensible. This fundamental distinction is carried out in literally hundreds of ways in everyday life, so that when persons or things are placed above others (such as social classes, victors in athletic competitions, officials who receive "groveling" supplicants), we signify that they are somehow better or more praiseworthy than those below them.

A contrast of this kind also exists between the world of culture and the world of nature. The animal kingdom serves in every society as a source of qualities that are considered to be the opposite of human virtues. The most frequent contrast is one that separates the moral world of human sympathy from the unfeeling world of nature. Thus to characterize a person as an "animal," "brute," or "beast" is to assign him infrahuman qualities. But the contrast can also be seen in the dichotomy of tamed/untamed, so that all that is social is conceived of as domesticated, cultivated, and controlled, and all that is identified with nature is thought of as wild and unrestrained. The word *culture* itself derives from the Latin root *colere*, meaning to till, cultivate, or nurture like a plant.

If this is a correct assessment it explains a great deal of the symbolism described above. The reader may have noticed how frequently the identification with animals appeared in the description of individuals who stand apart from the social order: the horns worn by certain Hebrew prophets, John the Baptist's animal skins, the anchorites eating grass like cattle, and many other examples can be found.

An almost identical motif occurs in religious rituals, most notably in certain kinds of initiation and life crisis ceremonials known to anthropologists as *rites of passage*. These rituals are found in virtually all societies, and an anthropologist (Turner 1974: 252–53) who has analyzed the rites in various parts of the world has shown that whenever there is an attempt to detach initiates from the social order—in order to provide them a symbolic rebirth—the detachment is characteristically represented by a profusion of animal and natural symbolism: the neophytes are dressed in bird feathers, animal masks, and garments made of grasses and leaves. It thus seems that whenever there is an effort to express radical separation from society, nature is seized upon as the logical contrast; and this is because nature is the symbolic obverse of culture in the same sense that low is the opposite of high, or as left is treated as the opposite of right.

The hair symbolism that was discussed above can also be interpreted in this light. Since hairiness (i.e., furriness) suggests the animallike nature of the individual, long and unkempt hair in males can easily signify that the person belongs to an unruly natural order rather than to the controlled arena of human society: he appears less domesticated by social constraints than the average citizen.

Another illustration of the opposition between culture and nature is the effort made by all socialized individuals to conceal, or even to deny, the purely creatural aspects of the human body. In our Euro-American society biological processes are considered to belong to the "natural" order, and as such must be separated off from ordinary social intercourse (Douglas 1973: 101). The most evident of these processes are those associated with excretory functions and sexual relations. Both are so hidden away that they remain entirely private acts; any intrusion of nakedness or of bodily elimination into the public domain is a serious offense, occasionally punishable by law. In addition, these same organic processes are the source of all of our most powerful expletives and four-letter words, none of which are to be used in polite company.

The need to disguise our creatural nature is also pointed up by the embarrassment caused when we fail to do so. Everybody is familiar with the "creature releases" (flatulence, belching, digestive rumble, yawns, sneezes, itches, etc.) that can intrude into social interaction at inopportune moments. We are all taught from early childhood to suppress or limit the salience of these eruptions. But despite precautions, the individual occasionally fails. Trapped in a crowded elevator, or seated in a dentist's waiting room, a stomach begins to emit clearly audible sounds. Regardless of the fact that the owner of the stomach has committed no willful offense, he or she suffers embarrassment. The shame is apparently due to the fact that the rumble presents fleeting evidence of our animal nature, every reminder of which should ideally be suppressed (Goffman 1963: 68).

But perhaps the most telling evidence of the culture/nature contrast is the fact that much of our social hierarchy is constructed along this same gradient. The people who are considered to rank highest in terms of social class are those who make the greatest effort to deemphasize their animallike qualities. Aristocrats, as Mary Douglas (1973: 101–02) has pointed out, tend to place great store in manners that project a modulated refinement: they try to minimize the noise and obtrusiveness in eating, they stress formality in dress, control over immediate impulses, soft understatement of voice, and the like. Our manuals of etiquette, many of which are written by ladies of the upper class, constantly reiterate these same values. For example, the table manners that are considered proper in polite society are clearly designed to conceal the more physical aspects of eating, such as slurping, gnawing, chewing, and disgorging food from the mouth. One authority on etiquette states (Post 1955: 485):

> All rules of table manners are made to avoid ugliness. To let anyone see what you have in your mouth is offensive, to make noise is to suggest an animal; to make a mess is disgusting.

And another (Shaw 1958: 146):

> The purpose behind all "how to eat" rules is to keep us from making unsightly spectacles of ourselves to others. Eating is not a pretty performance at best, but eat we must, so every effort should be made to do so in as polite and unobtrusive a way as possible.

What is true of table manners also characterizes all formal etiquette: there is an effort to deemphasize the purely physical aspects of the person and to project an image of composure, self-restraint, and grace.

An image that is frequently advanced of the lowest classes, on the other hand, is one of raw physicality and of animallike qualities. The description of Stanley Kowalski, the proletarian hero of Tennessee Williams's play *A Streetcar Named*

Desire, provides an apt illustration. In the following passage Kowalski and his poker buddies are seen through the eyes of Blanche, a woman with aristocratic pretentions (Nelson 1961: 140):

> He acts like an animal, has an animal's habits! Eats like one, moves like one, talks like one! There's even something—subhuman —something not quite to the stage of humanity yet! Yes, something—ape-like about him, like one of those pictures I've seen in—anthropological studies! . . .Night falls and the other apes gather! There in front of the cave, all grunting like him, and swilling and gnawing and hulking! His poker night!—you call it—this party of apes! Somebody growls—some creature snatches at something—the fight is on! God!

Similar characterizations of the lower classes can be found in studies by sociologists and anthropologists of American communities. When members of the upper classes are called upon to describe the lower elements of their communities they frequently resort to animal imagery. Thus a prominent citizen of "Elmtown," a midwestern community, says (Hollingshead 1949: 48):

> There is a really low class here that is a lulu. It is made up of families who. . . . simply don't have any morals. They have animal urges and they respond to them. They're like a bunch of rats or rabbits.

And in general assessments by Elmtown's upper classes the lowermost group is accused of committing frequent incest, of being loud and coarse in speech, and of rarely rising above a physical level of existence (1949: 78). Nor is the situation of this community atypical. In the American farm community described by James West in *Plainville, U.S.A.*, the lowermost members of the community are routinely spoken of as "people who live like animals."

There is of course no effort to contend that such portrayals are accurate; they are little more than class stereotypes. Nevertheless, the widespread occurrence of this pattern points to the considerable symbolic significance of the culture/nature distinction. It would appear that wherever society is divided into social classes, the upper ranks of the hierarchy appropriate to themselves symbols of disembodiment, thereby separating themselves from the animal/physical plane, and they leave the lower ranks of the hierarchy in varying degrees of association with corporality and nature.

Finally, it should be noted that this is an expression of the same theme regarding marginality, discussed above. Since the lowest classes are in a very real sense marginal to society, it is fitting that they are associated with the symbols common to other examples of social marginality, or what the anthropologist Victor Turner calls social "outsiderhood" (1974: 233). Like prophets, hermits, and initiates in religious ceremonies, and other socially marginal types, they are draped in the symbols of animality and natural processes.

Conclusion

In this chapter, two different modes of anthropological understanding have been addressed. The first is what can be called an *actor-oriented* perspective, or what is known in technical anthropological language as an "emic" approach. Here the aim is to understand the native categories of thought and to know how the natives divide up their social and natural universe. The anthropologist tries to peer inside the culture to determine, to the best of his ability, how that world appears from the native's perspective. As Bronislaw Malinowski expressed it: "This goal is, briefly, to grasp the native's point of view, his relation to life, to realise *his* vision of *his* world" (Malinowski 1922: 25).

The other mode of understanding, the *observer-oriented* perspective, has a different aim. This is known in technical language as an "etic" approach, and the goal is to provide an analysis of the society from an exterior, scientific observer's point of view. Here we typically want to determine the basic architecture of a social system, the systematic relationships between its parts, and the normative principles that underlie social action and belief. The natives generally do not grasp this larger picture. Malinowski understood this aim of anthropological work as well as the other. Writing of the Trobriand Islanders, he remarked that the natives (1922: 83)

> . . . have no knowledge of the *total outline* of any of their social structure. They know their own motives, know the purpose of individual actions and the rules which apply to them, but how, out of these, the whole collective institution . . . [is shaped], this is beyond their mental range. . . . For the integral picture does not exist in . . . [the native's] mind; he is in it, and cannot see the whole from the outside.

The message is clear: an observer-oriented approach probes deeper into the structure of the society than is necessary for those who merely live in it. The observer's perspective has been illustrated in this chapter by concentrating on some of the symbolic meanings found in the Western cultural tradition—elements of everyday experience and a code of meanings that we all employ at one time or another. These illustrations have demonstrated that there is a more profound level of meaning, a deeper structure, in some of our expressive behavior than is apparent on the surface of things.

But a cautionary word is necessary: one should not assume that an observer-oriented approach is always, or necessarily, a symbolical one. The latter is just one, among many theoretical designs that permit anthropologists to surpass the natives' limited vision of their own society.

Suggested Readings

Douglas, Mary, *Purity and Danger: An Analysis of Concepts of Pollution and Taboo*. London: Routledge and Kegan Paul, 1966.
   Douglas's writings embody the most significant new approach to religion and cosmology that has emerged in anthropology since the work of Durkheim and his students at the beginning of this century. A genuine classic.

Douglas, Mary, *Natural Symbols: Explorations in Cosmology*. New York: Pantheon Books, 1970.
   The author argues that our physical bodies provide a system of "natural" symbols that are used to express similar ideas all over

the world. The arguments are daring, speculative, occasionally fuzzy, and controversial. The book is hard going in places, but well worth the effort.

Evans-Pritchard, E. E., *Witchcraft, Oracles and Magic Among the Azande*. Oxford: At the Clarendon Press, 1937.
A classic study of the belief system of a tribal people. With wit and charm, the author shows how Azande beliefs in witches and magic form a consistent, logical, and ideologically defensible system of explanation.

Hallpike, C. R., Social Hair, *Man*, Vol. 4, No. 2, June, pp. 256–64, 1969.
This is a response to Edmund Leach's more famous essay "Magical Hair." Hallpike rejects Leach's psychological interpretations of the meaning of hair symbolism and substitutes some social explanations. My own interpretations owe a great deal to this essay.

Chapter 7

Intracultural Variation

At various points in the preceding chapter's discussion of symbolic themes it was necessary to insert remarks such as, "there is a tendency," "in general," or "admitting many exceptions." These remarks were essential in order to point out that there is always some discrepancy between the abstract or structural characterizations drawn by anthropologists and the concrete reality that is observed in any particular instance. After all, not all women who enter the predominantly male occupational domain wear their hair short; nor do members of the upper classes always behave as the authorities on etiquette might lead one to believe. These are merely tendencies that can be charted, or, if we want to measure them more accurately, that can be expressed in terms of statistical frequencies. Anthropologists write in these general terms because they are concerned primarily with *shared* aspects of behavior, with patterns and regularities, rather than with the exceptional or distinctive qualities.

Be this as it may, anthropologists have not been unconcerned with the question of how their general descriptions relate to the behavior of individuals in living situations. The fact that many persons, in various contexts, do not behave according to sociocultural expectations has always been one of the more intriguing lines of anthropological inquiry. Particularly if we are to understand how societies change over time, then this variation in behavior takes on special significance.

In this chapter we will, therefore, take up the large matter of *intracultural variation* (i.e., the diversity of conduct within particular societies) and look at some of the implications that such variation has for anthropological theory. The general theme was touched upon in Chapter Three, but because of its general importance it merits more detailed consideration.

Diversity of Temperament and Belief

No careful observer of American society would be likely to deny that there is considerable variation of belief and behavior in our everyday life. We take it for granted, for instance, that a committed member of the Mormon Church and a Marxist intellectual would be likely to disagree on a wide variety of social issues. Nor do we expect a member of Boston's upper classes to prefer the same foods, speak, or behave in ways that are characteristic of dirt farmers in Mississippi. Our society is divided by regional, ethnic, occupational, religious, and class lines, and each of these dimensions has a discernible impact on behavior.

But is the same true of all societies? Is this diversity in attitudes and beliefs also characteristic of the small-scale tribal and peasant societies studied by anthropologists and which are *not* cross-cut by regional, class, or occupational divisions? Anthropologists have taken different positions on the matter. The anthropologist Robert Redfield, following in a long tradition of European social thought, argued that homogeneity of belief and behavior is indeed characteristic of isolated tribal—or what he called "folk"—societies. In his global description of such communities he said (1947: 297):

> The people who make up a folk society are much alike. Having lived in long intimacy with one another, and with no others, they have come to form a single biological type. . . . what one man knows and believes is the same

as what all men know and believe. . . . In real fact, of
course, the differences among individuals in a primitive
group and the different chances of experience prevent this
ideal state of things from coming about. Nevertheless, it is
near enough to the truth for the student of a real folk society to report it fairly well by learning what goes on in the
minds of a few of its members, and a primitive group has
been presented, although sketchily, as learned about from a
single member.

Thus while Redfield does qualify his remarks, the thrust of
the statement is to argue that there is little differentiation,
of outlook or character, in simpler societies.

A similar view was often expressed in the early studies
(ca. 1930–50) of the relationship between culture and personality. In these investigations it was commonly assumed
that, due to the uniformity in preliterate societies of the
agents and conditions of socialization, most personalities
were destined to turn out very much alike. It was recognized,
of course, that it was more difficult to assimilate certain
temperaments to a particular cultural pattern than to others,
and that the former would remain the abnormals or deviants
in that society. But these deviant personalities were considered to be relatively few in number, and it was thought that
a vast majority of the adults in any small community would
be found to share the same basic personality type. This was
a widely accepted dogma in the anthropology of the 1930s
and 40s, and the general viewpoint was eloquently expressed
in Ruth Benedict's *Patterns of Culture* (1934).

Thus we have two closely related assertions: that members
of preliterate communities tend to think alike, and that they
share a similar personality type. But years before Redfield
wrote the passage quoted above, the anthropologist Edward
Sapir had argued that even in the simplest societies one finds
significant differences of outlook and opinion (Sapir 1949:
569–77 [first pub. 1938]). Sapir illustrated his point by
referring to one of the classics of early American anthropology, the study of the Omaha Indians in the 1880s by the
Reverend J. O. Dorsey.

The Omaha tribe consisted of only about 1,100 persons when Dorsey lived with them, yet in his interviews he found that the individuals often differed with one another in attitudes and in the recital of ethnographic facts. And since Dorsey was a rigorously truthful soul, he incorporated most of these discrepancies into his account. The modern reader is therefore somewhat disconcerted to find at the end of many passages a caveat to the effect that certain Indians of the tribe (particularly La Fleche and Two Crows) disagreed with many of the facts as written. One Omaha told Dorsey, for example, about a ceremony addressed to the thunder god that was supposed to stop the rain, and this man added that it was invariably successful. But Dorsey adds, "This is denied by Joseph La Fleche and Two Crows, who say, 'How is it possible for them to stop the rain?'" (1884: 227). And another informant asserted that when a war party returned the men stopped for the night some distance from the village. But, "La Fleche and Two Crows deny this, saying that the warriors come into the village when they please, as they are hungry and wish to see their wives and children" (1884: 328). And so the account proceeds, with informants disagreeing over the names of clans and of ceremonies, over the substance of ceremonies, and even over the mundane activities of everyday life.

Sapir made the point, therefore, that even in this tiny and apparently culturally homogenous group, the individuals did not think alike. Nor were the differences merely matters of detail, since they extended to questions of religious conviction and disbelief. As we have seen, the idea that a ceremony could be used to suspend the rain struck one pious informant as unquestioned, whereas the skeptical La Fleche and Two Crows found the same notion ridiculous.

Since Sapir's time an impressive amount of ethnographic detail has accumulated that tends to support his position rather than the homogeneity postulate of Redfield (see Edgerton 1976: 12–17, 64–74). There are many things that the "average" person cannot tell the ethnographer even in very small communities. Leopold Pospisil, working with a tribal people of highland New Guinea, found that when he asked questions about the supernatural, or inquired into their views of the universe, the response from a large majority was an apathetic "I do not know" (1963: 93). These tribesmen are an exceptionally practical and materialistic people, and are simply not inclined to philosophize. Pospisil was able, nevertheless, to record a cogent cosmology and world view because certain individuals went counter to the trend and devoted themselves to speculative philosophy. These persons were thus able to discuss metaphysical themes with him in vastly greater detail than the average individual (1963: 83). The example demonstrates again that one man is not "everyman" in tribal societies.

The second notion, that uniform socialization in small communities tends to produce a common personality type, has not fared any better. Time and again researchers who have looked closely at this matter have found that there is as much personality variation in tribal communities as in comparably sized groups in our own technologically advanced society.

One of the early critics of the uniformity assumption was C.W.M. Hart, an anthropologist who had lived among the Tiwi, a small tribe (population 1,062) of Australian Aborigines who live by hunting and foraging and are classed among the world's simplest societies. During two years of fieldwork in the 1920s Hart lived in daily association with these nomadic hunters and came to know many of the men extremely well. Given this intimate knowledge, he was struck by the wide differences in the personalities of many of his close associates, and he noted that such differences occurred in spite of the fact that all were reared under similar conditions and exposed to the same cultural influences. To illustrate the range of variation he analyzed the personalities of five brothers, all of whom had been raised in the same household and by the same mother (Hart 1954: 243).

The three eldest brothers had been fathered by a man of great political skill and reputation, and the first of the sons, Antonio, was expected to follow in the great man's footsteps. This was not to be, however, for Antonio was temperamentally unsuited for leadership. Hart tells us that he was a man who seemed perpetually unsure of himself. If he acted out a public role it was because it was thrust upon him, never because he sought it. When he was obliged to speak publicly he voiced the opinion of the majority, rarely expressing an idea of his own. He followed opinion but could never guide it. At the first opportunity to relinquish the light of public attention he did so, escaping into the bush to the company of his children and hunting dogs. He was, in short, an irresolute and retiring personality, with absolutely no thirst for political power.

Mariano, Antonio's younger brother, was an individual of very different stripe. Assertive, domineering, and convinced of his own self-importance, he was a formidable presence in any company. Early in life he became a kind of political intermediary between the Australian white community and members of his own tribe, constantly exhorting his fellows to adopt white ways. He held definite opinions on every political issue, which he expressed with outspoken vehemence and conviction. Nor did he shrink from adopting stands that were unpopular with his associates, and to which he adhered uncompromisingly. If others did not agree with him, and could not be persuaded, he would wash his hands of them, confident that they would see the greater wisdom of his view in the end. As Hart expressed it, Mariano was as humorless and dedicated as an Old Testament prophet, "and just as difficult to like" (1954: 290).

The third brother, Louis, shared none of Mariano's political interests or ambitions. He was, in fact, an almost entirely antisocial individual, seeming to care little for his fellow men. He did, however, have one central, abiding concern, and this was the seduction of other men's wives. At the time that Hart studied them (1928–30), Tiwi marriage regulations had the effect of concentrating almost all the nubile women in polygynous households controlled by elderly men. Thus if young bachelors were to satisfy their sexual desires they were bound to prey upon this illicit community of married women. And while nearly all bachelors engaged in seduction at one time or another, Louis outdid them all. Hart says that Louis had been "publicly accused of adultery with

almost every possible woman for miles around" (1954: 251).
Moreover he dedicated himself to the task with remarkable
singleness of purpose. Little else interested him; he took no
part in council debates, did not seek friends or try to influence others, and had absolutely no sense of humor. He was,
in fact, a gloomy, taciturn, and introverted individual. If
other qualities appeared during his trysts with women in the
bush, the anthropologist was unable to record them.

Louis's dour character provides a striking contrast to that
of his younger brother, Tipperary. The outstanding characteristic of this young man was his gaiety and lively sense of
humor. He tended always to look on the bright side of things
and could make a joke of any situation. Hart tells of a typical
incident (1954: 254):

> On one occasion a camp I was in was badly scared by a
> ghost appearing in the middle of the night in the midst of
> the camp fires. Everybody, anthropologist included, hud-
> dled around their fires, not daring to look. . . . Finally the
> apparition seemed to have gone and there were low whis-
> pers from various firesides of, "Has it gone?—I think it's
> gone—it doesn't seem to be there now." "Perhaps it's gone
> to Port Darwin to see a movie," said Tip[perary], loudly,
> and immediately the tension was broken and the whole
> camp shouted with laughter.

His was an infectious, good-natured humor that made others
laugh with him, and he was one of the most well liked men
of the tribe. Whereas his older brothers tended to be solemn
and introverted, Tipperary was cheerful, outgoing, and
sociable.

The final brother, Bob, was a man of about twenty-eight
years when Hart knew him, and his most obvious characteristic was a kind of yielding tractability. He seemed always
to conform to the expectations of others, rarely deviating
from the norms or attracting public notice. Hart says that he
was the kind of person, found in every society, who simply
fits into the background, unnoticed and wholly uninfluential
with his fellows.

These, then, are thumbnail sketches of the five brothers. The fact that they were reared in a tribal setting, and in the same household, did not prevent them from developing radically different personalities. They ranged from the morose introversion of Louis to the happy gregariousness of Tipperary; and from Bob's pliant conformity to Mariano's headstrong independence. The material thus throws doubt on the notion that similar socialization necessarily molds personalities to a common pattern.

Complexities of a similar nature have developed whenever anthropologists have collected detailed life-history materials. These data have frequently brought to light characteristics that are difficult to reconcile with dominant patterns of the culture. An outstanding example is the account by Regina Flannery of Coming Daylight, a Plains Indian woman of the Gros Ventre tribe. This was a woman who had experienced the nomadic life on the Plains before the disappearance of the buffalo, and consequently was raised in a society that was engaged in active warfare with its neighbors. As one would imagine, great emphasis was placed in this community on spirited aggressiveness toward enemies, and all acts of personal bravery, heroism, and sacrifice were exalted. Yet Coming Daylight possessed none of these qualities: she was timid and sensitive; she could not withstand physical suffering, either in herself or in others; she was repelled by the sight of blood; and she was so pacific in temperament that she was unable to react aggressively even when physically abused.

When still a child she was requested by her grandmother to sacrifice a finger-joint for a sick relative, since it was believed that her act of suffering would aid in his recovery. But Coming Daylight refused, and ran away when her grandmother threatened her. She wandered alone in the hills for two days, and by the time she was discovered the relative had died. In adult life she witnessed an attack on their camp in which one of the enemy warriors was shot and scalped almost in her presence. The man was not yet dead when she came upon him and he was bleeding profusely. Two women of the camp were already on the scene, striking him with

the side of an axe and laughing each time he tried to rise.
Coming Daylight stood some distance off, afraid to approach.
Then (Flannery 1960: 91):

> When one of [the two women] . . . , Woman Chief by
> name, saw her she ran to her saying: "Why are you stand-
> ing so far off?" She grabbed her by the arm and pushed a
> big club into her hand, saying: "He is still alive—you will
> do a great thing. *Ahe ya'*!" Woman Chief forced Coming
> Daylight to strike him.

It is important to note that despite these personal qualities,
Coming Daylight was not considered a deviant or misfit in
Gros Ventre society. This was because, Flannery tells us
(1960: 91), she generally lived up to what was expected of
her, even when to do so ran counter to her natural inclinations.

If we ask how she developed these traits in the first place,
there is no obvious answer. It is clear from Flannery's account
that the person with greatest responsibility for her upbringing
was the grandmother. Yet this woman apparently did nothing
to encourage these characteristics of timidity and squeam-
ishness, and in fact strongly disapproved when they pre-
vented the child from meeting her obligations. Add to this
the general emphasis on courageousness in the society as a
whole, and we must wonder why these forces were insufficient to mold her character along conventional lines.

The foregoing data are admittedly impressionistic and based
on observations in only two societies. Nevertheless, they
accord with the findings of other investigators who have
employed more systematic tools of research.

Various anthropologists have, for example, used psychological testing devices (especially the Rorschach ink blot test
and the Thematic Apperception Test, or TAT) to determine
the most common, or typical, personality characteristics in
various preliterate societies. These tests are based on the
Freudian notion of projection. The subjects are confronted
with an image of ambiguous content (e.g., a symmetrical
ink blot or an enigmatic drawing) and are asked what it
suggests to them, or to tell a story about it. It is thought that

in their responses subjects will "project" their personal needs (motives, fears, aspirations) into the situations and thus reveal hidden dimensions of personality.

When these tests have been administered in preliterate communities they have revealed a wide range of personality types. In the famous study by Cora Dubois of the people of Alor, a small island of what is now Indonesia, the Rorschach protocols of thirty-seven natives displayed greater personality differences than are found within an average European population (Oberholzer in DuBois 1944: 630)! And another study employing Rorschachs among the Tuscarora Indians of New York state disclosed surprising diversity. The author, Anthony Wallace (1952: 749), tells that he began with the

> . . . naive initial hypothesis . . . that there would be a clearly homogenous personality type, recognizable even by superficial inspection of the [Rorschach] records. The problem actually became one of defining any common structure at all.

In order to determine a common tendency, Wallace created a modal class based on the statistically most frequent Rorschach responses. He found that 37 percent of the sample fell into this modal range; another 22 percent fell outside of this range but were similar to the modal class; and a full 40 percent were so far removed from the modal personality type that he classed them as "deviant" (Wallace 1952: 78).

We must ask, therefore, what kind of "typical" personality is manifest in a society where less than half of the population falls into the dominant class? And in a situation where 40 percent of the individuals must be classified as deviants, the whole notion of a common personality type appears to have very little meaning (see Kaplan 1957: 119).

Two Sources of Conformity

The above findings, and others like them, have led anthropologists gradually to abandon the notion that the shared patterns of behavior found in any society arise from the fact that the individuals are fundamentally alike. All of the data point to a very different conclusion: that the individuals of *all* societies are heterogeneous and diverse. And if this is true, the problem then is to understand how behavior becomes standardized; how, if the people themselves are not alike, they come to behave, most of the time, in roughly equivalent ways.

Anthropologists have offered two general answers to this question. The first is a variant of the socialization argument. Many scholars, while willing to concede that the personalities in a society are diverse, maintain nevertheless that individuals experience a process of socialization that is sufficiently similar, so that they learn the same general norms, standards, and customs. Accordingly, behavior in a society approximates a common standard because individuals have learned so many of the same things.

The second answer to the question, by no means inconsistent with the first, is that diverse individuals, with their varying interests and motivations, remain within the bounds of acceptable conduct by adjusting their behavior to social conventions, or to the expectations of others. This argument will be developed shortly; but first let us return to the socialization thesis.

It is not necessary to describe socialization in any detail here, since that was accomplished in Chapter Three. One aspect of it deserves mention, however, and that is what is often referred to as the "internalization of norms." As stated previously, the basic aim of socialization, or enculturation, is to teach persons the norms, attitudes, and beliefs that prevail in their society. As many writers have pointed out, this process is frequently so effective, particularly the portion of it that occurs during childhood, that individuals genuinely internalize certain of the standards; that is they adopt them as their own. For example, if a little boy is taught to wash his hands before eating, and is told that it is done to eliminate germs, he may adopt the practice as a personal habit and continue to wash even when adults are not present. We are then justified in saying that he has internalized the norm. Another familiar example is the Protestant work ethic.

It is often maintained that among the early Protestants hard work and business success were interpreted as signs of divine grace, and the persons who lived diligent but austere lives were held in highest esteem. Children in these communities were constantly admonished, in both word and deed, that idleness was sin and frivolity even worse. It is little wonder, therefore, that work became a compulsion for many, and the Protestant faithful were known to drive themselves in their worldly callings long after their material needs were satisfied (Weber 1904). It seems clear that some of the latter accepted the obligation to work as an individual standard.

The concept of internalization is significant because it is considered by many scholars to be the crucial link between the individual and society. By means of internalizing society's standards it is possible to argue that social ideals are no longer merely "out there," apart from the individual, but are infused in his innermost being; society is, as Peter Berger has stated, "in man" (1963: 93, 121).

If this point of view is followed to its logical conclusion there can be little conflict between the individual and society, since individuals identify with the norms and consequently *want* to do what society expects of them. As the psychologist-author Erich Fromm has stated the case, by means of internalization individuals develop the "social character" demanded by their society (1941: 311):

> . . . by adapting himself to social conditions man develops those traits that make him *desire* to act as he *has* to act. . . . In other words, the social character internalizes external necessities and thus harnesses human energy for the task of a given economic and social system.

This is an extreme statement of the view. Many authors, like Fromm, seem virtually to equate socialization and internalization, yet the two are by no means identical. An individual can be well socialized, in the sense of being obedient to group standards, without genuinely internalizing any of the norms. This can be made clear by reverting back to the hand washing example.

It will be recalled that the aforementioned child developed the desire to wash his hands before eating. Our knowledge of children suggests, however, that not many will behave in this fashion. Even when similarly cautioned about germs most will not find the admonition compelling. They will wash their hands when specifically reminded to do so, or if they fear parents will notice the omission, or when they want to bring their good manners to the attention of others.

What is interesting is that the actual behavior observed in the two cases can be identical despite the fact that in the first instance the norm is upheld because the child *wants* to be clean, whereas in the second it is observed because the child knows that *others respect cleanliness*. The distinction may appear trivial, but it is an important one. It demonstrates that socialization, and the conformity that it engenders, can be accomplished in two ways: by convincing individuals of the compelling reality of the norms (thus achieving internalization), or by simply teaching them *what norms exist* and the importance that these apparently have for others (Kaplan 1957: 105). An individual, therefore, who knows the conventions of his society, and how others are liable to react to infractions, will be able to regulate his conduct appropriately whether he respects the norms or not. This is the way persons in multiethnic communities cope with the plurality of customs all the time; and it is of course standard practice for enlightened missionaries and anthropologists in the field.

What these facts demonstrate clearly is that individuals often act in ways that have nothing to do with their own psychological predispositions, or even with what they personally judge to be proper. They behave much of the time as they are *expected* to behave; and to the extent that this is true, we can expect social action to be frequently "out of character." Let us look at some commonplace illustrations.

When we meet an acquaintance on the street, and eye-contact is established, we find it necessary to offer some greeting: a nod, a smile, or "how are you?" These cordial gestures are forthcoming even if we do not particularly like the person or have an interest in his wellbeing. Likewise, if at the end of a social gathering the hostess enquires if we have had a good time, we summon the enthusiasm to say that we have indeed, even if the party was very dull. Both are examples of behavior that accords with expectations: individuals sense the conduct that is demanded in particular circumstances, and they comply.

Another more vivid instance is provided by mourning customs among the Kiowa Indians, as observed by Weston LaBarre (1947: 54–55):

> Consider old Mary Buffalo at her brother's funeral: she wept in a frenzy, tore her hair, scratched her cheeks, and even tried to jump into the grave (being conveniently restrained from this by remoter relatives). I happened to know that she had not seen her brother for some time, and there was no particular love lost between them: she was merely carrying on the way a decent woman should among the Kiowa. Away from the grave, she was immediately chatting vivaciously about some other topic.

As a final example, a young lady from the American deep South tells of a party she attended in a northern city where Negroes were present (Goodman 1967: 191):

> I found it not at all difficult to accept them socially much to my surprise. In that atmosphere it seemed very natural. I talked to them and felt no discomfort at all. Then a girl I had known at [a southern] college showed up. Everything changed the minute I saw her. Somehow or other we infected one another with prejudice. We became self-conscious about the Negroes and couldn't talk to them as social equals again.

The preceding illustrations all have one thing in common: the individuals are coerced by social conventions. Their conduct would presumably be very different if they could act from the heart, but each finds it expedient to do what is socially appropriate under the circumstances.

Here, then, we have one answer to the question of how the diversity of personalities, along with individualistic modes of thinking and motivation, can give rise to a semblance of social uniformity. People do what others do in order to fit in and to be approved by their fellows. As one sociologist has remarked, this is one of the primary injunctions of all social life (Goffman 1963: 11):

> The rule of behavior that seems to be common to all situations . . . is the rule obliging participants to "fit in." The words one applies to a child on his first trip to a restaurant presumably hold of everyone all the time: the individual must be "good" and not cause a scene or disturbance; he must not attract undue attention to himself, either by thrusting himself on the assembled company or by attempting to withdraw too much from their presence. He must keep within the spirit or ethos of the situation; he must not be *de trop* or out of place.

The fact that individuals usually do adjust to the spirit of the situation does not mean that they endorse the circumstances or would not have them otherwise. It is simply that most social situations are too powerful to be challenged, and the individual therefore appears to go along with them but with considerable grimacing and a great deal of private digression. It is this "pattern of outward conformity and inner rebellion," as Bert Kaplan has phrased it, that makes individuals in any society *appear* to be more alike than they actually are (Kaplan in Singer 1961: 40).

The two very different views of socialization that have been outlined lead to varying interpretations depending on where the emphasis is placed. If we take the internalized actor point of view, conformity is the result of individuals who believe in their customs and are obedient to them. If we adopt the other perspective we tend to see customary behavior as maintained by external constraint; that is, participants are obliged by an institutional structure and a common set of norms that are external to the individuals themselves.

Anthropological literature abounds with situations that present the ethnographer with a choice between the two interpretations. Take, for example, the widespread custom of sharing among simple hunting and gathering societies. Anthropologists who have worked among the Eskimo, Bushmen, Ituri Pygmies, and other foraging groups have described customs that attest to remarkable generosity. When game is killed in these societies the successful hunter does not eat the meat alone with his family, but distributes it within a wide circle of kin. The few material goods that are possessed also tend to change hands readily; it is often sufficient for one person to ask the owner for an item and it is given. Moreover, ethnographers can generally point to specific socialization practices that instill these values early in life. Bushmen mothers, for example, constantly enjoin their children to be generous, to give gracefully, and to be sensitive to the needs of others. The infants are frequently decorated with strings of beads which they wear for about a year, and then the mother encourages the child to give them away as a gift to another. This is only the first step in a lifelong cycle of giving that engages the attention of every Bushman throughout life.

This magnanimity can be interpreted as stemming from the nature of the individuals themselves: they have been taught the virtues of generosity from childhood and so the sentiments of egotism and niggardliness have little hold on them.

But this interpretation runs counter to facts that appear in many of the ethnographic accounts. First of all, one of the most frequently heard reproaches in either an Eskimo or Bushman camp is the imputation of stinginess (Briggs 1970; Thomas 1958; Lee 1979); and it is clear from the following account that Bushmen sometimes share because they are forced to, not because it gives them pleasure. Lee tells us that (1979: 458)

The most serious accusations one !Kung [Bushman] can level against another are the charge of stinginess and the charge of arrogance. To be stingy, or far-hearted, is to hoard one's goods jealously and secretively, guarding them "like a hyena." The corrective for this, in the !Kung view, is to make the hoarder give "til it hurts," that is, to make

him give generously and without stint until everyone can
see that he is truly cleaned out. In order to ensure compliance with this cardinal rule, the !Kung browbeat each other
constantly to be more generous and not to hoard.

And anthropologists who have conducted detailed studies
of gift-giving among Bushmen agree that the principal reason that goods are given away is to avoid arousing jealousy
in others (Marshall 1961; Draper 1978); a person who possesses a cherished item becomes the immediate object of
envy from virtually everyone in camp. Nor do Bushmen
keep their envious thoughts to themselves; they badger the
person incessantly. Thus a woman who wears an attractive
necklace is likely to hear (Draper 1978: 45),

"How is it that you are a person whose neck is nearly broken with the weight of all those necklaces and I am here
with only sweat on my own neck?"

And Thomas (1958: 22) gives the example of a man who
comes into possession of a particularly good knife and would
like nothing more than to keep it, but

. . . as he sits by himself polishing a fine edge on the blade
he will hear the soft voices of the other men in his band
saying: "look at him there, admiring his knife while we
have nothing." Soon somebody will ask him for his knife,
for everybody would like to have it, and he will give it
away.

If he should unwisely persevere and resists the clamor, he
will likely become the target not only of jealousy but hostility
as well. It is considered far better to make a gift of the item
and thereby preserve amicable relations. Moreover, if the
individual is clever he can use the forced exchange for his
own benefit, since all gifts necessitate eventual reciprocity.
Thus one man confided to Lorna Marshall that when he had
something particularly desirable to give, like eland's fat, he
would take "shrewd note of certain objects he might like to

have and gave their owners especially generous gifts of fat"
(1961: 243); he would then hint to of the various items
he sought in return.

These data therefore cast doubt on the notion that sharing
among Bushmen arises because they act selflessly, or even
because they are particularly charitable towards one another.
Marshall, who knows them well, has concluded that despite
the institutionalized generosity that is so much a part of their
lives, Bushmen *as individuals* are not particularly magnan-
imous. She says, in fact, that "altruism, kindness, sympathy,
or genuine generosity were not qualities which I observed
often in their behavior" (1961: 231). If they act as if they
are generous it is because the group requires that they share,
or suffer the consequences.

The Need for Flexible Behavior

In the Bushman example an external constraint interpretation
seems to fit the facts better than the socialized actor point
of view, and the case was obviously chosen to show that
there are alternatives to an internalization hypothesis. For if
we regularly make the assumption that people behave as they
have been taught to behave, we produce an image of individuals as far more acquiescent, and far less flexible, than
they probably are. It leads inevitably to what one author has
called the "oversocialized conception of man " (Wrong 1961);
i.e., the notion that social norms gain such a hold on individuals that they behave almost as programmed actors in a
large social drama.

But this is clearly a misrepresentation of how the bulk of
human conduct is ordered. Much animal behavior, it is true,
can be founded upon programming of this sort: on genetic
codes that provide fairly standard responses for most of life's
contingencies. But human life is far too complex for this,
too burdened with problematic situations that demand choice
and situationally appropriate behavior. It is hardly possible
to believe that the malleable and protean types of conduct
that are demanded in every human society can be based on
norms internalized in childhood, or that these varied responses
are somehow embedded in the individual personality (Stokes

and Hewitt 1976: 847). The latter circumstances would seem
to lead to rigidity of behavior rather than the reverse.

What is meant, then, by behavioral flexibility, and why is
it important? It is important because wherever men and women
are organized in society we find that they must play a series
of highly differentiated social roles, each of which makes
different demands on behavior. This is as true of simpler
societies as it is in our own Western culture. In tribal communities these roles are typically allocated according to an
elaborate system of kinship, so that appropriate conduct is
specified for each role relationship. The individual must behave
in a carefully circumspect manner with a mother-in-law, for
example, being unable to speak to her or even to meet face-
to-face. With a particular aunt it is necessary to joke, snatch
at her breasts, and be intentionally flippant. With another
relative one must be cool and reserved. Margaret Mead gives
an impression of the complexity of these demands in a New
Guinea society, the Mundugumor (1935: 194):

> The world is early presented to the child as one in which
> there are a large number of such fixed relationships, with a
> separate behaviour-pattern appropriate to some and highly
> inappropriate and insulting to others, a world in which one
> must be always upon one's guard, and always ready to
> respond correctly and with apparent spontaneity to these
> highly formal demands. . . . Even gaiety is not in any
> sense a relaxation for a Mundugumor; he must always be
> gay on the right occasions and addressing the right persons;
> he must always be watchful that none of the persons toward
> whom, or in the presence of whom, such behavior would
> be incorrect are anywhere about. This gives a tight-rope
> quality to all jest and laughter.

Thus to be a Mundugumor is to "be" different things at
different times. The individual must have the capacity to
assess various circumstances and to act according to the
needs of the situation.

Or let us take another example, that of the Cheyenne warrior. Here were men who were noted for their bellicosity and
unremitting aggressiveness. As members of a society that

was bound into relations of perpetual hostility with neighboring tribes (see Chapter Four) the men were frequently called upon to display qualities of militancy, cunning, and reckless daring. And this, of course, is the dominant image that has come down to us of these men and of their social character.

It should not be forgotten, however, that there were circumstances in the life of the same warriors in which they were expected to be mild, self-effacing, and unemotional. This was particularly true in relations with their own kin and, to a somewhat lesser extent, with all other Cheyennes. Thus Hoebel states that (1960: 49):

> . . . Cheyenne basic values are contradictory at certain points. On the one hand, the individual is trained and encouraged to be militarily aggressive. He is publicly rewarded with many ego-satisfying reinforcements for sterling performance on the battlefield. . . . At the same time, he must repressively control his sex drives, and he is trained in social altruism and mild demeanor within the camp.

A considerable effort was thus manifest in Cheyenne legal practices to ensure that the violent behavior appropriate to war and military training did not spill over into relations with other Cheyennes. Furthermore, the highest status to which a male could aspire was to become a "peace chief," a person whose behavior and demeanor were virtually the opposite of those of the hot-tempered warrior. In fact, becoming a peace chief entailed relinquishing certain military duties due to the perceived polarity between civilian and military interests. And the chief's ideal characteristics have been described as "an even-tempered good nature, energy, wisdom, kindliness, concern for the well-being of others, courage, generosity, and altruism" (Hoebel 1960: 37).

All Cheyennes were exposed, therefore, to contradictory values; and the task for the individual was to apply them in the proper situations. The threat to the system came, of course, from the few individuals who had difficulty segregating their behavior as required.

Turning to our own society we find that the situation is not materially different. Every person must play various roles in a lifetime, and must juggle the values and behavior appropriate in each context. An individual may become, at one time or another, obedient child, teenage lover, parent, car salesman, scoutmaster, elder of the church. Some of the roles will be learned with very little effort, while others, like successful lover or car salesman, may require considerable on-the-job training. But whatever the combination of roles, the individual will find that each demands a different pattern of conduct, and that characteristics displayed in one role cannot be transferred directly to another. Thus five-year-old boys get into predictable trouble when they bring friends home from school, since they try to maintain the image of cheeky insolence affected on the playground but mother will have none of it. The army officer who exacts strict obedience from the men of his company is in proper role, but if he demands the same respect from wife and children he is frowned upon as a martinet. And the renowned surgeon, obeyed almost like God in the hospital, becomes a meek and bumbling novice at his weekly cello lesson.

There are even times when the identities that an individual assumes in different roles are so discrepant, so suggestive of separate characters, that the differences can become a source of embarrassment. In these circumstances the individual may try to segregate his audiences: he will want to prevent those familiar with one of his roles from witnessing his performance in the next (Goffman 1959: 137). An illustration is a military officer who is a model of resolution and self-assurance in his military duties, but is under the thumb of a domineering wife at home. It could be acutely embarrassing, therefore, if the men of his company should chance to observe him in the supermarket being ordered about by his exacting spouse. Anticipating such circumstances, he might try to avoid all occasions in which the two audiences—his troops and his wife—could possibly come together.

This is a striking example, but is not different in kind from the many occasions when people do not want to be seen in a particular place by a particular audience. And much of our humor dwells precisely on those unexpected occurrences that suddenly strip away social masks, permitting an audience to "see through" characters and images that individuals were trying to sustain up to that point. Indeed, the sociologist Erving Goffman has argued that this is what embarrassment essentially *is*: it occurs when an individual projects a certain role identity, that is, he claims to be a particular type of person, but events transpire which discredit his claim to be what he says he is (Goffman 1967: 107–08). Thus if I am overheard "talking behind someone's back," I suffer embarrassment. This is because to the person's face I acted in a friendly and well-intentioned manner, but my behavior with others shows that the first display was nothing but pretense. And if we think of other examples of embarrassment we find that most of them have to do with attempts to "be" a character of a certain kind, and then failure to live up to the expectations aroused.

These data should be convincing evidence that individuals have multiple selves and that they can become different persons depending on the situations they confront. Moreover this *must* be the case because society requires that we fit into an elaborate series of statuses and roles that make inconsistent and frequently contradictory demands.

We begin to understand, therefore, why the conception of socialization as a process designed to produce a few standard personality types, or as a means of inculcating deeply internalized values, is such a fiction. Values are not intrinsically good or equally applicable to all situations. Parents in our own society are frequently aware, if only intuitively, that an overweening stress on obedience and formal behavior can stifle a child's spontaneity, but an upbringing that allows an extraordinary degree of personal freedom can lessen the child's respect for authority and may even erode the capacity for self-discipline. Honesty, too, is self-limiting. The child who is taught that truthfulness is always and everywhere the best policy soon discovers that it is simply not the case; that there are many situations in which a *dis*honest action or comment, often for the sake of politeness, causes less disruption than an honest one.

Socialization is most successful, therefore, when it frees individuals from a series of fixed responses that would reduce

their capacity to cope with the many problematic and ambiguous situations of everyday life. In the words of one authority (Brim 1960: 138):

> . . . the function of the socialization process is not to pro-
> duce for society something such as the "dominant" individ-
> ual or "dependent" person; socialization instead is aimed
> at producing individuals equipped to meet the variety of
> demands placed upon them by a life in a society. . . . It
> does this by increasing a person's repertoire of behavior;
> extending the range and increasing the complexity of
> responses which he has at his command; freeing him from
> a limited series of stereotyped responses: [and] providing
> him with a richer set of discriminations between various
> social situations.

This pronouncement is not very different, in fact, from the
advice given in our various etiquette manuals. There we are
told that "well-bred" individuals are those who behave with
discretion and tact. They are persons with a keen sense of
the conduct required in any set of circumstances, who can
respond with the behavior and emotions—sometimes acted,
sometimes genuinely felt—that match the occasion.

These data on behavioral flexibility would thus seem to
argue *against* the notion that socialization fosters a "basic
personality," which thereafter prepares individuals to function successfully in their society. It is simply not possible to
fully equip people for the variety of roles and situations that
they are likely to encounter. The best that can be done is to
provide a few general orientations and models for conduct.
Individuals are then expected to creatively "fill in," to extend
the bits and parts of roles that have already been mastered
to new and problematic situations (Goffman 1959: 72–73).

Routine Deviance and Social Change

But there is still another reason to insist upon the importance
of behavioral diversity, and this is due to the relationship
that it bears to social change. As many students of society

have remarked, if everybody consistently adhered to the norms and standards that they were taught, there could be very little cultural change. For change generally entails a substitution of standards: practices that are considered appropriate to one generation are rejected as old-fashioned or irrelevant by the next. If change is to occur, therefore, people must at some point fail to conform to prevailing standards.

The observation was made in Chapter Three that nonconformity and deviant activities are universal features of human society, and there is no need to cover that ground here. What does deserve emphasis, however, is both the *routine* nature of nonconformity and the extent to which it is *actively promoted* in perhaps every society. The meaning of this statement can best be illustrated by referring to a distinction that the anthropologist Morris Freilich has drawn between what he calls "smart" behavior and "proper" behavior (Freilich 1972: 286).

Proper behavior, in this formulation, needs very little explication: it is conduct that follows closely on cultural guidelines, the way things *ought* to be done from the point of view of cultural ideals. Smart behavior, on the other hand, is any form of practical, resourceful, or innovative conduct that is *not* guided by established rules; the aim is simply to solve problems in a practical manner. Thus when individuals face unprecedented circumstances for which there are few or no cultural guidelines, they must cope with the situations as best they can. In so doing they will frequently hit upon culturally unorthodox solutions. If other people then follow this precedent, their solutions may become the normal way of handling that problem in the future.

But smart behavior can also refer to conduct that, despite the existence of rules, ignores, evades, or "gets around" the prescribed ways of doing things. Thus the conduct of *realpolitik* figures like Talleyrand or Bismarck fits the definition, since their policies were guided by opportunism, the realities of power, and the claims of national interest far more than by the moral principles that they may have annunciated in public. Thus smart behavior encompasses all conduct that places greater emphasis on expediency and on "getting the job done" than on culturally sanctioned principles.

At first sight the distinction between smart and proper
appears to be a mere restatement of the disapproved and the
approved. But, as Freilich points out, it is not so simple.
Despite official pronouncements, it is possible to be *too* proper,
too faithful to cultural norms. This is illustrated by the persons in every society who are criticized and even punished
for unswerving loyalty to a moral code (Williams 1951: 355).
The bureaucrat who applies the letter-of-the-law to every
situation in his jurisdiction, with no regard for extenuating
circumstances, is a figure of contempt in our literature and
cinema. Politicians who commit themselves to fixed ideals
often find that their constituents are concerned about the
"political pies" that naive dedication to principle may lose
for the district. The motorist who drives only at the posted
speed or who waits at a lingering red light long after other
drivers have concluded that it is probably out of order can
become the target of obscenities and abuse.

These examples show that rules, like values, are not to
be applied unquestioningly. Individuals are expected to exercise judgement and initiative in dealing with them. The person must decide in each case if the circumstances warrant a
loose or narrow construction of the rule, or if they invalidate
it altogether.

In making these judgements a guide that is of utmost
importance is what other people appear to do in similar situations. People in all societies continuously monitor their
behavior by observing how the influential people around
them seem to uphold or disregard various rules. Thus when
a teen-age girl in our society chafes against a regulation
enforced by her parents, she often appeals to the fact that
"Patty's mother lets *her* do it." By saying this she makes the
implicit argument that what people actually *do* is more
important than rigorous adherence to principle.

A similar ambivalence toward social rules is reflected in
the respect that is often shown for people who cut corners,
for clever politicians, and for shrewd entrepreneurs and
"operators" of various kinds. In his travels in the United
States in the 1840s, Charles Dickens thought that the appreciation for astute but unprincipled dealings was one of the

chief characteristics of Americans of that period. He remarked (n.d.: 218):

> Another prominent feature [of Americans] is the love of "smart" dealing: which gilds over many a swindle and gross breach of trust . . . and enables many a knave to hold his head up with the best. . . . The following dialogue I have held a hundred times: "Is it not a very disgraceful circumstance that such a man as So-and-so should be acquiring a large property by the most infamous and odious means, and notwithstanding all the crimes of which he has been guilty, should be tolerated and abetted by your Citizens? He is a public nuisance is he not?" "Yes, sir." "A convicted liar?" "Yes, sir." "He has been kicked and cuffed, and caned?" "Yes, sir," "And he is utterly dishonourable, debased, and profligate?" "Yes, sir." "In the name of wonder, then, what is his merit?" "Well sir, he is a smart man."

Of course the appreciation for corner-cutting does not normally reach these extremes. But it is safe to say that there is toleration in most societies for ambitious individuals who creatively hedge on the rules. It is their enterprise that so frequently opens up opportunities for others.

Nor should we overlook the fact that there are spheres in all technologically advanced societies in which the creation of novelty and the deviation from established practice are positively encouraged (Blake and Davis 1964: 467–68). This is most obvious in domains such as science and medicine where the greatest kudos go to individuals who make original contributions to their fields. Just as striking is the promotion of originality in all artistic endeavors. In every contemporary society, painters, writers, composers, and sculptors are expected to take existing forms and to develop them in new ways. An artist who claimed that he intended only to imitate the great masters would not be taken seriously as an artist. Moreover, this spirit of originality tends to foster a critical attitude toward all received wisdom, and, as noted in the previous chapter, artists tend to stand somewhat apart from the larger society and to be nonconformist in dress and demeanor. It is part of their accepted role, in fact, to constantly survey, comment upon, and criticize the society in which they live (Turner 1977: 73).

In tribal societies individual nonconformity and the deliberate pursuit of originality are certainly far less common. There is, however, something that can be regarded as an equivalent. Anthropologists have long remarked the significance of "rituals of rebellion" in simpler societies. These are ceremonial occasions in which sweeping status reversals take place: the weak are given license to insult and revile the powerful; normally decorous women act lewdly or take on the roles and behavior of men; and the normal order of things is reversed in various other ways. Much the same occurs during life crisis and initiation ceremonies. In these rites the initiates are dressed up as fantastic beings and exposed to unfamiliar images in which the everyday world is often suspended and deliberately subverted.

The question that occurs, then, is why do these contranormative tendencies exist in virtually all societies? If social life is based upon adherence to fairly consistent rules for behavior, why is lax compliance so frequently tolerated, and why are the rules themselves subjected to recurrent criticism?

The answer, perhaps obvious at this point, is that without some social elasticity cultural change could occur only with great difficulty. All of the elements that have been discussed—the respect for smart behavior, the disapproval of those who slavishly follow custom, the criticism of the taken-for-granted world so often reflected in art, literature, and ritual—all can be thought of as means of mitigating cultural rigidity. By constantly reminding individuals that their reality is not the only possible one, they are better prepared to explore in new directions. For the general circumstances that any society must face inevitably undergo change. Individuals must not be so fettered by rules, so mired in the cake of custom, that they cannot meet changing conditions with situationally appropriate behavior. Thus when Émile Durkheim, almost ninety years ago, tried to explain why crime and nonconformity *must* exist in every society, he linked them directly to the requirements of change (1895: 71):

Nothing is good indefinitely and to an unlimited extent. The authority which the moral conscience [system of social sanctions] enjoys must not be excessive; otherwise no one would dare criticize it, and it would too easily congeal into an immutable form. To make progress, individual originality must be able to express itself. In order that the originality of the idealist whose dreams transcend his century may find expression, it is necessary that the originality of the criminal, who is below the level of his time, shall also be possible. One does not occur without the other.

Thus every society faces a joint task: it must engender conformity to the existing order, but must allow for those "heretics of each age, the men with outlandish ideas and customs, [who] have often become the heroes of the next" (Lewis in Schorer 1961: 107).

Suggested Readings

Berger, Peter, *Invitation to Sociology: A Humanistic Perspective*. New York: Doubleday, 1963.
    Many of the issues of this chapter are dealt with in Berger's wonderful statement on the meaning of sociology. The entire book is good, but see in particular the chapter "Sociological Perspective— Society as Drama."

Edgerton, Robert B., *Deviance: A Cross-Cultural Perspective*. Menlo Park, Calif.: Benjamin/Cummings, 1976.
    This is a brief and cogent discussion of what anthropologists and sociologists have learned about deviant behavior in various societies around the world.

Freilich, Morris, Manufacturing Culture: Man the Scientist, in Morris Freilich, ed., *The Meaning of Culture: A Reader in Cultural Anthropology*. Lexington, Mass.: Xerox College Publishing, 1972.
    This wide-ranging article is an attempt to reconcile the cultural determinist point of view with the facts of individual creativity. If individuals are merely products of their culture (as determinists contend), where do the forces of creativity arise? Freilich finds one answer to the question in his dichotomy of "smart" and "proper" behavior.

Goffman, Erving, *Behavior in Public Places: Notes on the Social Organization of Gatherings*. New York: The Free Press, 1963.

All of Goffman's works focus on self-interested individuals in our Anglo-American society who are suspended in systems of rules that require them to act, or to give the appearance of acting, contrary to personal interests. Goffman deals masterfully with the strategems individuals devise to handle this ever-present dilemma. Here he looks at "gatherings" and depicts the subordination that individuals are expected to assume in relation to these august bodies.

Turner, Victor W., Passages, Margins, and Poverty: Religious Symbols of Communitas, in Victor Turner, *Dramas, Fields and Metaphors: Symbolic Action in Human Society*. Ithaca, N.Y.: Cornell University Press, 1974.

Turner is another scholar who has greatly advanced our understanding of social symbolism. He has argued that in all societies there are antistructural tendencies that oppose formal, structural relations. In this essay he describes the forms of symbolism that become apparent in situations in which antistructural tendencies (or "communitas") are expressed.

Wallace, Anthony F., *Culture and Personality*. New York: Random House, 1963.

One of the best studies of the relationship between culture and personality. Wallace disputes the notion that societies are composed of individuals of similar personality traits. All societies include a wide range of characters and temperaments. Behavior is standardized in them *not* because the individuals are similar, but because the institutions and normative order channel behavior along customary lines.

Chapter 8

Epilogue

An epilogue provides an author the opportunity to complete or to round out some of the ideas developed in foregoing chapters; it is also a place where the implications of certain concepts can be drawn out and underlined. It is the latter goal that I have particularly in mind in writing this final chapter, for some of the points of view that have been delineated have implications that will not be immediately apparent. This is because most readers are not conversant with the controversies that have erupted about these or similar ideas in the past.

This is not to say that what has been written is particularly controversial; most of the ideas are rather conventional, widely accepted in the discipline. Nevertheless, there are certain points at which the interpretations contradict or run counter to notions fostered by others. I want to take the opportunity, therefore, to place some of the ideas in a frankly controversial context, so that readers may better appreciate the implications of adopting one position rather than another.

British Steel and Sacred Cows

One of the points at which the preceding account differs from many others is in the degree of emphasis placed on the persistence of customs that do not contribute to the successful adaptation of a society to its environing context (see especially Chapter Five). Many of my colleagues, particularly those with a rationalist-materialist bias, tend to avoid this form of argument. They are likely to contend that a majority of human customs can be explained in practical, materialist terms, and that customs that do not contribute in some way to efficiency, or to sound accommodation to circumstances, tend rather quickly to be discarded. The well-known anthropologist Marvin Harris takes just such a position. In his popular *Cows, Pigs, Wars and Witches: The Riddles of Culture*, he supplies some seemingly sensible, down-to-earth explanations for customs that often perplex practical-minded Westerners, such as the religious prohibition on consumption of beef in India, or pork avoidance among Moslems and Jews, or witchcraft beliefs in various parts of the world (1974: 4–5):

> . . . the solution to each of the riddles examined in this book lies in a better understanding of practical circumstances. I shall show that even the most bizarre-seeming beliefs and practices turn out on closer inspection to be based on ordinary, banal, one might say "vulgar" conditions, needs, and activities.

In pursuing such a strategy, Harris arrives at interpretations that stand in sharp contrast to the way that apparently retrograde and inefficient customs were handled in Chapter Five above. Let us look, then, at Harris's approach. His explanation for the taboo on beef consumption in contemporary India can be taken as representative of his general point of view.

For anyone who believes that human behavior must make sense in practical terms, the Hindu beef taboo cries out for explanation. As is well known, Hindus consider cows sacred animals and are extremely reluctant to kill them or to consume their flesh. In many Indian states cows are protected by antislaughter laws. Hindus have felt so deeply about the issue in the past that violent demonstrations and riots have erupted against the Moslems in India who do not venerate cows and fail to abide by such restrictions. Cow veneration is also manifest in the religious rites performed for cattle throughout India, and in the freedom cows are given to wander in the towns and countryside, grazing where they will. Government agencies even provide old-age homes for decrepit animals whose owners find it uneconomical to continue to care for them but will not resort to slaughter.

It is estimated that there are some 120 million cows in the country as a whole, yet the religious taboos drastically curtail the utilization of their meat. Even poor and undernourished Indians refuse to eat beef that is readily available. Nor do cattle make an impressive contribution in terms of dairy products. The average American or European dairy cow yields about twelve times more milk yearly than does the average Indian cow. And since the animals are allowed to survive long past their age of prime usefulness, they consume precious fodder and grains while giving little in return. These facts have been considered by many a scandalous waste of resources, particularly in a country where hunger and malnutrition have been endemic features.

Harris answers, however, that this is merely a shortsighted Western view of the matter. The main economic contribution of Indian cattle, he points out, is not as producers of food, but as draft animals in the agricultural cycle. Cows are needed to produce the bullocks that every male peasant requires to plow his fields, thresh the grain, and draw his cart. The dung of the cattle is also the primary source of fertilizer for the fields. Dried cattle droppings are employed by Indian women as the principal fuel for cooking, an important resource in a country that has limited wood supplies and almost no resources of coal and oil. Cattle dung is also frequently made into a paste and used as a flooring material in rural homes. Harris points out in addition that even the meat of the animals is not entirely wasted, since members of low-ranking castes and untouchables usually take possession of the animals after they die; and these people generally eat the meat since their low position in the caste hierarchy cannot be further debased by doing so. The same groups also make use of the hides in a flourishing leathercraft industry.

Even more intriguing is Harris's assertion that Indians make more efficient use of their cattle—in an energy yield versus cost assessment—than do Americans of their beef cattle. Such a determination is derived by dividing the total number of useful calories the cow produces per year by the calories the cow consumes over the same period. The calculation shows a 17 percent efficiency rating for Indian cattle, meaning that they produce 17 percent more valued resources than they consume, whereas beef cattle in the western United States receive only a 4 percent rating. The expert cited by Harris (Odend'hal 1972) who computed these figures adds, however, that the difference is not due to the greater productivity of Indian cattle, which is low. It is because in a poor country like India people must make use of every available resource (dung, milk, tilling power, hides, etc.), none of which are much utilized in American beef farming due to the availability of energy alternatives (gas, coal, chemical fertilizers, tractors, etc.).

Harris's various arguments have been attacked and defended for over a decade now, and there exists an extensive literature on the subject by Indianists, geographers, economists, and anthropologists. The main point of contention has always been Harris's assertion that the taboo on cattle slaughter is a "positive-functioned" trait, the resultant of ecological pressures which, by safeguarding the economically indispensable cow, contributes to the material welfare of the Indian masses. He says (1974: 21):

> The taboo on slaughter and beef eating may be as much a product of natural selection as the small bodies and fantastic recuperative powers of the zebu breeds.

This interpretation was formulated, moreover, as a direct challenge to the many experts from developmental and agricultural agencies who have long maintained that a change in Hindu attitudes toward cattle could result in a far more economical and productive use of bovine resources.

How are two such different assessments possible? They occur, above all, because the contending parties view the cattle complex from different perspectives. The agronomical engineer who criticizes Indian practices compares their system with the use of cattle in other modernizing countries. He advises Indians that there are better, scientifically tested, ways of doing things; and furthermore, if they are able to institute certain basic reforms, heretofore inhibited by religious attitudes toward cattle, they can gradually lay the foundation for a more advanced agricultural economy.

Harris, on the other hand, only considers the *system as constituted*. By concentrating on the various ways in which cattle are integrated into an elaborate agricultural scheme, he points up the indispensable role that they play in maintaining that system. But what he does *not* do is question the system itself. He argues instead that because the agricultural economy is a finely tuned mechanism of intermeshing parts in which cattle play a central role, the use of cattle is therefore rational or efficacious. Let us look briefly at some of his arguments (Harris 1974: 14–30).

A central element in his contention is that since Indian farmers require oxen to plow their fields, and since cows produce the necessary bullocks, any unnecessary cow slaughter will inevitably reduce the precarious quantity of draft animals available to Indian peasants. Nor can bullocks easily be replaced by tractors, says Harris; first, because poor peasants generally cannot afford them; and second, because so much more land can be cultivated by tractors than by oxen, the general use of tractors would leave millions of Indian peasants redundant on the land. The inevitable consequence would be a catastrophic emigration to the already overburdened cities.

Another fact of significance cited by Harris is that tractors do not yield byproducts useful to peasants. Cows, on the other hand, produce both fertilizer and cooking fuel. Moreover, the dung-fuel is wonderfully adjusted to the peasants' routine: it burns with a low, long-lasting flame that permits Indian housewives to tend to children while preparing meals, in much the way that electronic appliances give Western women similar freedom. Finally, Harris argues, Indian cows live at very little expense to humans. They get much of their food by scavenging grass along roadsides, railroad tracks, and canal banks, and by consuming agricultural waste products, such as rice straw and sugar cane tops, that cannot directly be consumed by humans. In sum, Harris demonstrates how the various elements of the complex fit together as a whole. He says as much: "What I am saying is that cow love is an active element in a complex, finely articulated material and cultural order" (1974: 30).

It *is* a finely articulated order, and Harris's demonstration of that order is remarkably convincing. But Harris wants to proceed further; he wants to say that the Indian use of cattle is rational or "positive-functioned" (he sometimes says "adaptive"); but all he is justified in saying is that their use is rational *from the point of view of that system*. This same observation has been made by one of Harris's critics (Friedman 1974: 458):

> It is dangerous to take as given the entire system within which the element 'cattle' operates. Once one has described the actual state of affairs it is tautological to say that a particular variable is adaptive simply because it has a necessary function in the total system. It is the system [itself] which defines the necessary function of its elements. . . . It is a deadly weakness of functionalism that it identifies the rationality of the element while ignoring the rationality of the system.

Or to place the discussion in light of the examples dealt with in Chapter Five, Harris is like the individual who justifies the use of *kanji* (Chinese characters) in Japanese writing, or the American who argues in favor of the English system of weights and measures by insisting on the intricate connectedness of these elements to other parts of the cultural whole. Such elements do make sense form this internal perspective; but this does not by any stretch of the imagination make them "adaptive" or "positive-functioned." Compared to alternative ways of doing things—alphabetization in the case of Japanese writing, and metrication in the American case—both are costly and inefficient. The same can be said for Indian utilization of cattle: compared to the way they are employed in other developing countries, or to the possibilities inherent in the application of science, Indian practices are clearly obsolete.

Harris certainly recognizes this. But at the same time he insists on the near impossibility of reform, stressing particularly the difficulties of replacing bullocks by tractors. In this respect his discussion is reminiscent of the British steelmen of the past century who argued against innovations in steelmaking because of the dislocating impact the advances would have on the industry as a whole; hence their claim that the innovations were "not suitable to English conditions" (see Chapter Five). From the standpoint of maintaining an antiquated system, in which these steelmen had vested interests, it was a perfectly reasonable argument. But of course it had disastrous consequences for British industry in relation to world markets and competition from other countries. The same might be said if Indian officials should retard agricultural modernization in order to protect the vested interests that Indian peasants have in postage-stamp agriculture and the cattle complex; it would simply weaken India's competitive position in the world economy.

All of these arguments can be clarified, therefore, if we make a distinction between the external environment for a custom and its internal place-in-the-system context. In the first perspective a custom or way of doing things is evaluated in relation to competing alternatives; only when it is compared to more efficient means of accomplishing the same ends do we perceive the inadequacy of a given practice. This is what Veblen had in mind when he described the backward British railways of his day. He wrote of the (1915: 130)

. . . silly little bobtailed carriages [freight cars] used in British goods traffic; which were well enough in their time,

before American or German railway traffic was good for
anything much, but which have at the best a playful air
when brought up against the requirements of today.

He refers here to the external context. If it had not been for
the German and American competition, better equipped for
twentieth century industrial traffic, English railways might
never have been considered obsolete.

But then Veblen turned to the internal context of the same
English freight cars (1915: 130–31):

Yet the remedy is not a simple question of good sense. The
terminal facilities, tracks, shunting facilities, and all the
ways and means of handling freight on this oldest and most
complete of railway systems, are all adapted to the bobtailed car. So, again, the roadbed and metal, as well as the
engines, are well and substantially constructed to take care
of such traffic as required to be taken care of when they
first went into operation, and it is not easy to make a piecemeal adjustment to later requirements.

Here we have the entire distinction. From the external
perspective, and relative to the competition of the day, the
cars could be considered "silly" and out-of-date. But if we
view the matter from an internal vantage point the existence
of the antiquated cars is at least understandable: we perceive
why they have persisted and the enormous difficulties entailed
in their replacement.

The upshot of all of this is that if we are to speak intel-
ligibly about the adaptiveness or survival value of customs,
it is the external, competitive relationship that is most relevant. Analysis of the internal coherence or "functionality"
of a system tells us almost nothing about its adaptiveness.
Indeed, in an entirely different context, Harris has argued
in a similar vein, maintaining that the adequacy of any system cannot be assessed by examining its internal coherence.
Employing a biological analogy he notes that, "Dinosaurs
were no less a marvel of consistency, coordination, and continuity than the mammals which replaced them" (1968: 535).

Thus, extending his analogy a bit, if it had been possible for a modern biologist to examine the earth's last living dinosaur, he would probably have found nothing in its *internal* structure that would explain the species' imminent extinction. The heart would have pumped blood to the lungs, the liver would have secreted bile, the stomach, digestive tract, and other internal organs would have performed their functions as adequately as they do in any healthy animal. The answer to the question of why the species verged on extinction simply could not be discovered there. It would only be revealed by analyzing the relationship between the animal and its environment: the changing climate, competition for food, predators, parasites, and the like.

The same argument applies to India and the cattle complex. By showing how the system operates we say nothing about its ultimate efficiency or adaptiveness. These are matters that can only be assessed in relation to the competition the system must face. And in this connection it is certain that the diffusion of scientific farming throughout the world makes the Indian use of cattle increasingly obsolete. This does not mean, however, that Indians necessarily will abandon their practices. In other countries the use and disposition of cattle are economic considerations, based almost entirely on marketplace values. In India, due to the close relationship of cow love to conceptions of ritual purity and caste position, a great deal more is involved. Any change in the use of cattle brings highly charged social and religious issues directly to the fore. Therefore, even in the face of striking inefficiencies, Indian farmers are not likely to embrace radical reform. They are much more likely to continue to make do, to compensate here for any inefficiencies there. Indeed, it is this quality of makeshift expediency, so ably described by Harris, that accounts for the system's viability even now. The peasant, driven to the wall by poverty, and constrained by socioreligious considerations he cannot alter or disregard without penalty, does the best he can under the circumstances. We marvel, therefore, *not* at the rationality of the system, but rather, as in the case of Japanese writing, at the ingenuity that makes such a bad system work at all.

The Autonomy of Culture

The reason for this extended discussion of the sacred cow is not because the argument is in itself of great significance; it is employed rather as a vehicle to point up an important difference in theoretical orientation. It should be obvious that the preceding account argues to a certain extent against the concept of adaptation, or at least against excessive reliance on such a notion.

There was a period in American anthropology, in the early part of this century, when the whole concept of environmental adaptation was disparaged and little utilized. Then, beginning with the influential writings of Julian Steward on cultural ecology (see especially *Theory of Culture Change*, 1955) a significant reorientation took place, and adaptation became an important tool of understanding and interpretation. In the last thirty years the pendulum has swung very far in this direction, to the point that many anthropologists utilize the concept of ecological adaptation to a far greater extent than is justified. (And that, of course, is the reason that Chapter Five of this book was written.)

The argument is an important one because it deals with the question of the origin of sociocultural traits. The adaptationists employ, implicitly or explicitly, a natural selection model for society. They conceive of social institutions as arising, in the main, out of the practical adjustment of individuals and groups to external circumstances. Thus, Steward argued that when people make adjustments to environmental conditions they are forced to adopt novel practices; once these practices are regularized, they become the basis for new culture to be passed on to the succeeding generation. He gave high priority in his scheme, therefore, to efficiency. Practices and institutions that are most effective or advantageous in particular circumstances tend to survive, whereas those that do not contribute some advantage are discarded or eliminated. This occurs, Steward believed, because humans are basically practical and they try to optimize their material and economic conditions. By means of such practical decision-making, societies come to possess the customs and behaviors that make good sense in the environments in which they are located. Steward's followers reason similarly. Here is a recent statement of the point of view (Netting 1974: 485):

> No one but an arch determinist would claim that an environment demanded one and only one adaptation, but among the social and technological alternatives available, those that negatively affected the viability of the population adopting them would either be eliminated over time or cause the extinction of the population.

But an argument such as this is only valid if we grant the same importance to efficiency as do ecologists such as Steward, Harris, and Netting. And what about different degrees of efficiency or inefficiency? In reference to the above quotation one anthropologist has remarked that we need to know what is meant by the "negative" impact of traits (Hallpike 1974: 488):

> If "negatively affect" means "to make the population's survival impossible" then the proposition is tautologous; if it just means "create hardship" or "lower the birthrate, but not sufficient to cause extinction" then the conclusion does not follow.

Hallpike would place far less stress on efficiency and contends that "the inefficient society and its institutions are perfectly capable of surviving in many natural and human environments" (1974: 488).

If we therefore discount, as Hallpike does, the principle of efficiency, we have to ask what prevents societies from achieving an optimal, or near optimal, relationship to their environmental situations. Or we might ask the question in another form: What prevents individuals from making the optimal choices that Steward thought they would tend to make?

The answer is obvious: it is structure—constituted structure. When individuals confront a new situation they invariably do so in a context of already existing sociocultural constraints. Americans are not free to choose the metric system over the traditional one, even though many individuals reasonably conclude that the former is better. The choice, however, is not determined by rationality alone, since important vested interests are involved. The same is true of the Indian farmer with his cattle: how he might choose without the load of socioreligious institutions is one matter; how he chooses in their presence is quite another. As indicated earlier, once a set of sociocultural relationships becomes integrated into a set pattern, or structure, it is difficult to modify any of the elements without affecting other parts of the whole. These systemic properties thus constitute a conservative influence, so that even when societies change they tend to do so in ways that conserve the fundamental pattern.

This difference in outlook between those who think of culture as arising out of practical activity and those who attach greater significance to structure has been a source of debate in anthropology during the entire twentieth century. As Sahlins has recently shown (1976: 57–73), this was a crucial contrast in the outlook of two of the founding fathers of American anthropology, Morgan and Boas; it has been a continuing point of contention between American and British anthropology; and it was the main difference that Steward noted between his cultural ecology and the "historical" anthropology of many of his contemporaries.

In the period that Steward worked out his perspective, American anthropology was under the forceful influence of Boas and his principal students. Boas had taught that the impact of physical environment on culture, while always measurable, was not of primary significance. The more important elements in culture change, he believed, were located internally and consisted of certain dominant interests or cultural biases that could be found in every society. He arrived at this conclusion through various detailed studies of cultural borrowing. He discovered that when a society borrowed customs or institutions from neighboring societies, these institutions were inevitably recast and reinterpreted according to the dominant interests or "genius" of the borrowing society (Stocking 1968: 214). The new elements were made to conform, in other words, to already existing patterns. This was the basis of his famous concept of integration, reflecting the tendency for elements in a cultural system to become mutually consistent and reinforcing.

These ideas were taken up by Boas's principal students, particularly Benedict and Kroeber, but also by others like Leslie White, and given elaborate expression. These authors spoke of enduring patterns, themes, styles, and cultural configurations, and claimed a tendency for any culture to develop autonomously, or as White expressed it, "in terms of its own principles and laws" (White 1949: 167). Elsewhere White says (1949: 339):

> If, then, we cannot explain cultures in terms of race or physical type, or in terms of psychological processes, and if appeal to environment is equally futile, how *are* they to be accounted for and made intelligible to us?
>
> There seems to be only one answer left and that is fairly plain. . . . Cultures must be explained in terms of culture.

As might be expected, Steward was highly critical of this point of view and dismissed it as entailing "the fruitless assumption that culture comes from culture" (1955: 36).

But what a remarkable similarity this debate bears to the more recent one, referred to above, between Netting and Hallpike! Netting argues on the one hand in favor of adaptation and the importance of the environment, whereas Hallpike counters with his assertion that the main characteristics of human society arise internally, from "the systems properties internal to societies" (Hallpike 1974: 488–89).

It is an interesting commentary on this discussion that a remarkably similar debate is taking place in contemporary biology (see Lewin 1980: 886). For years the main interpretive tools in that science have been adaptationism and natural selection. Recently, however, a number of scholars have challenged the preponderant role accorded adaptationism in biological explanation. It is instructive that they cite the same limitations that were stressed in Chapter Five: prior structure, and the interconnectedness of (organic) systems.

Referring to the limitations set by prior structure, it is noted that selection must necessarily work with materials already at hand. These starting points or ancestral designs with which selection operates are frequently unpromising for future developments. Nevertheless they are all that exist—the only genetic materials available—meaning that all subsequent changes tend to appear as variations on the original framework. Thus, one writer poses the question (Lewin 1980 886):

> Why do most land vertebrates have four legs? The seemingly obvious answer is that this arrangement is the optimal design. This response would ignore, however, the fact that the fish that were ancestral to terrestrial animals also had four limbs, or fins. Four limbs may be very suitable for locomotion on dry land, but the real reason that terrestrial animals have this arrangement is because their evolutionary predecessors possessed the same pattern. . . . Evolutionary history is clearly a potent force in determining evolutionary future.

Using similar illustrations, Gould makes an identical point about antecedent structure (1981: 36):

> Why should a rat run, a bat fly, a porpoise swim, and I type this essay with structures built of the same bones unless we all inherited them from a common ancestor? An engineer, starting from scratch, could design better limbs in each case. Why should all the large native mammals of Australia be marsupials, unless they descended from a common ancestor isolated on this island continent? Marsupials are not "better," or ideally suited for Australia; many have been wiped out by placental mammals imported by man from other continents.

Another restraint on adaptation recognized by biologists is the influence of integration. Since all organisms are to some extent integrated systems, an adaptive change in one feature frequently has undesirable consequences for other parts of the system. These are what Darwin referred to as "correlations of growth" (Gould 1980: 50). Thus animal breeders often find that when they select for a desired trait, like increased milk production in cows or thicker fur in minks, they often enhance undesirable and even deleterious characteristics that are genetically correlated with the first.

Even more significant, however, is the diminished reproductive capacity of highly selected lines (Wallace and Srb 1961: 107). It has been repeatedly demonstrated, for example, that in animal populations selected for a specific trait, the individuals that are the best exemplars of the trait in question produce fewer offspring than those that are average for that same characteristic. Thus, if one selects for hens that lay large eggs, experiments have shown that the larger eggs are less likely to hatch than eggs that are average or smaller-than-average for that population. The most likely explanation for this is that rapid selection tends to upset the balance, or integration, that has been achieved within a constellation of genes. Two biologists write (Wallace and Srb 1961: 107):

. . . in the evolutionary history of a population, natural selection has consolidated a constellation of genes, producing individuals of high fitness. The proper interactions of these genes in governing developmental, physiological, and biochemical processes are extremely important. . . . Any change, therefore, is opposed by a tendency to maintain previously selected, *well-integrated combinations of genes*, and, consequently, restraint is imposed on the ability of a population to respond to the new situation. If this restraint is too severe, and if the demand for the new phenotype must be met, the population cannot succeed in meeting the new circumstance. It becomes extinct. [Emphasis added.]

We see that in biology, therefore, just as in culture, there are structural constraints on change; and that the changes that take place are likely to be ones consistent with previously established relationships.

Much the same can be demonstrated for language: the evolutionary changes that occur in any speech community are to a certain degree directional, controlled by the morphological characteristics of the language itself. This was demonstrated years ago by the eminent linguist-anthropologist Edward Sapir. He noted that English and German, daughter languages of a common ancestral stock, have independently experienced some remarkably similar phonological changes. He argued that these parallels were due to the limitations set by the morphological characteristics of the ancestral language. One finds, for example, an identical pattern of irregular plurals in both dialects. The English plural for foot is feet, and for mouse, mice, which are direct parallels to *Fuss/Fusse* and *Maus/Mause* in German (Sapir 1921: 184). Since the forms were not present in the ancestral protolanguage, Sapir reasoned that there was some momentum or structural tendency at work "that eventually drove both of these dialects along closely parallel paths" (1921: 182). Here again we see that new material is made to fit the mold of prevailing structure.

Democracy and the American Frontier: Adaptation or Ancestral Design?

But while there can be little doubt that languages and organisms often develop according to immanent designs, what evidence can be adduced to show that societies betray a similar tendency? (And the word "tendency" is used advisedly here, since it is not the intention to argue that societies are characterized by the same degree of internal coherence as are either languages or organisms.)

An argument that can throw some light on this question is the longstanding controversy among students of American history regarding the role of the frontier in generating American democracy. The argument was opened in 1893 with a seminal paper by the historian Frederick Jackson Turner on "The Significance of the Frontier in American History" (see

Billington 1966: 9–20). Turner argued that the principal
elements of American democracy such as individualism,
exaltation of the common man, hostility toward hierarchical
control, and vigorous local government were all born of the
frontier experience. The need to constantly build society
anew in the wilderness reduced the scope of inherited priv-
ilege and of all established institutions. The new society
grew in circumstances of abundant land and vast opportunity
so that no individual had to look to any other as an irrev-
ocable master or superior. The result was a society based on
equality, economic mobility, and individual freedom. In a
famous passage Turner summarized his thesis (Turner in
Billington 1966: 29):

> American democracy was born of no theorist's dream; it
> was not carried in the *Sarah Constant* to Virginia, not in
> the *Mayflower* to Plymouth. It came out of the American
> forest, and it gained new strength each time it touched a
> new frontier. Not the constitution, but free land and an
> abundance of natural resources open to a fit people, made
> the democratic type of society in America. . . .

This was therefore an environmentalist argument: Turner
thought of American institutions as growing out of a struggle
with nature and with the conditions of frontier settlement.
He reasoned additionally that if the frontier had such an
impact in America, it may have had similar effects elsewhere. He called, therefore, for comparison of the pioneer-
ing experience in countries such as Canada, Australia, South
Africa, and Russia, to determine if similar causes had everywhere generated similar institutions.

In the many years since it was propounded, Turner's thesis
has met vigorous challenge. There are various facets to the
controversy, but certainly the most telling criticisms have
centered on Turner's attempt to isolate western American
history from its institutional precedents. As mentioned above,
Turner thought that the newness of the frontier communities
was an important key: the necessity of creating society from
virtually nothing in the wilderness encouraged the settlers

to innovate, to create original institutions that would meet their special needs. But is this what we find? Did westerners fashion new institutions in the wilderness?

Not according to those who have made detailed studies of institutional history. With the minor exception of some zealous religious sects (Mormons, Hutterites, Amish, etc.) the sociopolitical institutions established in western America were almost without exception modeled on precedents established earlier in the East. The constitutions that were written in every western state incorporated the familiar patterns of the single executive, bicameral legislature, the principle of separation of powers, bills of rights, and other well-established standards of American democracy (Wright 1934: 15–29). And while there was a tendency to extend suffrage in the West and to eliminate property qualifications to vote, none of these programs exceeded the reforms undertaken earlier in the most progressive eastern states. Indeed, in the matter of extending the vote to free Negroes, the western states generally lagged behind New England. The testimony of political institutions suggests, therefore, that the settlers were rather more imitative than original.

The same can be said for architecture and the arts that developed in the West. Almost every settlement began with stark cabins and farm buildings that were utilitarian responses to frontier conditions. But this period of spartan circumstances was generally of short duration. Most settlers were anxious to improve their situation and to import the amenities of civilization as soon as possible. So when they set about enlarging their homes, or were able to construct public buildings, they frequently adorned them in the style of Greek architecture with neoclassical facades and Ionic columns, so that one finds scattered "from Ohio to Puget Sound, pioneer-period buildings with the fine proportions and restful dignity of Greek temples" (Agard 1957: 168). This style represented to them, as to most Americans of that time, the height of civilized taste.

The books that they read also reflected the larger European civilization. Tocqueville remarked in the 1830s that English literature was widely read in America, even in the recesses of the forest. "There is hardly a pioneer's hut," he tells us, "that does not contain a few odd volumes of Shakespeare," and adds that he himself first read *Henry V* in an American log cabin (Tocqueville 1835: 58). There are also the accounts of many visitors who noted the inordinate pride that westerners took in their modest cultural accomplishments. Travelers were incessantly prevailed upon to assure the locals that a certain opera house, theater company, or musical troupe was "just as good as anything you could find in the East." Thus, the portrayal of the frontier as a new beginning, or as somehow constituting a "lapse in civilization," is more misleading than real.

A truer picture would show how the settlers gradually transformed the wilderness into replicas of the towns and villages they had left behind in the East. Turner missed this point because his attention was focused on the effects of environment on society, and not on how society could shape the environment. As Owen Lattimore has noted, he reversed the causal sequence (1962: 490):

> Turner, in fact, was an acute observer; but what he saw so clearly, he saw while standing on his head. In large measure, when he thought he saw what the frontier did to society, he was really seeing what society did to the frontier. That he was standing on his head accounts for the fact that he touches only glancingly on the American frontiers of the French and Spanish. . . . Yet why was it that the Spanish and French frontiers in America (especially the frontier in Canada, so close geographically to New England) did not create societies more like that of the United States—except, significantly, in Canada west of Quebec, where the settlers were British? What can account adequately for the great differences, unless it be the differences in cultural momentum and impact of the Spanish and French who came to the Americas?

Lattimore makes a crucial point here, for if the frontier situation was decisive, we would expect it to have exerted a similar influence on the French settlers as on the English.

But even in Tocqueville's day it was obvious that this was not the case. When Tocqueville visited Quebec in 1831 he was impressed by the great similarity of the French-Canadians to his countrymen back in France, though they maintained virtually no contact with the mother country. "They are still Frenchmen, trait for trait," he wrote, "not only the old ones, but all, even to the *bambin* twisting his forelock" (Pierson 1959: 224). Their form of settlement also struck him forcefully, for they lived in closely knit parishes while farming small tracts of land, apparently uninterested in the open territories to the west. This was such a remarkable contrast to the bustling westward march of the Americans, and even to the English settlers in Ontario, that he was led to enquire about it. When he asked a *habitant* "why the [French] Canadians let themselves be hemmed in their narrow fields when at twenty leagues they could find fertile and uncultivated land," the peasant replied: "Why do you prefer your wife even though your neighbor's has prettier eyes?" (Pierson 1959: 224–25). Later when he wrote *Democracy in America* Tocqueville reflected on this experience (1835: 332):

> I have met with men in New England who were on the
> point of leaving a country where they might have remained
> in easy circumstances, to seek their fortune in the wilds.
> Not far from that region I found a French population in
> Canada, closely crowded on a narrow territory, although
> the same wilds were at hand; and while the emigrant from
> the United States purchased an extensive estate with the
> earnings of a short term of labor, the Canadian paid as
> much for land as he would have done in France. Thus na-
> ture offers the solitudes of the New World to Europeans
> also; but they do not always know how to make use of her
> gifts. Other inhabitants of America have the same physical
> conditions of prosperity as the Anglo-Americans, but with-
> out their laws and their customs; and these people are
> miserable.

What Tocqueville learned from this experience is that the laws and customs—or culture—that a people brings to a situation is crucial. The environment merely provides a set of possibilities that can be shaped in various ways depending on cultural predispositions. In establishing their kind of society the French made different use of available resources than did the Anglo-Americans, and two quite different civilizations were able to evolve out of remarkably similar physical conditions.

This example should make clear what is meant by saying that societies develop to a certain extent autonomously, or according to their "own principles and laws." For how else are we to explain the similarities that can still be found between modern Quebec and France? And what about the institutional parallels between Australia, New Zealand, Canada (excluding Quebec), and the United States? Is not the most plausible explanation simply that British settlers brought to each of the latter areas a common sociocultural design that has worked its way out in reasonably similar ways?

The Lasting Imprint of Origins

A perspective of this kind, one that recognizes the significance of original design, has been developed by various students of European colonization. Societies transplanted to the New World are of considerable interest to anthropologists, as well as to historians, because they afford well-documented examples of what occurs to cultural traditions that are wrenched free of their original contexts.

The historian Louis Hartz has coined a meaningful term for these transplanted communities, calling them "fragment" cultures, expressing the idea that only a portion of the European whole is ever transmitted to the new lands. Whole classes and certain institutions are inevitably left behind. In the founding of colonial America, for example, the English aristocracy and the peasantry played only minor roles, and these strata exerted almost no influence in the settlement of Australia.

But what is most intriguing about fragment cultures is how they can be shown to bear the continuing imprint of their origins. Hartz has even argued that each fragment is a kind of embodiment, or unfolding, of the stage of European history at which it became separated from the larger whole (1964: 3–10). Let us examine this proposition in the context of two contrasting cases: the founding of New France and the settlement of Australia.

When France colonized Lower Canada in the seventeenth century, she was a strongly centralized and hierarchical society, but one that retained many elements from the recent feudal past. Institutions of representative government were either nonexistent or very weakly developed. It was essentially this structure of government that was transferred to the new colony: a political absolutism that granted the settlers few democratic freedoms and in which authorities in the mother country attempted to regulate all significant matters of the colony, even the "minor details of rural life" (McRae 1964: 224).

Colonization also provided the French crown an opportunity to establish a "purer" society than existed in the mother country. By careful screening of applicants for emigration, only those who fit into the absolutist scheme were admitted to the colony. Catholic orthodoxy was a prime consideration, so that Protestants were excluded; the policy also meant that French freethinkers, soon to become so important in the Enlightenment at home, were totally unrepresented in New France. What is more, the forces that *did* play important roles in settlement—the peasantry, military, lesser nobility, and clergy—were a selection of some of the most conservative elements of seventeenth century France, persons "who overwhelmingly adhered to the standards of feudalism" (Finlay 1975: 317).

We can understand, therefore, what is meant by the partial or "fragmentary" nature of the new society: important segments of Old France never crossed the ocean, and those that did were representative of a society that was already in decline in the old country. Add to this the relative isolation and poverty of the settlement, and the result was a society of almost medieval simplicity and immobility. The Catholic Church assumed control of education, and parish priests became the most influential figures throughout the rural districts. The aim of the schools, the historian Parkman tells us, was "first, to make priests; and secondly, to make obedient servants of the Church and King. All the rest was extraneous and of slight account" (1901: 426). He adds that there was little reading material in the colony "except formulas of devotion and lives of the saints" (425). If he exaggerates he does not stretch the matter far, for we learn that no printing press operated in New France during the entire period of French control, and that the first newspaper appeared in Quebec only after the English conquest in 1759 (Parkman 1901: 425).

From this we can understand what is meant by saying that French Canada had almost no experience of the Enlightenment (Hartz 1964: 26–33). There was no indigenous criticism of the absolutist regime, and no social ferment that could lead, as it did in France itself, to a democratic transformation of society. The fact is that Quebec remained in unruffled political backwardness until the British took possession of the country and gradually introduced democratic reforms. It is for this reason that European visitors in the nineteenth century saw in Quebec a vestige of a way of life that had disappeared throughout most of Europe. Tocqueville said as much. Referring to his visit to Canada he remarked, "Everywhere we were received like compatriots, children of *old France*, as they say here. To my mind the epithet is badly chosen. Old France is in Canada; the new is with us" (Pierson 1959: 210).

It is little wonder, therefore, that the men and women of the St. Lawrence did not react to the opportunities of the frontier in the same manner as the Anglo-Americans around them. The colonists that France sent to the New World were essentially medieval men imbued with precapitalist attitudes and outlooks. Their reaction to landed property was entirely consistent with this scheme: land was regarded by them almost as a family heirloom, to be possessed, harbored, and passed on to the next generation. It was generally *not* treated in the manner of the capitalistic Anglo-Americans, as a commodity to be bought and sold like any item of merchandise (Gerhard 1959: 208–12).

In turning to the peopling of Australia we encounter an entirely different set of founding conditions. Whereas French Canada was struck off from a semifeudal European stem, the whole impetus of Australian development took place after the beginnings of the Industrial Revolution. The men and women who peopled the continent were largely representatives of the British working classes, most of whom had experienced the grim conditions of industrial labor in England and were critical of any society that allowed such conditions to exist. This fact, that Australian institutions took shape "in a period in which traditional and aristocratic values were under sharp attack" (Lipset 1967: 291), has had enormous influence on Australian development.

As is well known, white settlement began in 1788 with the establishment of a British penal colony, and many of the first permanent settlers were emancipated convicts. Historians have long debated the influence that these men may have exerted. It is surmisable, however, that they harbored little affection for the society, and particularly the authority structure, that had cast them off.

Voluntary migration was also encouraged before the end of the eighteenth century, but due to the high cost of the voyage (eight times more expensive than the trip to North America) it did not at first result in a steady stream of immigrants. But in 1831 the British Colonial Office initiated a policy of "assisted migration," which was designed to reduce the burden of the indigent and unemployed population in England. Under this policy the government paid the fare to Australia of anyone who chose to emigrate. Parishes throughout England responded by sending their paupers to the ports of embarkation. The plan substantially boosted the flow of emigrants; it also assured that a majority of those who landed in Australia were members of the British lower classes (Nadel 1957: 27).

Gold was discovered in Australia in 1851 and precipitated a great influx of fortune seekers. In the following ten years about 600,000 persons entered the country; about a third were assisted immigrants, the others being able to pay their way. But since the gold was in alluvial deposits, and its mining did not require much capital, it could be sought by the average man. Moreover, there were many English Chartists and European radicals among the newcomers. These were men who had participated in the struggles in England and on the continent to improve the wretched conditions of the working masses and were usually bitterly opposed to the inequalities of the old society. The following is an excerpt from a political document of the gold rush period that well expresses these attitudes (Nadel 1957: facing 18):

> We must direct our efforts to the obtaining of a better system than we left behind, where class legislation and misrule have brought the people to the starvation point. It has ever been the practice of the wealthy to oppress the poor, and the custom of kings to deprive by fraud and plunder the people of the land, and parcel it out to an aristocracy, who degrade the people to the level of serfs. . . .

Working class sentiments such as these, and particularly the intense dislike of class distinctions, became part of the Australian national temper in this early period and have never been erased. All of the noted observers of Australian society have remarked this characteristic. James Bryce commented, "Nowhere can one find a stronger sentiment of equality, that antagonism between the wage-earning and the employing class which the traveller feels in the atmosphere as soon as he lands in Australia" (1921: 171). In the United States the ideal of greatest emotional appeal has always been liberty (or freedom); in Australia that place of honor is held by equality (Lipset 1967: 288–89).

Moreover, it is an equalitarianism tinged with militancy. There is deep distrust of laissez faire economics in Australia, a belief that an unfettered economy merely allows the rich to press their advantages over the poor. Thus, Australians have long accepted the need for governmental intervention to protect the working classes, to redistribute income, and to prevent economic disparities from becoming rigid class distinctions. These sentiments also partly explain why the well-to-do have made only limited contributions to Australian politics. Wealth arouses such suspicion that affluent candidates are at a disadvantage. It has been said, with only slight exaggeration, that "it is harder for an industrial mag-

nate to enter [Australian] politics than for a camel to pass
through the eye of a needle" (quoted in Rosecrance 1964:
306). An upper class participation in government, therefore,
so noteworthy a feature of both English and American
democracy, has never been characteristic of Australia.

This gives some idea, then, of what is meant by saying
that Australia was "born radical" (Rosecrance 1964: 304).
The conditions of capital and labor that existed in England
in the early industrial revolution, and which generated radical protests there, became the founding conditions for Australian democracy. And it explains why an essentially agrar-
ian society has nurtured political developments that are
elsewhere associated with advanced industrialism. For when
the Labour Party came to power in Australia in 1911 it became
the world's first working-class government. As Bryce
remarked (1921: 257):

> Thus for the first time in history (apart from moments of
> revolution) executive power passed legally from the hands
> of the so-called "upper strata" to those of the hand-work-
> ers. Australia and the world saw a new kind of government
> of the people by a class and for a class. Instead of the land-
> owners or the richer people governing the landless or the
> poorer, the position was reversed: the latter imposed the
> taxes and the former paid them.

What better demonstration could we find of the perpetuation of cultural design? Once the Australian fragment crystallized about a working-class ethos, derived ultimately from
European conditions, it became a factor in all future developments. Nationalism itself became closely tied to an ideal
of solidarity between equals in the class struggle, known
throughout Australia as the bond of "mateship" (Hartz 1964:
12).

If the reader still is tempted to believe that these qualities
must somehow be related to environment, then it becomes
necessary to explain how it all occurred not once, but twice.
For much of what has been written about Australia could be
applied to New Zealand as well. In a land with an environ-

ment and aboriginal population wholly different from those
of Australia, we find almost the same complex of values.
There is in New Zealand the same passion for equality over
liberty, the populist rejection of laissez faire, and an insist-
ence that government take an active role in the economy,
both to secure justice for the working masses and to ensure
that economic disparities do not become acute (Coleman
1958: 224, 235). A historian writes (Coleman 1958: 236):

> . . . another thread running through New Zealand history
> was . . . a pervasive fear of the recurrence in New Zealand
> of all those features of the Old World which men found ob-
> noxious: the poverty, sweated labor, unemployment, slums,
> industrial strife, land monopoly, rack-renting, absentee-
> ism, and serfdom. Such aspirations and fears were not born
> in the crucible of the frontier but were the unhappy heri-
> tage that the settlers brought with them from the mother
> country.

Thus, the political culture that the countries share is largely
a product of their common history. They were colonized at
about the same time and by similar social classes. Having
separated from the same European stem, they embodied a
particular moment of the European experience, which they
were to elaborate in very different settings.

A Summing Up: Stability and Change

The historical examples that have been reviewed here, and
also in Chapter Five, stand in sharp contrast to the case made
for adaptation (on the Great Plains) in Chapter Four. Is there
not a paradox here, some basic contradiction? How can
adaptation emerge triumphant in one set of circumstances
and its virtual opposite, continuity of tradition, be promoted
in others?

If there is a paradox it arises from a tendency to think in
either/or terms: *either* adaptation is the key to our explanations *or* cultural continuity is, but not both. But why must
this be true, since they are not mutually exclusive? The reader

will recall that at various points in the book it was suggested that two opposed tendencies, or processes, can be distinguished in every society and in every historical period. These tendencies were referred to in the Preface (following Moore 1976) as processes of regularization and processes of situational adjustment.

Processes of regularization refer to the various means by which humans attempt to impose order, pattern, and stability on everyday experience. This is accomplished most frequently by the imposition of rules and regulations, making behavior conform to general expectations. Thus when a mother teaches her child the proper way to greet adults, or to set places at a dinner table, or how to pronounce the word "repertoire," she is an agent of regularization; she imposes cultural order on experience. The same may be said of the legislative process, though on a grander scale: the aim is to formulate general rules, or guides, for conduct. And of course the great benefits of regularization are order and harmony: the predictability of interaction in all societies is based on acknowledgement, by individuals, of common sets of rules (see Chapter Three).

When harmony and order are highly valued, therefore, regularization can be carried to great lengths. Utopian planners, in their efforts to establish ideal communities, often envision a world in which social relations are ordered according to plan. An anthropologist has described the utopian impulse evident in Spain's colonization of the New World in the sixteenth century (Wolf 1959: 163–64):

> The New World would not have to grow, piecemeal, in the shadows of ancient complexities: it would be a planned world, projected into reality by the royal will and its executioners. Thus utopia would become law, and law utopian. . . . was it true that many Indians lived in scattered hamlets instead of stationary, circumscribed, concentrated settlements? Then let there be a law to force them to live in nucleated towns, each with its own church, each surrounded by its own fields—within a measured radius of 560 yards from the church steeple—so that they could

learn to order their lives to the tolling of church bells and to the commands of royal officers. . . . Let each Indian keep twelve chickens and six turkeys and sell them for no more than 4 reales per turkey and 1 1/2 reales per chicken; let each Indian working in a textile mill receive a daily ration of eighteen tortillas or fourteen tamales, plus chili, chickpeas, and beans. No problem was too insignificant to demand solution, and all solutions were solutions of law.

This was a grandiose effort to regulate and stabilize human relations. It will come as no surprise, however, to learn that elements of the scheme were unworkable. How could these very specific laws apply to the multiplicity of conditions found in the new lands? Were nucleated settlements equally feasible everywhere? Did some Indians not keep more than twelve chickens? Did the currency maintain a constant value in relation to domestic fowl? In short, there must have been hundreds of specific situations that encouraged evasion. And that is of course what happened: the reality of everyday life eventually grew around and over such laws, leaving in most instances "a hollow shell of words" (Wolf 1959: 164). Local officials, faced with the dilemma of applying specific laws that bore almost no relationship to real conditions, adopted a motto that became famous throughout the empire: *obedezco pero no cumplo*, "I obey [the rule] but I do not carry it out."

Here then we have a classic conflict between the attempt to impose cultural order and the conditions that render the order obsolete. The clash was exacerbated in this instance due to the visionary nature of Spanish law; but a conflict of this kind is endemic to all societies. No matter how sensibly the rules are drawn, they must be applied to complex and untidy circumstances. Moreover the circumstances do not remain constant: new techniques and resources are discovered; groups that once were marginal rise to prominence; former enemies join in an alliance against a common threat. And each interest group that appears on the scene interprets the existing rules to its own advantage, often altering them (or their application) in the process. By such means rules and practices that are taken seriously in one period become dead letters in the next.

We can discern the outline of the same process in our own society. If we compare any etiquette manual written in the 1940s with one written today, we find that many behavioral standards have been drastically revised. The change is clearly connected with the fact that individuals and groups have generally ignored the rules in the interim; and the authorities who must decide what is and what is not proper social form have had to change their prescriptions. Here Amy Vanderbilt explains why she found it necessary to revise her book on American etiquette rather extensively between the 1962 and 1972 editions (Vanderbilt 1972: vii):

> This major revision has been much more difficult to do
> than was the first major one ten years ago because the
> sixties and early seventies have been a period of social
> upheaval. I have certainly had to consider the Sexual Revo-
> lution which in many cases merely reflected what many
> people were doing all along but were not prepared publicly
> to admit. There has been a great change in language and
> the way we handle it. . . . Many things once automatically
> considered unshakably correct have been changed drasti-
> cally under direct assault by the young.

In other words, if there is a great deal of on-the-ground change, or change in what people actually do, the rules are frequently altered to reduce the disparity between dictum and practice. When dealing with processes of situational adjustment, therefore, we see how rules *follow* behavior; how our cultural standards tend to accommodate to circum- stances. And that of course is what the adaptive framework in anthropology is mainly about.

It is only half the story, however, for rules can also guide and structure behavior; or we might say that in a certain sense they *precede* it. Rules are frequently imposed on peo- ple that constrain them to do things they would never do in the absence of the rules. Many of the aforementioned Indi- ans of sixteenth century New Spain were actually uprooted from their homes and congregated in centralized villages

(Gibson 1964: 282–87). The law, dictated by authorities across an ocean, preceded the social form. The same has occurred in the spread of great religious movements: newly Christianized or Islamicized natives adopt a way of life different in many respects from that of pagans around them. And in the contemporary world the establishment of a Marxist ideology can result, as it has in Cuba, in an extensive reorganization of the society.

Thus when we speak of processes of regularization, we refer to the effort to impose rules and order, and to make the rules binding on others. Rules in this sense have an inhibiting, channeling, or deterrent effect on behavior. And it is important to note in this connection that rules are not always abandoned simply because they are flouted in practice. The incidence of drunk-driving offenses in the United States has increased in the past twenty years, but such dereliction has not led to abandonment of the laws. On the contrary, the statutes and penalties for violation have become increasingly severe in the same period.

Now that these two processes have been described, how does the dichotomy help resolve the conundrum of adaptation versus cultural continuity alluded to above? It can be of assistance, it seems, if we are willing to make one basic assumption: that the two processes do not operate with equal force in all cultural spheres and in all historical periods. There may in fact be circumstances in which processes of situational adjustment are vastly more important for a particular cultural outcome than are processes of regularization; and there are other times and places in which the opposite may occur.

For illustration let us return to the Plains Indians used earlier as an example of adaptation. As we have seen, the period from about 1680–1880 A.D. was one of tremendous on-the-ground change in the region. The acquisition of the horse induced groups from adjacent areas to migrate into the High Plains to take up mounted nomadism. In most instances the new life was a radical turnabout from their former existence. Each of the societies had to work out, by trial and error and by borrowing from neighboring groups, the techniques that contributed to success; and we must assume that each group was required to make countless adjustments in technology, organization, and attitudes in the process.

But this initial and momentous adjustment was simply one among many. New groups constantly entered the area to challenge those already there. The intruders included various Indian tribes that had been displaced by white encroachment in the east, and finally the white settlers and soldiers themselves. The newcomers invariably brought with them advanced technology, particularly weaponry, that intensified an already tumultuous military situation. Societies that had held their own as mounted archers had to meet the sudden challenge of enemies armed with rifles. They either acquired the new weapons or were ejected from the territories they had won. Equally important, they had to devise military tactics appropriate to each change in armament, and such knowledge was often gained through bitter experience. The Cheyennes suffered severe defeats in the 1850s at the hands of various eastern tribes (Sac, Fox, Delawares) who possessed long-range rifles and whose approach to battle rendered Cheyenne tactics obsolete (Hoebel 1960: 69).

The situation was, in other words, highly unstable. Hard and fast cultural schemes could not become established under such conditions. No sooner did one set of rules and practices come into being than they were invalidated by the rapidly changing circumstances. The need, therefore, was for resourceful and experimental types of behavior that allowed each society to cope with the fluidity of actual conditions. And this is generally what we find in characterizations of Plains societies. We learn that the Comanche, for example, were relatively free of binding rules (Kardiner 1945: 81):

> The opportunistic character of this society makes itself felt everywhere, be it in the adaptability, the readiness for change, the contempt for death, or the tenuous character of its religion.

It is for these reasons that an approach that emphasizes how culture *follows* behavior is fruitful in the Plains context. The situation that individuals and groups faced were extremely compelling. The predatory warfare and competition between societies made the circumstances "more than superficially analogous to . . . natural selection in the biological world" (Secoy 1953: 94). Opportunistic types of behavior were tolerated and encouraged because the guidelines from the cultural past—the elements of traditional wisdom—could not meet the needs of a truly dynamic situation. We must recognize, of course, that not everything changed, and that certain elements persisted from the past (see Chapter Five); nevertheless, a great deal *did* change, and a perspective that focuses on the processes by which this occurred cannot fail to be enlightening.

But what about situations that bear no resemblance to that of the Plains? Would we expect the same analysis to apply to circumstances in which stability is far more conspicuous than change? Or, to express it another way, would it apply to situations in which processes of regularization are clearly ascendant over those of situational adjustment?

One of the societies mentioned in the treatment of persistence in Chapter Five was ancient Egypt. Here was a society noted for the continuity of its tradition. Certain basic patterns developed early in its history (during the Old Kingdom, ca. 3000–2200 B.C.) and were then maintained with remarkable consistency for about fifteen hundred years (Wilson 1951: 49). This is not to deny that changes occurred, but the truly impressive fact is how little was altered in this enormous stretch of time.

The geographical isolation of Egypt was undoubtedly a factor. The Nile river creates a ribbon-like oasis in the midst of a desert, so that the lands to the east, west, and south of the valley were sparsely inhabited. The occupants of these regions were mainly tribal peoples who did not constitute a serious threat to early Egyptian society. The Red Sea provided a natural barrier as well, so that the only invasion route for the civilizations to the east was over the difficult Sinai Peninsula. Conquerors eventually came from this direction, but only very late in Egyptian history. For the first two thousand years of her existence, Egypt suffered only one period of foreign domination (by the Hyksos ca. 1730–1570 B.C.).

The culture that emerged in this protected environment came to center about values of stability, order, and permanence. Such values were closely associated with the powerful divine monarchy that made its appearance at the dawn of Egyptian civilization. These rulers, or pharaohs, were considered god-kings who governed on earth according to divine plan. Moreover this plan was thought to be fixed and valid for all time. A great deal of the creative energy of the civilization, therefore, can be understood as an attempt to confirm and legitimate both the established order and its view of the world.

Architecture is a prime example. It has often been noted that when a society places the interests of the state far above the interests of its subjects, the scale of state buildings tends to increase accordingly (Burns 1973: 40). In ancient Egypt the scale was tremendous; one has only to think of the giant pyramids and the temples, with their colossal statues, hewn from stone cliffs. Furthermore, virtually all the buildings were for purposes of state; to commemorate the pharaohs or their royal relatives. The massiveness and solidity of these monuments were expressive both of the power of the rulers and of their imperishability. The art and sculpture suggests much the same. The pharaohs are portrayed not as flesh-and-blood figures, but as impassive and serene beings, as eternal as the gods they claimed to be.

Similar notions received explicit expression in literature and philosophy. A concept that was central to much Egyptian thought was the principle of *ma'at*. This was a moral precept variously translated as "justice," "righteousness," or "goodness." Its true meaning, however, was more akin to "the proper order of things." Egyptian philosophers insisted that there was a principle of harmony in the universe, established at creation, to which men should strive to adjust. An act that was considered good, or true, was one that was in harmony with this appropriate order; a baneful act was one that was out of place, or that upset established relations. It is of course not difficult to understand how a principle of this kind served to reinforce the constituted order. One authority remarks (Wilson 1951: 48):

Ma'at, then, was a created and inherited rightness, which tradition built up into a concept of orderly stability, in order to confirm and consolidate the *status quo*, particularly the continuing rule of the pharaoh.

These, then, are what are meant by processes of regularization. A firm framework of cultural rules was laid down by which social relations were ordered and patterned. Due to the sheltered nature of the civilization there were few influences from the outside that could challenge the order once it came into being, or that might serve as catalysts for change. As a consequence, the wisdom of the past was rarely invalidated by changing circumstances; or if this did gradually occur the pace was so slow that it was not conspicuous. Each generation of Egyptians found that the culture acquired from the anterior generation required only slight modification to meet the needs of everyday life. Under these conditions the traditional order came to be greatly revered as a model for the present, and cultural rules and categories became virtually unassailable. The Greek historian Herodotus, who visited Egypt in the fifth century B.C., considered Egyptians "the most conservative of all nations" (1906: 119); and a modern scholar writes of "the extraordinary attachment to the traditional as opposed to the actual" as a distinguishing characteristic of ancient Egyptian life and thought (Gardiner 1961: 56).

The ultimate result of such commitment to tradition was stagnation, since it discouraged the innovative and experimental forms of behavior that provide a basis for change. Except for the brief and unsuccessful attempt to revitalize Egyptian culture under Pharaoh Amenhotep (ca. 1375–1355 B.C.), the society remained much the same for centuries. A famous scholar has remarked that late Egyptian civilization was like a carcass that continued to exist long after all life had departed from the body (Toynbee 1962: 136). And of course the price for stagnation was high. When Egypt eventually came into contact with more dynamic societies—Persians, Greeks, Romans—she succumbed militarily and became a satellite in far-flung empires. What remained of the ancient culture was gradually abandoned under foreign domination.

These two case examples, Plains Indians and Ancient Egypt, have been juxtaposed because they exemplify opposite historical tendencies. In the first instance the sociocultural order was continuously revamped by processes of situational adjustment; efficiency became a dominant concern for all Plains tribes, while order, stability, and harmony were sacrificed. In the Egyptian case, once the basic pattern was established, all subsequent events were assimilated to a common mold. Stability and order were emphasized to such a degree that the society lost contact, as it were, with the real world around it.

Both are extreme cases, and as such they cast light on underlying processes. Most human history, however, is an admixture: individuals embark in new directions through creative adjustment to circumstances; and at the same time, but in different spheres of their lives, they conform to the past. It is for this reason that the examples of cultural continuity discussed earlier in this chapter (in the United States, French Canada, and Australia) may appear to bear little resemblance to the stultifying conservatism of ancient Egypt.

Yet there is a similarity that should not be lost to view. All are cases in which processes of regularization, the imposition of cultural form, are of great significance. Each demonstrates also that cultural rules and patterns are not merely epiphenomenal, not simply derivative or caused by something else. Culture in all of these cases is portrayed as an active principle, preceding, guiding, and channeling human action.

A lesson to be learned from this discussion is that what we see depends to a great extent on where we look. If our attention is caught by processes of situational adjustment, we understand clearly how culture can be regarded as epiphenomenal, as a product of on-the-ground arrangements. And in certain respects this is an accurate perception.

But when we focus on processes of regularization we confront a different reality: we recognize culture as a force in its own right, and we understand how sociocultural systems can have a momentum of their own, and how they can assimilate foreign material and impose upon it a characteristic design (Murphy 1970: 169).

This latter point sounds more complex than it is. It is really little more than the observation that societies can transform environments (as well as be transformed by them). The principle is illustrated charmingly in the classic film *2001: A Space Odyssey*. There is a scene that depicts Howard Johnson restaurants operating in outer space, much as they do in the contemporary United States. While the scene is an exercise in imagination, it is probably fantasy of a prescient kind. For Americans will likely "Americanize" space in ways similar to this, just as the Japanese will be capable of imposing a rather different organization on areas that come under their control. Space will probably constitute no more of an obstacle to the transformative effects of culture than were the New World environments occupied by Europeans of distinct national traditions.

Suggested Readings

Harris, Marvin, *Cultural Materialism: The Struggle for a Science of Culture*. New York: Vintage Books, 1980.

For those interested in the point of view that attempts to make practical, materialist sense out of human customs, this book provides a philosophical rationale.

Hartz, Louis, *The Founding of New Societies*. New York: Harcourt, Brace and World, 1964.

Here Hartz develops the concept of "fragment" cultures and the way in which their elements unfold in new environments. The writing is not always clear, and Hartz expects more historical knowledge from the reader than most of us have. But the discussion is remarkably suggestive. There are contributions by other scholars as well.

Lipset, Seymour, *Revolution and Counterrevolution: Change and Persistence in Social Structures*. New York: Basic Books, 1968.

Lipset, like Hartz, has maintained an interest in the persistence of cultural traditions over time. This is a collection of various of his papers on the themes of persistence and change in Western societies. All of his interpretations are scholarly, lucid, and perceptive.

Simoons, Frederick J., Questions in the Sacred-Cow Controversy, *Current Anthropology*, Vol. 20, No. 3, September, 1979, pp. 467–93.

For those interested in the sacred-cow question this is an excellent review of the controversy. Simoons is critical of Harris's position, and he brings together an impressive amount of scholarly evidence.

Wright, Benjamin F., American Democracy and the Frontier, *Yale Review*, Vol. 20, winter, 1931, pp. 349–65.

This is a cogently argued paper that takes issue with Turner's interpretation of the role of the frontier in American democracy.

References

Agar, Michael
   1973   *Ripping and Running: A Formal Ethnography of Urban Heroin Addicts*. New York: Seminar Press.

Agard, Walter A.
   1957   Classics on the Midwest Frontier, in Walker D. Wyman and Clifton B. Kroeber, eds. *The Frontier in Perspective*, Madison: The University of Wisconsin Press.

Balikci, Asen
   1970   *The Netsilik Eskimo*. New York: The Natural History Press.

Barry, Herbert, Irvin L. Child, and Margaret K. Bacon
   1959   Relation of Child Training to Subsistence Economy, *American Anthropologist*, Vol. 61, pp. 51–63.

Beals, Alan
   1970   Gopalpur, 1958–1960, in George Spindler, ed., *Being an Anthropologist: Fieldwork in Eleven Cultures*, New York: Holt, Rinehart & Winston, pp. 32–57.

Beardsley, Richard K., John W. Hall, and Robert E. Ward
   1959   *Village Japan*. Chicago: University of Chicago Press.

Benedict, Ruth F.
   1934   *Patterns of Culture*. New York: Mentor Books.
   1946   *The Chrysanthemum and the Sword: Patterns of Japanese Culture*. Boston: Houghton Mifflin Co.

Berger, Peter
   1963   *Invitation to Sociology: A Humanistic Perspective*. New York: Doubleday.

Berreman, Gerald D.
   1962   *Behind Many Masks: Ethnography and Impression Management in a Himalayan Village*. Ithaca, New York: Society for Applied Anthropology, Monograph 4.
   1968   Ethnography: Method and Product, in James A. Clifton, ed., *Introduction to Cultural Anthropology*. Boston: Houghton Mifflin Co., pp. 337–73.

Billington, Ray A., ed.
   1966   *The Frontier Thesis: Valid Interpretation of American History?* New York: Holt, Rinehart & Winston.

Blake, Judith and Kingsley Davis
   1964   Norms, Values, and Sanctions, in R. Faris, ed., *Handbook of Modern Sociology*. Chicago: Rand McNally.

Bohannan, Paul
   1963   *Social Anthropology*. New York: Holt, Rinehart & Winston.

Briggs, Jean L.
   1970   *Never in Anger: Portrait of an Eskimo Family*. Cambridge:
          Harvard University Press.
Brim, Orville G.
   1960   Personality Development as Role-Learning, in Ira Iscoe and
          Harold W. Stevenson, eds., *Personality Development in Chil-
          dren*, Austin: University of Texas Press.
Brinton, Crane
   1952   *The Anatomy of Revolution*. New York: Vintage Books.
Bryce, James
   1921   *Modern Democracies*. New York: Macmillan Co.
Bunzel, Ruth
   1929   *The Pueblo Potter: A Study of Creative Imagination in Prim-
          itive Art*. New York: Columbia University Press.
Burn, D. L.
   1940   *The Economic History of Steelmaking, 1867– 1939: A Study
          in Competition*. Cambridge: Cambridge University Press.
Burns, Edward M.
   1973   *Western Civilizations: Their History and Their Culture*. New
          York: W. W. Norton.
Burns, Edward M., Robert E. Lerner, and Standish Meacham
   1980   *Western Civilization*. 2 Vols. New York: W. W. Norton.
Calverton, Victor F., ed.
   1931   *The Making of Man: An Outline of Anthropology*. New York:
          The Modern Library.
Chagnon, Napoleon A.
   1968   *Yanomamo: The Fierce People*. New York: Holt, Rinehart &
          Winston.
Coleman, Peter J.
   1958   The New Zealand Frontier, *Pacific Historical Review*, Vol.
          27, pp. 221– 37.
DaCunha, Euclides
   1944   *Rebellion in the Backlands*. Chicago: University of Chicago
          Press.
Davis, Kingsley
   1940   Extreme Social Isolation of a Child, *American Journal of
          Sociology*, Vol. 45, No. 4, Jan., pp. 554–65.
Dean, John P., Robert L. Eichhorn, and Lois R. Dean
   1967   Observation and Interviewing, in John T. Doby, ed., *An Intro-
          duction to Social Research*. New York: Appleton-Century-
          Crofts.
Dickens, Charles
   n.d.   *American Notes*. New York: World's Popular Classics.

Dorsey, J. O.
  1884 *Omaha Sociology*. Bureau of American Ethnology, 3rd Annual
         Report, 1881–82. Washington, D.C.: U. S. Government
         Printing Office.
Douglas, Mary
  1966 *Purity and Danger: An Analysis of Concepts of Pollution and
         Taboo*. London: Routledge & Kegan Paul.
  1973 *Natural Symbols: Explorations in Cosmology*. New York:
         Vintage Books.
Downs, James
  1973 *Human Nature: An Introduction to Cultural Anthropology*.
         Beverly Hills, Calif.: Glencoe Press.
  1975 *Cultures in Crisis*. 2nd ed. Beverly Hills, Calif.: Glencoe
         Press.
Draper, Patricia
  1978 The Learning Environment for Aggression and Anti-Social
         Behavior Among the Kung, in Ashley Montagu, ed., *Learn-
         ing Non-Aggression: The Experience of Non-Literate Socie-
         ties*. New York: Oxford University Press.
DuBois, Cora
  1944 *The People of Alor*. 2 Vols. New York: Harper & Row.
Durkheim, Émile
  1895 *The Rules of Sociological Method*. Chicago: The University
         of Chicago Press.
  1912 *The Elementary Forms of the Religious Life*. New York: Col-
         lier Books.
Eames, Edwin, and Judith G. Goode
  1977 *Anthropology of the City: An Introduction to Urban Anthro-
         pology*. Englewood Cliffs, N.J.: Prentice-Hall.
Edgerton, Robert B.
  1976 *Deviance: A Cross-Cultural Perspective*. Menlo Park, Calif.:
         Benjamin/Cummings.
Eggan, Fred R.
  1966 *The American Indian: Perspectives for the Study of Social
         Change*. Chicago: Aldine.
Ember, Carol R., and Melvin Ember
  1981 *Cultural Anthropology*. 3rd ed. Englewood Cliffs, N. J.:
         Prentice-Hall.
Evans-Pritchard, E. E.
  1937 *Witchcraft, Oracles and Magic Among the Azande*. Oxford:
         At The Clarendon Press.
Fernea, Elizabeth W.
  1965 *Guests of the Sheik: An Ethnography of an Iraqi Village*. New
         York: Anchor Books.

Finlay, John L.
    1975   *Canada in the North Atlantic Triangle: Two Centuries of Social Change*. Toronto: Oxford University Press.
Firth, Raymond
    1973   *Symbols: Public and Private*. Ithaca: Cornell University Press.
Flannery, Regina
    1960   Individual Variation in Culture, in Anthony Wallace, ed., *Men and Cultures*. Philadelphia: University of Pennsylvania Press.
Florinsky, Michael T.
    1969   *Russia: A Short History*. London: Macmillan Co.
Foster, George
    1960   *Culture and Conquest: America's Spanish Heritage*. Viking Fund Publications in Anthropology, No. 27, New York: Wenner-Gren.
Frankel, Marvin
    1955   Obsolescence and Technological Change in a Maturing Economy, *American Economic Review*, Vol. 45, June, pp. 296–319.
Freilich, Morris
    1972   Manufacturing Culture: Man the Scientist, in Morris Freilich, ed., *The Meaning of Culture: A Reader in Cultural Anthropology*. Lexington, Mass.: Xerox College Publishing.
Friedman, Jonathan
    1974   Marxism, Structuralism and Vulgar Materialism, *Man*, Vol. 9, pp. 444–69.
Fromm, Eric
    1941   *Escape From Freedom*. New York: Farrar & Rinehart.
Gans, Herbert J.
    1962   *The Urban Villagers: Group and Class in the Life of Italian Americans*. New York: The Free Press.
Gardiner, Alan
    1961   *Egypt of the Pharaohs*. London: Oxford University Press.
Geertz, Clifford
    1963   *Agricultural Involution: The Processes of Ecological Change in Indonesia*. Berkeley: University of California Press.
    1973   *The Interpretation of Cultures*. New York: Basic Books.
General Accounting Office
    1978   *Getting a Better Understanding of the Metric System: Implications if Adopted by the United States*. Report to the Congress. Washington, D.C.: U.S. Government Printing Office.
Gerhard, Dietrich
    1959   The Frontier in Comparative View, *Comparative Studies in Society and History*, Vol. 1, pp. 205–29.

Gibson, Charles
1964   *The Aztecs Under Spanish Rule: A History of the Indians of the Valley of Mexico, 1519–1810.* Stanford: Stanford University Press.

Gladwin, Thomas
1957   Personality Structure in the Plains, *Anthropological Quarterly*, Vol. 30, pp. 111–24.

Goffman, Erving
1956   The Nature of Deference and Demeanor, *American Anthropologist*, Vol. 58, June, pp. 473–502.
1959   *The Presentation of Self in Everyday Life.* New York: Doubleday.
1963   *Behavior in Public Places: Notes on the Social Organization of Gatherings.* New York: The Free Press.
1967   *Interaction Ritual: Essays in Face-to-Face Behavior.* Chicago: Aldine.

Goodenough, Ward
1956   Residence Rules, *Southwestern Journal of Anthropology*, Vol. 12, pp. 22–37.

Goodman, Mary E.
1967   *The Individual and Culture.* Homewood, Ill.: Dorsey Press.

Gould, Stephen J.
1980   *The Panda's Thumb: More Reflections in Natural History.* New York: W. W. Norton.
1981   Evolution as Fact and Theory, *Discover*, May, pp. 34–37.

Gregg, Dorothy, and Elgin Williams
1948   The Dismal Science of Functionalism, *American Anthropologist*, Vol. 50, pp. 594–611.

Hall, Edward T., and William F. Whyte
1960   Intercultural Communication: A Guide to Men of Action, *Human Organization*, Vol. 19, No. 1, Spring, pp. 5–12.

Hall, Robert K.
1949   *Education for a New Japan.* New Haven: Yale University Press.

Hallpike, C. R.
1969   Social Hair, *Man*, Vol. 4, No. 2, June, pp. 256–64.
1974   Correspondence: Functions of War, *Man*, Vol. 9, No. 3, pp. 488–89.

Harlow, Harry F., and Margaret K. Harlow
1962   Social Deprivation in Monkeys, *Scientific American*, Vol. 207, No. 5, pp. 136–46.

Harris, Marvin
1956   *Town and Country in Brazil.* New York: Columbia University Press.

1968   *The Rise of Anthropological Theory*. New York: Thomas Y. Crowell.

1971   *Culture, Man, and Nature*. New York: Thomas Y. Crowell.

1974   *Cows, Pigs, Wars and Witches: The Riddles of Culture*. New York: Vintage Books.

Hart, C.W.M.

1954   The Sons of Turimpi, *American Anthropologist*. Vol. 56, pp. 242–61.

Hartz, Louis

1964   *The Founding of New Societies*. New York: Harcourt, Brace & World.

Hatch, Elvin

1973   *Theories of Man and Culture*. New York: Columbia University Press.

Herodotus

1906   *Histories: Books I to III*. Translated by G. Woodrouffe Harris. New York: Macmillan Co.

Hertz, Robert

1909   *Death and the Right Hand*. London: Cohen & West.

Hoebel, E. A.

1960   *The Cheyennes: Indians of the Great Plains*. New York: Holt, Rinehart & Winston.

Hoebel, E. E., and Ernest Wallace

1952   *The Comanches: Lords of the South Plains*. Norman: University of Oklahoma Press.

Hollingshead, August B.

1949   *Elmtown's Youth*. New York: John Wiley & Sons.

Hsu, Francis L.

1969   *The Study of Literate Civilizations*. New York: Holt, Rinehart & Winston.

Hymes, Dell, ed.,

1969   *Reinventing Anthropology*. New York: Vintage Books.

Kaplan, Bert

1957   Personality and Social Structure, in Joseph B. Gittler, ed., *Review of Sociology: Analysis of a Decade*. New York: John Wiley & Sons.

Kaplan, David, and Robert A. Manners

1972   *Culture Theory*. Englewood Cliffs, N. J.: Prentice-Hall.

Kardiner, Abram

1945   *The Psychological Frontiers of Society*. New York: Columbia University Press.

Keiser, Lincoln

1969   *The Vice Lords: Warriors of the Streets*. New York: Holt, Rinehart & Winston.

Kluckhohn, Clyde
   1949   *Mirror for Man*. New York: Premier Books.
Kobben, A.J.F.
   1967   Participation and Quantification: Field Work Among the Djuka
          (Bush Negroes of Surinam), in D. G. Jongmans and P.C.W.
          Gutkind, eds., *Anthropologists in the Field*. Assen, Nether-
          lands: Van Gorcum.
Kroeber, Alfred
   1917   The Superorganic, *American Anthropologist*. Vol. 19, pp.
          163–213.
   1939   *Cultural and Natural Areas of Native North America*. Berke-
          ley: University of California Press.
   1948   *Anthropology*. New York: Harcourt, Brace & World.
Kuhn, Thomas
   1962   *The Structure of Scientific Revolutions*. Chicago: University
          of Chicago Press.
LaBarre, Weston
   1947   The Cultural Basis of Emotions and Gestures, *Journal of
          Personality*, Vol. 16, Sept., pp. 49–68.
Lattimore, Owen
   1962   *Studies in Frontier History: Collected Papers 1928–1958*.
          London: Oxford University Press.
Lee, Richard E.
   1979   *The !Kung San: Men, Women and Work in a Foraging Society*.
          New York: Cambridge University Press.
Levine, A. L.
   1967   *Industrial Retardation in Britain: 1880–1914*. New York: Basic
          Books.
Lewin, Roger
   1980   Evolutionary Theory Under Fire, *Science*, Vol. 210, Nov.,
          pp. 883–87.
Liebow, Elliot
   1967   *Tally's Corner: A Study of Negro Streetcorner Men*. Boston:
          Little, Brown and Co.
Lipset, Seymour M.
   1967   *The First New Nation: The United States in Historical and
          Comparative Perspective*. New York: Doubleday.
   1968   *Revolution and Counterrevolution: Change and Persistence
          in Social Structures*. New York: Basic Books.
   1972   *Rebellion in the University: A History of Student Activism in
          America*. London: Routledge & Kegan Paul.

Malinowski, Bronislaw
  1922 *Argonauts of the Western Pacific*. New York: Dutton.
  1926 *Crime and Custom in Savage Society*. New Jersey: Littlefield,
         Adams.
Marriott, Alice
  1953 *Greener Fields: Experiences Among the American Indians*.
         New York: Thomas Y. Crowell.
Marshall, Lorna
  1961 Sharing, Talking, and Giving: Relief of Social Tensions Among
         !Kung Bushmen, *Africa*, Vol. 31, pp. 231–49.
McRae, Kenneth D.
  1964 The Structure of Canadian History, in Louis Hartz, *The
         Founding of New Societies*. New York: Harcourt, Brace &
         World.
Mead, Margaret
  1935 *Sex and Temperament in Three Primitive Societies*. New York:
         W. Morrow.
Miller, Roy A.
  1977 *The Japanese Language in Contemporary Japan: Some
         Sociolinguistic Observations*. Washington: American Enter-
         prise Institute for Public Policy Research.
Miller, Walter B.
  1955 Two Concepts of Authority, *American Anthropologist*, Vol.
         57, April pp. 271–89.
Mooney, James
  1907 The Cheyenne Indians, Memoirs of the American Anthro-
         pological Association. Vol. 1, Pt. 6, pp. 357–442.
Moore, Sally F.
  1976 Epilogue: Uncertainties in Situations, Indeterminacies in Cul-
         ture, in Sally Falk Moore and Barbara Meyerhoff, eds., *Sym-
         bol and Politics in Communal Ideology: Cases and Questions*.
         Ithaca: Cornell University Press.
Murdock, George P.
  1965 *Culture and Society*. Pittsburgh: University of Pittsburgh Press.
Murphy, Robert F.
  1970 Basin Ethnography and Ecological Theory, in Earl H. Swan-
         son, Jr., ed., *Languages and Cultures of Western North Amer-
         ica: Essays in Honor of Sven S. Liljeblad*, Pocatello, Idaho:
         The Idaho State University Press.
Nadel, George
  1957 *Australia's Colonial Culture: Ideas, Men and Institutions in
         Mid-Nineteenth Century Eastern Australia*. Cambridge: Har-
         vard University Press.

Nadel, S. F.
  1954 *Nupe Religion*. London: Routledge & Kegan Paul.
Nelson, Benjamin
  1961 *Tennessee Williams: The Man and his Work*. New York: Ivan Obolensky.
Netting, Robert McC.
  1974 Correspondence: Functions of War, *Man*, Vol. 9, No. 3, pp. 485–87.
Newcomb, W. W.
  1950 A Re-examination of the Causes of Plains Warfare, *American Anthropologist*, Vol. 52, July–Sept., pp. 317–30.
Norbeck, Edward
  1970 Changing Japan: Field Research, in George Spindler, ed., *Being an Anthropologist: Fieldwork in Eleven Cultures*. New York: Holt, Rinehart & Winston.
Odend'hal, Stewart
  1972 Energetics of Indian Cattle in Their Environment, *Human Ecology*, Vol. 1, No. 1, pp. 3–21.
Ogburn, William F.
  1922 *Social Change with Respect to Culture and Original Nature*. New York: B. W. Huebsch.
Oliver, Douglas
  1955 *A Solomon Island Society: Kinship and Leadership Among the Siuai of Bougainville*. Cambridge: Harvard University Press.
Oliver, Symmes C.
  1962 Ecology and Cultural Continuity As Contributing Factors in the Social Organization of the Plains Indians, *University of California Publications in American Archeology and Ethnology*, Vol. 48, No. 1.
Parkman, Francis Jr.
  1856 *The California and Oregon Trail: Being Sketches of Prairie and Rocky Mountain Life*. New York: Hurst.
  1901 *The Old Regime in Canada*. Boston: Little, Brown and Co.
Pelto, Pertti J., and Gretel H. Pelto
  1978 *Anthropological Research: The Structure of Inquiry*. 2nd ed., Cambridge: Cambridge University Press.
Perry, John
  1955 *The Story of Standards*. New York: Funk & Wagnalls.
Pierson, George W.
  1959 *Tocqueville in America*. New York: Doubleday.
Porac, Clare, and Stanley Coren
  1981 *Lateral Preferences and Human Behavior*. New York: Springer-Verlag.

Pospisil, Leopold
1963 *The Kapauku Papuans of West New Guinea*. New York: Holt, Rinehart & Winston.

Post, Emily
1955 *Etiquette: The Blue Book of Social Usage*. New York: Funk & Wagnalls.

Powdermaker, Hortense
1966 *Stranger and Friend: The Way of an Anthropologist*. New York: W. W. Norton.

Radcliffe-Brown, A. R.
1952 *Structure and Function in Primitive Society*. London: Cohen & West.

Radin, Paul
1927 *Primitive Man as Philosopher*. New York: D. Appleton.

Rappaport, Roy
1968 *Pigs for the Ancestors: Ritual in the Ecology of a New Guinea People*. New Haven: Yale University Press.

Rasmussen, Knud
1931 *The Netsilik Eskimos: Social Life and Spiritual Culture*. Report of the Fifth Thule Expedition, 1921–24. Copenhagen: Glydendalske Boghandel.

Redfield, Robert
1947 The Folk Society, *American Journal of Sociology*, Vol. 52, No. 4, Jan., pp. 293–308.
1960 *The Little Community and Peasant Society and Culture*. Chicago: University of Chicago Press.

Reischauer, Edwin O., and John K. Fairbank
1958 *East Asia: The Great Tradition*. Boston: Houghton Mifflin Co.

Richardson, Miles
1970 *San Pedro, Colombia: Small Town in a Developing Society*. New York: Holt, Rinehart & Winston.
1975 Anthropologist—The Myth Teller, *American Ethnologist*, Vol. 2, No. 3, Aug., pp. 517–32.

Rosecrance, Richard N.
1964 The Radical Culture of Australia, in Louis Hartz, ed., *The Founding of New Societies*. New York: Harcourt, Brace & World.

Sahlins, Marshall D.
1964 Culture and Environment: The Study of Cultural Ecology, in Sol Tax, ed., *Horizons of Anthropology*, Chicago: Aldine.

Sansom, George
1928 *An Historical Grammar of Japanese*. Oxford: At the Clarendon Press.

1976 *Culture and Practical Reason*. Chicago: University of Chicago Press.

Sahlins, Marshall D. and Elman R. Service
1960 *Evolution and Culture*. Ann Arbor: University of Michigan Press.

Sapir, Edward
1921 *Language: An Introduction to the Study of Speech*. New York: Harcourt, Brace.
1949 Why Cultural Anthropology Needs the Psychiatrist, in David G. Mandelbaum, ed., *Selected Writings of Edward Sapir in Language, Culture, and Personality*. Berkeley: University of California Press.

Schorer, Mark
1961 *Sinclair Lewis: An American Life*. New York: McGraw-Hill.

Secoy, Frank R.
1953 *Changing Military Patterns on the Great Plains*. Monographs of the American Ethnological Society, Vol. 21. New York: J. J. Augustin.

Service, Elman R.
1960 The Law of Evolutionary Potential, in Marshall D. Sahlins and Elman R. Service, *Evolution and Culture*. Ann Arbor: University of Michigan Press.

Shaw, Carolyn H.
1958 *Modern Manners: Etiquette for All Occasions*. New York: E. P. Dutton.

Simmons, Jack
1978 *The Railway in England and Wales, 1830–1914: The System and its Working*. Leicester University Press.

Singer, Milton
1961 A Survey of Culture and Personality Theory and Research, in Bert Kaplan, ed., *Studying Personality Cross-Culturally*. New York: Harper & Row.

Skorupski, John
1976 *Symbol and Theory: A Philosophical Study of Theories of Religion in Social Anthropology*. New York: Cambridge University Press.

Spradley, James
1970 *You Owe Yourself a Drunk: An Ethnography of Urban Nomads*. Boston: Little, Brown and Co.

Spradley, James, and David W. McCurdy
1972 *The Cultural Experience: Ethnography in Complex Society*. Chicago: Science Research Associates.

Steward, Julian H.
1938 *Basin-Plateau Aboriginal Sociopolitical Groups*. Bureau of

American Ethnology bulletin No. 120. Washington, D.C.: U.S. Government Printing Office.

1955   *Theory of Culture Change*. Urbana: University of Illinois Press.

Stocking, George

     1968   *Race, Culture, and Evolution: Essays in the History of Anthropology*. New York: The Free Press.

Stokes, Randall, and John P. Hewitt

     1976   Aligning Actions, *American Sociological Review*, Vol. 41, No. 5, Oct., pp. 838–49.

Thomas, Elizabeth M.

     1958   *The Harmless People*. New York: Knopf.

     1965   *Warrior Herdsmen*. New York: Vintage Books.

Tindall, William Y.

     1967   *The Literary Symbol*. Bloomington: Indiana University Press.

Tocqueville, Alexis de

     1835   *Democracy in America*. 2 Vols. New York: Knopf.

Toynbee, Arnold J.

     1962   *A Study of History*. Vol. 1. New York: Oxford University Press.

Treat, Charles F.

     1971   *A History of the Metric System Controversy in the United States*. National Bureau of Standards Special Publication 345–10. Washington, D.C.: U.S. Government Printing Office.

Turnbull, Colin

     1961   *The Forest People*. New York: Simon and Schuster.

Turner, Frederick J.

     1966   The Significance of the Frontier in American History, in Ray A. Billington, ed., *The Frontier Thesis: Valid Interpretation of American History?* New York: Holt, Rinehart & Winston.

Turner, Victor W.

     1974   *Dramas, Fields and Metaphors: Symbolic Action in Human Society*. Ithaca: Cornell University Press.

     1977   Process, System, and Symbol: A New Anthropological Synthesis, *Daedalus*, Vol. 106, No. 3, Summer, pp. 61–80.

Valentine, Charles

     1968   *Culture and Poverty: Critique and Counter-proposals*. Chicago: University of Chicago Press.

Vanderbilt, Amy

     1952   *Amy Vanderbilt's New Complete Book of Etiquette: The Guide to Gracious Living*. New York: Doubleday.

     1972   *Amy Vanderbilt's Etiquette*. New York: Doubleday.

Veblen, Thorstein

     1915   *Imperial Germany and the Industrial Revolution*. Ann Arbor: University of Michigan Press.

Wallace, Anthony F.
  1952 *The Modal Personality Structure of the Tuscarora Indians As Revealed by the Rorschach Test*. Bureau of American Ethnology bulletin No. 150. Washington, D.C.: U.S. Government Printing Office.

Wallace, Bruce, and Adrian M. Srb
  1961 *Adaptation*. Westport, Connecticut: Greenwood Press.

Wax, Rosalie
  1971 *Doing Fieldwork: Warnings and Advice*. Chicago: University of Chicago Press.

Weber, Max
  1904 *The Protestant Ethic and the Spirit of Capitalism*. New York: Scribner.

  1952 *Ancient Judaism*. Glencoe, Ill.: The Free Press.

West, James
  1945 *Plainville U.S.A.*. New York: Columbia University Press.

Weyer, Edward M.
  1932 *The Eskimos: Their Environment and Folkways*. New Haven: Yale University Press.

White, Leslie A.
  1949 *The Science of Culture: A Study of Man and Civilization*. New York: Grove Press.

  1962 *The Pueblo of Sia, New Mexico*. Bureau of American Ethnology bulletin No. 184. Washington, D.C.: U.S. Government Printing Office.

Whyte, William F.
  1955 *Street Corner Society: The Social Structure of an Italian Slum*. 2nd ed. Chicago: University of Chicago Press.

Williams, Robbin M.
  1951 *American Society: A Sociological Interpretation*. New York: Knopf.

Williams, Thomas R.
  1967 *Field Methods in the Study of Culture*. New York: Holt, Rinehart & Winston.

Wilson, John A.
  1951 *The Burden of Egypt: An Interpretation of Ancient Egyptian Culture*. Chicago: University of Chicago Press.

Wolf, Eric R.
  1959 *Sons of the Shaking Earth*. Chicago: University of Chicago Press.

Wright, Benjamin F.
  1931 American Democracy and the Frontier, *Yale Review*. Vol. 20, Winter, pp. 349–65.

  1934 Political Institutions and the Frontier, in Dixon R. Fox, ed.,

Sources of Culture in the Middle West. New York: Appleton-Century.

Wrong, Dennis H.
  1961 The Oversocialized Conception of Man in Modern Sociology, *American Sociological Review*, Vol. 26, pp. 183–93.

Yang, Ch'ing-k'un
  1961 *Religion in Chinese Society*. Berkeley: University of California Press.

Index